Industrial Tribunals

Preparing and presenting your case

by
John Angel LLB MSc *Solicitor*

Tolley Publishing Company Limited
AN EXTEL GROUP PUBLICATION

Published in association with
the Institute of Personnel Management

Published by
Tolley Publishing Company Ltd
Tolley House
17 Scarbrook Road
Croydon
Surrey CR0 1SQ England

Typeset by Kerrypress Ltd
Luton, Beds., England

Printed in
Great Britain at
Heffers Printers Ltd
Cambridge, England

Cover design by Jonathan Newdick

*The first edition of this book was published by the Institute of
Personnel Management in 1980 under the title
'How to Prepare Yourself for an Industrial Tribunal'*

In memory of my father

Acknowledgements

I am very grateful to a number of people for their help, in particular to Sally Harper for encouraging me to write the second edition of this book. I would also like to express my gratitude to David Maier for his painstaking research, David Lewis for his constructive criticism and help in updating the Tribunal Table and Barry Mordsley for his valuable comments on practice.

Also my thanks go to the staff of the English, Welsh and Scottish Industrial Tribunals and of ACAS who, as with the first edition, have been ever helpful.

The Crown Copyright material in Appendices B and C and the specimen forms in the text are reproduced by kind permission of the Controller of Her Majesty's Stationery Office.

Stop Press

The Redundancy Rebate Regulations 1984 (SI 1984 No 1066) came into force on 1 October 1984, revoking and replacing the Redundancy Payments Rebate Regulations 1965 (SI 1965 No 1893). (See **Appendix A, claim 15, column 9.**)

Foreword

It is a matter for satisfaction that the success of the first edition of this book has led to the production of a second. It was never the intention that the industrial tribunals should be the sole preserve of the lawyers: rather the reverse in fact. The aim has always been that the tribunals should be seen so to conduct their hearings that those with business before them should feel sufficient confidence to present their cases without recourse to the services of a trained lawyer. The achievement of this aim has not always been easy. Difficult points of law, mainly where questions of jurisdictions are involved, can and do arise. In such cases the help of a lawyer will be an advantage. But more commonly there are no legal complications. In the great majority of cases it should be possible for the intelligent layman or the lay representative to present his case with clarity and confidence. To this end, John Angel's excellent book is extremely helpful. Case references have been kept to a minimum, which is as it should be. It is an unfortunate fact that tribunal cases, whether at first instance or on appeal, suffer from over-reporting. To his credit John Angel has not fostered that trend. Where he has cited legal authorities it has been in the context of matters affecting procedure and in that area he could scarcely have avoided doing so.

The legal position, as stated in this edition, is as at 1 July 1984. This has meant that the author has been obliged to deal with the new equal pay procedures which stem from the amendments to the Equal Pay Act 1970, namely the Equal Pay (Amendment) Regulations 1983 (SI 1983 No 1794), enacted in order to comply with EEC law. These procedures are indeed complicated and their operation is only now being treated for the first time. John Angel has dealt with this subject in a helpful manner in Appendix C to this edition. Both employers and employees will obtain enlightenment from a study of the analysis of the various steps in the process which John Angel sets out with clarity.

I wish this edition success. It should be of assistance to those for whom it is primarily intended. If this proves to be the case, as I hope it will, it will also help the tribunals themselves in securing a speedy and just disposal of their business.

Sir Jack Rumbold QC
President
The Industrial Tribunals
(England and Wales)

August 1984

Contents

Contents

List of Figures

Table of Cases

Table of Cases

Abbreviations

Legislation

EA 1980	Employment Act 1980
EA 1982	Employment Act 1982
EPA	Employment Protection Act 1975
EPCA	Employment Protection (Consolidation) Act 1978
EqPA	Equal Pay Act 1970
HSWA	Health and Safety at Work Act 1974
ITA	Industrial Training Act 1982
RRA	Race Relations Act 1976
SDA	Sex Discrimination Act 1975

General

ACAS	Advisory, Conciliation and Arbitration Service
CAB	Citizens' Advice Bureau
COIT	Central Office of Industrial Tribunals
CRE	Commission for Racial Equality
DE	Department of Employment
DHSS	Department of Health and Social Security
EDT	Effective date of termination (of employment)
EOC	Equal Opportunities Commission
HMSO	Her Majesty's Stationery Office
PHA	Pre-hearing assessment
SSAT	Social Security Appeal Tribunal
ROIT	Regional Office of Industrial Tribunals
TU	Trade Union

Courts

CA	Court of Appeal
EAT	Employment Appeal Tribunal
HC	High Court
HL	House of Lords
IT/tribunal	Industrial tribunal
NIRC	National Industrial Relations Court
QBD	Queen's Bench Division of High Court

Law reports and other references

AER	All England Law Reports
CCR	County Court Rules
ICR	Industrial Court Reports (1972 – 74)
	Industrial Case Reports (1975 – present)
IRLIB	Industrial Relations Legal Information Bulletin
IRLR	Industrial Relations Law Reports
ITR	Industrial Tribunal Reports (1966 – 1978)
SI	Statutory instrument
WLR	Weekly Law Reports

Scope of the Book

Industrial Tribunal Rules

Industrial tribunal procedure for England and Wales is governed by a 1980 statutory instrument, the Industrial Tribunals (Rules of Procedure) Regulations (SI 1980 No 884). It is set out in full in Appendix B and the guidance on tribunal procedure given in this book is based on these Regulations. They are referred to as 'the Regulations' or 'the Tribunal Regulations' in the text.

The procedural regulations for Scotland (SI 1980 No 885) and Northern Ireland (SI 1981 No 188) are very similar. Most procedural differences for Scotland are referred to in the text. But for more specific guidance on procedures in these two parts of the United Kingdom the reader should look at the publications on these particular jurisdictions listed in Appendix E.

The 1980 Tribunal Regulations from 1 January 1984 have been extended to accommodate the new equal pay procedures in 'equal value' cases introduced as a result of amendments to the Equal Pay Act 1970. Appendix C describes these new procedures, and sets out the amending Regulations in full.

Jurisdiction of industrial tribunals

Since the establishment of industrial tribunals in 1964 for the purpose of hearing appeals against levy assessment made under the Industrial Training Act of that year the jurisdiction of tribunals has increased remarkably. There are now over 60 different claims which can be brought before an IT, and details of most of these can be found in Appendix A. The Employment Acts of 1980 and 1982 alone introduced nine new claims. The only obvious omission from their jurisdiction relates to claims for damages for breach of contract of employment (wrongful dismissal) which the Secretary of State for Employment has power to introduce at any time.

No doubt the jurisdiction will be further extended, thereby increasing the importance of ITs and the need to understand the procedures surrounding them.

Introduction

The first edition of this book was written primarily to encourage the parties themselves or lay representatives such as personnel officers to take or defend industrial tribunal cases.

This edition continues to encourage such representation but recognises that in practice a large percentage of parties are represented by lawyers (in 1982, 36 per cent of all applicants and 49 per cent of all respondents). This second edition, therefore, gives more in-depth guidance and will be useful equally to lawyers and to lay persons who are now experienced tribunal practitioners.

A framework for understanding industrial tribunal procedure

This book is written for anyone who may be involved with an industrial tribunal (IT), whether an employer, employee, trade union representative, an employers' association or a lawyer representing either side. It examines the procedures from both parties' point of view since, without an understanding of the other side's involvement a case cannot be adequately prepared. In other words, some degree of objectivity is essential. Moreover, the book does not try to indicate tactics to score points over the other side, for it is dangerous to assume that the other party is not as knowledgeable as you.

The book is divided into four sections. The *first* part considers the preparation of an IT case. It represents about half of the text because a properly prepared case is the key to the most satisfactory performance. If the case is suitably prepared then the presentation at the hearing, which is regarded by most lay persons as the most formidable part of the procedure, becomes that much easier.

The *second* section is concerned with presentation. It describes how tribunals deal with such matters as opening speeches, examination of witnesses, cross examination, re-examination and interruptions by the tribunal.

The *third* part of the book looks at the tribunal's decision and matters which follow from it: costs, expenses, enforcement of orders, awards and so on. The chapter on costs is particularly detailed because of the interest of both parties in this area. This part also summarises the remedies available to ITs in a way that can aid the preparation and presentation of a case.

Finally, the *fourth* section looks at the various ways of challenging a tribunal's decision through such means as a review or an appeal.

In a book of this size it would be impossible to describe the procedures for all tribunal claims. Therefore the guidance concentrates on claims for unfair dismissal, redundancy, sex and race discrimination and equal pay, which represent the vast majority of actual claims. The new equal value procedures are described in Appendix C.

Introduction

In order to make the guidance in the book more useful, the text is illustrated by a hypothetical unfair dismissal case using forms similar to those used by ITs in practice. The description of IT procedure is based on practice in England, Wales and Scotland. This book does not delve into substantive issues of employment law, except where it affects procedure. The legal position stated here is as it existed on 1 July 1984.

Part I

Preparing Your Case

Chapter 1

Before Commencing a Claim

Decide why you wish to bring the claim

1.1 Before making a claim to an industrial tribunal (IT), it is important to identify why the claim is being made; in other words what are the objectives for bringing proceedings? These objectives may take a variety of forms, for example:

— the desire to be re-instated;

— the wish to be compensated for loss suffered;

— the desire to be paid equally as much as a person of the opposite sex;

— an indirect means of applying pressure in an industrial dispute;

— the wish to clear one's name;

— as a matter of principle you do not want your employer to get away with discriminatory practices.

If the objective(s) can be established and understood (and these may change during the course of a case), there will be a *raison d'être* for bringing a claim which can then be handled in an appropriate way. For instance, if the only objective is monetary compensation, a settlement will be an acceptable outcome. However, if the case is being brought on a matter of principle, only a hearing will suffice.

Pros and cons

1.2 The intensity of the desire to achieve the objective can then be ascertained as against such matters as:

— the possible prejudicial effect on future employment if potential employers know you have gone to an IT (see 'Unfair Dismissal Applications and the Industrial Tribunal System' by Linda Dickens, Industrial Relations Journal 1979, Vol 9 No 4);

— the effect on the employment relationship after you have established your entitlement to time off for trade union duties;

— the mental anxiety suffered and the effect on family life during the conduct of a case;

— the cost in terms of professional fees if, say, lawyers are instructed;

3

— the effect in practical and psychological terms if you lose - no litigation is certain as to its outcome!

The objectives will need to be reappraised as the case proceeds. Although the vast majority of claims are brought by employees, it must be remembered that employers and others can also bring claims. (*See* the Tribunal Table in Appendix A, column 3.)

Decide whether there is a potential claim

1.3 Once the objectives have been clarified, you and your representative will need to consider whether there is a claim. Under the Regulations (Rule 1(1)(*c*)) you are required to give 'particulars' of the grounds for a claim. If these are insufficient there are various methods by which ITs can dissuade you from proceeding, which are described in later chapters.

Therefore, provided you are well within the time limits indicated in column 6 of Appendix A for bringing a particular claim, an investigation is recommended to:

(*a*) exhaust internal procedures;

(*b*) verify that you are qualified to bring a claim;

(*c*) ascertain the reasons for the employer's actions;

(*d*) identify the law involved;

(*e*) consider the available evidence;

(*f*) make a preliminary assessment of the grounds of the claim and the likelihood of it succeeding.

These are dealt with separately below.

Internal procedures

1.4 It may be possible to appeal against the employer's decision under an internal disciplinary procedure, or alternatively, under the terms of a grievance procedure. Where possible these procedures should be exhausted for a number of beneficial reasons, for example:

(i) the problem may be resolved by reinstatement; or

(ii) the employee can show he has done everything possible to resolve the matter (even though not under a legal obligation to do so: *Seligman and Late Ltd v McHugh [1979] IRLR 130)*; or

(iii) the employee may come to a better understanding of the reasons for his dismissal.

Are you qualified?

1.5 Each particular claim has its own qualifying requirements, which have to be fulfilled before the claim can be valid. For example, most actions require the claimant to have a minimum period of continuous employment before being eligible to claim. These periods are shown in column 5 of Appendix A. Qualifications can take a variety of forms. A trade union (TU) can bring a claim where it has not been notified of impending redundancies. However, that union has to be 'recognised' by the employer. [*EPA s 99(1)*]. Only an employee who is an official of a recognised 'independent' TU can apply for time off to carry out trade union duties. [*EPCA s 27(1)*].

Since this book does not deal with substantive matters outside procedure, it is not possible to discuss the qualifications relevant to each claim. You should, however, familiarise yourself with the qualifications applicable to the claim being made by referring to the numerous free guides readily available on these matters from the Department of Employment, ACAS, Equal Opportunities Commission, Commission for Racial Equality, Health and Safety Executive etc. (*See* also the reference books on employment law listed in Appendix E.)

Unfair dismissal case

1.6 As the guidance in this book is illustrated with a typical unfair dismissal case, the following list represents some of the qualifications the claimant must fulfil before being eligible to claim unfair dismissal. He/she:

— is an employee [*EPCA s 54(1)*];

— has been continuously employed for one year at the date of dismissal [*EPCA s 64 (1)(a)*], or two years where his employer has less than 21 employees [*EPCA s 64A*];

— is contractually obliged to work for 16 hours or more per week, or eight hours or more per week after five years of continuous employment [*EPCA s 146(4)-(7)*];

— has not reached the upper age limit [*EPCA s 64(1)(b)*];

— ordinarily works inside GB [*EPCA s 141*];

— is not expressly excluded from bringing a claim under a fixed term contract of one year or more [*EPCA s 142*];

— is not a registered dock worker or share fisherman [*EPCA ss 144, 145*];

— is not excluded by virtue of a designated dismissals procedure agreement or for reasons of national security [*EPCA s 65*];

— was not dismissed in connection with a strike, lock out or other industrial action taking place at the date of dismissal [*EPCA s 62*];

— was not employed under an illegal contract of employment (*see*, for example, *Coral Leisure Group Ltd v Barnett [1981] IRLR 204* and *Newland v Simmons and Willer (Hairdressers) Ltd [1981] IRLR 359*).

1.7   Before Commencing a Claim

The employer's reasons

1.7   Before you can appraise the grounds of your claim you must know the employer's reasons for your dismissal, or for not allowing you time off to participate in union activities, or for committing an apparent act of discrimination etc. This information may be found in a variety of sources such as a letter of dismissal. However, employers do not always provide information voluntarily or adequately. There are various statutory aids to help.

Written reasons

1.8   Section 53 of EPCA gives an ex-employee with six months' continuous service the right to ask his employer to set out *the reasons for dismissal in a written statement*. Although the request for written reasons does not itself have to be in writing, in order to activate the provisions of the statute the employee must make a clear request for the reasons for dismissal to be put in writing. (*Hanlon v Honda (UK) Ltd EAT 384/78*). Therefore, it is advisable to make the request in writing in a letter such as that shown in figure 1 on page 7. Where notice of dismissal is given, the employee can make the request any time from the date of the notice, even though he is still employed. [*EPCA s 53(1)(a)*].

The employer must provide the written reasons within 14 days of receiving the request and it is not enough merely to refer back to another document such as a letter of dismissal. The statement must be in such a form that anybody reading it would know why the dismissal had been made. (*Horsley Smith & Sherry Ltd v Dutton [1977] IRLR 172; Gilham v Kent County Council [1983] IRLR 353*). If the request is unreasonably refused or the reasons given are inadequate or untrue, then you may have another claim (see claim 13(a) in Appendix A) and could be awarded two weeks' gross pay by an IT. Where an employer replies outside the 14 day period, this does not automatically amount to an 'unreasonable refusal' particularly where there is only minimal delay. (*Charles Lang & Sons Ltd v Aubrey [1977] IRLR 354*, and see *Lowson v Percy Main & District Social Club & Institute [1979] IRLR 227*). The reply is admissible in evidence before an IT. [*EPCA s 53(3)*].

Questionnaire procedure

1.9   Under the SDA (Section 74) and RRA (Section 65) there are provisions to assist a person who considers that he or she may have been discriminated against in order to decide whether to start proceedings. (These are set out in the Sex Discrimination (Questions and Replies) Order 1975 (SI 1975 No 2048) and the Race Relations (Questions and Replies) Order 1977 (SI 1977 No 842) respectively.) These provisions take the form of a questionnaire which is sent by the aggrieved person to his or her employer or ex-employer. Figure 2 on pages 8–11 is an example of an abridged version of a race questionnaire which can be obtained from the Commission for Racial Equality (CRE), Elliot House, 10–12 Allington Street, London SW1E 5EH. Similar forms

24 Westmount Road
London NW11 9DX

22 January 1984

Dear Ms Hawkins,

Further to my dismissal on 13 January 1984 please send me particulars of the reasons for the dismissal.

I would refer you to Section 53 Employment Protection (Consolidation) Act 1978, under which you are required to provide me with written particulars of the reasons for my dismissal within 14 days of receiving this request.

Yours sincerely,

John Rider

TO: Ms J Hawkins
      Personnel Manager
      Mason (UK) Limited
      Units 10-14
      Humber Trading Estate
      Edgware Middlesex MS2 8SL

Figure 1
Letter requesting written reasons for dismissal

7

THE RACE RELATIONS ACT 1976 SECTION 65(I)(a)

QUESTIONNAIRE OF PERSON AGGRIEVED (THE COMPLAINANT)

Name of person to be questioned (the respondent)

Address

To THE COMPANY SECRETARY

of SALLWAY TUBE INDUSTRIES LTD

33-43 SMITH ST, COVENTRY, WEST MIDLANDS

Name of complainant

Address

1. I RANJIT SINGH

of 64 KENTON ROAD

WARLEY WEST MIDLANDS

consider that you may have discriminated against me contrary to the Race Relations Act 1976.

Give date, approximate time, place and factual description of the treatment received and of the circumstances leading up to the treatment (see paragraph 9 of the guidance)

2. On 1ST NOVEMBER 1983 I APPLIED FOR A VACANCY AS WELDER HAVING BEEN INTRODUCED BY THE JOB CENTRE. I WAS SEEN BY A MAN WHO IDENTIFIED HIMSELF AS MR SMITH AND HE TOLD ME THE VACANCY HAD BEEN FILLED THAT MORNING. MY APPOINTMENT WAS MADE WITHOUT MY NAME BEING GIVEN (I WAS REFERRED TO BY THE JOB CENTRE AS 'AN APPLICANT') AND IT WAS FOR 0930. A WHITE FRIEND ALSO A WELDER APPLIED THE SAME DAY WITHOUT INTRODUCTION FROM THE JOB CENTRE. HE WAS INTERVIEWED BY MR JONES AFTER LUNCH ON THAT DAY AND WAS OFFERED THE VACANCY TO COMMENCE WORK ON MONDAY 18TH NOVEMBER.

Complete if you wish to give reasons, otherwise delete the word "because" (see paragraphs 10 and 11 of the guidance)

3. I consider that this treatment may have been unlawful because

RR 65(a)

Reproduced by permission of HMSO

Figure 2: Race questionnaire (RR 65)

This is the first of your questions to the respondent. You are advised not to alter it

4. Do you agree that the statement in paragraph 2 is an accurate description of what happened? If not in what respect do you disagree or what is your version of what happened?

This is the second of your questions to the respondent. You are advised not to alter it

5. Do you accept that your treatment of me was unlawful discrimination by you against me? If not
    a   why not?
    b   for what reason did I receive the treatment accorded to me, and
    c   how far did considerations of colour, race, nationality (including citizenship) or ethnic or national origins affect your treatment of me?

Enter here any other questions you wish to ask (see paragraphs 12–14 of the guidance)

6. 1 WILL YOU PLEASE SUPPLY DETAILS OF ALL WELDER VACANCIES FOR OCTOBER AND NOVEMBER 1983?

6.2 WILL YOU PLEASE SUPPLY COMPLETE JOB DESCRIPTION?

6.3 WILL YOU PLEASE PROVIDE DETAILS OF ALL CANDIDATES INTERVIEWED OR OTHERWISE CONSIDERED FOR THE VACANCIES, BY RACE OR COLOUR, AGE, QUALIFICATIONS, PREVIOUS EXPERIENCE, DATE OF APPLICATION, DATE AND TIME OF INTERVIEW, BY WHOM REFERRED, WHETHER OR NOT ENGAGED, DATE ENGAGED AND DATE OF COMMENCEMENT OF EMPLOYMENT.

6.4 WILL YOU PLEASE STATE WHETHER OR NOT THE VACANCIES WERE ADVERTISED IF SO WHEN AND IN WHAT FORM?

6.5 PLEASE STATE DATE JOB PLACED AND CANCELLED AT JOB CENTRE

6.6 WILL YOU PLEASE IDENTIFY MR JONES' POSITION WITHIN YOUR COMPANY AND DETAIL THE RECRUITMENT PROCEDURE NORMALLY APPLIED?

6.7 WILL YOU PLEASE GIVE DETAILS OF YOUR WELDER WORK-FORCE BY RACE OR COLOUR AND LENGTH OF SERVICE

*Delete as appropriate
If you delete the first alternative, insert the address to which you want the reply to be sent

7. My address for any reply you may wish to give to the questions raised above is *~~that set out in paragraph 1 above~~/the following address

COMMISSION FOR RACIAL EQUALITY
DAIMLER HOUSE
33 PARADISE CIRCUS
QUEENSWAY
BIRMINGHAM B1 2BJ

Ranjit Singh.

See paragraph 15 of the guidance

Signature of complainant ....

Date 21ST DECEMBER 1983

NB   *By virtue of section 65 of the Act, this questionnaire and any reply are (subject to the provisions of the section) admissible in proceedings under the Act and a court or tribunal may draw any such inference as is just and equitable from a failure without reasonable excuse to reply within a reasonable period, or from an evasive or equivocal reply, including an inference that the person questioned has discriminated unlawfully.*

Reproduced by permission of HMSO

Figure 2 (continued)

THE RACE RELATIONS ACT 1976 SECTION 65(I)(b)

REPLY BY RESPONDENT

Name of complainant	To ....
Address	of ....
	....
Name of respondent	1. I ....
Address	of ....
	....
Complete as appropriate	hereby acknowledge receipt of the questionnaire signed by you and dated ....
	which was served on me on (date) ....
*Delete as appropriate	2. I *agree/disagree that the statement in paragraph 2 of the questionnaire is an accurate description of what happened.
If you agree that the statement in paragraph 2 of the questionnaire is accurate, delete this sentence. If you disagree complete this sentence (see paragraphs 21 and 22 of the guidance)	I disagree with the statement in paragraph 2 of the questionnaire in that
*Delete as appropriate	3. I *accept/dispute that my treatment of you was unlawful discrimination by me against you.
If you accept the complainant's assertion of unlawful discrimination in paragraph 3 of the questionnaire delete the sentences at a, b and c. Unless completed a sentence should be deleted (see paragraphs 23 and 24 of the guidance)	a My reasons for so disputing are

RR 65(b)

Reproduced by permission of HMSO

Figure 2 (continued)

b   The reason why you received the treatment accorded to you is

c   Consideration of colour, race, nationality (including citizenship) or ethnic or national origins affected my treatment of you to the following extent:—

Replies to questions in paragraph 6 of the questionnaire should be entered here

4.

Delete the whole of this sentence if you have answered all the questions in the questionnaire. If you have not answered all the questions, delete "unable" or "unwilling" as appropriate and give your reasons for not answering.

5.   I have deleted (in whole or in part) the paragraph(s) numbered .... above, since I am **unable/unwilling** to reply to the relevant questions of the questionnaire for the following reasons:—

See paragraph 25 of the guidance

Signature of respondent ....

Date ....

Reproduced by permission of HMSO

Figure 2 (continued)

relating to sex discrimination can be obtained from the Equal Opportunities Commission (EOC), Overseas House, Quay Street, Manchester M3 3HM or Caerways House, Windsor Place, Cardiff CF1 1LB. Although an exchange of letters would suffice, it is best to use the prescribed form for this purpose.

The idea of the questionnaire is to provide an exchange of questions and answers which focus attention on what would have to be shown in order to prove unlawful discrimination; but the main purpose is to establish as far as possible both the facts of the complaint and, in particular, the reasons why the employer took the action complained of. The questions and replies are admissible in tribunal proceedings.

There is no obligation upon an employer to answer a questionnaire, but the tribunal may draw an inference from a failure to reply, or from an equivocal or evasive reply, that the employer discriminated, and tribunals have been prepared to do this. In *Virdee v EEC Quarries Ltd [1978] IRLR 295*, the EAT upheld a decision by an IT that the employer's failure to answer all but one of nine questions put to them by Mr Virdee under Section 65 was an 'evasive reply'. The company were aware of Section 65 before replying and the tribunal concluded the evasion must have been deliberate. It was therefore just and equitable to draw an inference that the company had unlawfully discriminated against Mr Virdee in the arrangements they had made for determining who would be offered posts with the company.

It is always advisable for the employee to write to the employer who has failed to reply to a questionnaire, drawing his attention to the inference which a tribunal might draw. The employer should be informed that, if the matter proceeded to a hearing, the tribunal's attention would be drawn to the failure to reply and to the correspondence, and that the tribunal would be asked to draw the inference that this was deliberate, and that the employer discriminated unlawfully against the complainant. The purpose of such a letter is to make clear to the tribunal that the full consequences of failing to reply to the questionnaire were drawn to the employer's attention, so that he cannot later claim that he did not know or understand the consequences of failing to reply.

Whether or not such an inference will be made will of course depend on the relevance of the questions. Only information requested which is relevant and necessary for the fair disposal of a case or the savings of costs will qualify. What is meant by 'relevant' and 'necessary' is up to the tribunal to decide and is discussed in Chapter 13.

Although the questions procedure is generally invoked before a complaint is presented to an IT, it may still be used up to 21 days after a claim has been made.

Conciliation officer

1.10   A conciliation officer can be involved with an employment problem at the request of either the employer or the employee or on his own initiative from the time the employee has been given notice and before he has left employment or filed a complaint for unfair dismissal. [*EPCA s 134(3)*]. Even though he may not be able to resolve the problem both parties are likely to learn more about the reasons for the act complained of. The conciliation officer's functions are more clearly explained in Chapter 20, and a list of ACAS addresses can be found in Appendix D.

Unemployment questionnaire

1.11   A dismissed ex-employee may have applied for unemployment benefit and been refused. It is likely that a person considering an IT claim will also wish to appeal against a decision disqualifying him from unemployment benefit because of alleged misconduct or voluntary leaving. Such an appeal will result in the employer receiving a questionnaire from the Department of Employment (DE) (form UB 86). The questions asked include:

— Did you discharge the claimant; if so on what date?

— If so, was he discharged because of unsatisfactory conduct of any kind?

— If so, please give full details of the incident(s) which led to his discharge.

A copy of the replies to these questions is then sent to the former employee, possibly giving him another insight into the reasons for the employer's action.

Identify the law

1.12   It is necessary to identify the law in order to establish what matters have to be proved. The majority of actions are relatively straightforward and the layperson will have very little difficulty identifying the relevant law from the comprehensive set of guides on many aspects of employment law available from the Department of Employment (DE), Health and Safety Executive, ACAS, EOC and CRE (*see* Chapter 12). However, there are four sources of free (or nearly free) legal advice available to potential claimants.

(*a*) Most trade unions have specialists who regularly take legal information journals and bulletins. If you are a member, approach your union and seek its advice and help.

(*b*) Legal aid is not available for legal representation before an IT. However, under the Legal Aid Act 1974, a person whose income and capital are within certain prescribed limits can obtain (at present) up to £50 worth of *legal advice* from a solicitor on what is called 'the Green form' in England and Wales or 'the Pink form' in Scotland, for little or no cost. Under this scheme a solicitor can also do most of the *preparatory work* up to the tribunal hearing, and in a difficult case the £50 limit can be extended so that, for example, the solicitor can get a barrister's opinion on a complex issue. If you do not qualify for the legal advice scheme you can ask the solicitor for a fixed fee interview. Some solicitors will give you half an hour's advice for approximately £5. (The Legal Aid Act which came into force on 6 April 1979, gave power to the Lord Chancellor to extend the Green or Pink form to cover legal costs in presentations before ITs. Although The Royal Commission on Legal Services recommended in 1979 that legal aid be extended to ITs in certain circumstances this has not yet happened.)

A list of solicitors providing such advice may be obtained from a local Citizen's Advice Bureau (CAB) (and *see* 'Where to find names of solicitors' in Appendix D, on page 285).

(*c*)   The CRE [*RRA s 66*] and the EOC [*SDA s 75*] have certain powers to assist individual complainants where this is justified by special considerations, such as:

— where the case raises a question of principle;

— where it is unreasonable, having regard to the complexity of the case, to expect the individual to deal with the case unaided.

It is necessary to write to the appropriate Commission at the addresses given in Appendix D asking for assistance. The Commission is required within two months to consider the request, decide whether to grant it and inform the complainant. Even if the Commission does not give formal assistance it will normally be prepared to give informal advice.

(*d*)   There are several voluntary organisations who can provide legal advice. These include local CABs and neighbourhood law centres.

Evidence to support your case

1.13   Once it has been established that you are qualified, that you know the employer's reasons for his action and what you have to prove, you must then establish what evidence is available to support your case. This will involve interviewing and taking statements from potential witnesses (*see* Chapter 15) and examining documents (*see* Chapter 13). This must be done sufficiently thoroughly to make your preliminary analysis meaningful. However, at this stage it does not mean that witness statements have to be typed or bundles of documents prepared. That will only be necessary if the claim proceeds. What is important is to establish that there is evidence to support what you have to prove, although it will only be possible to assess the strengths and weaknesses of the evidence once the claim has been commenced.

The decision as to whether to bring the claim

1.14   When the recommended investigation has been completed you will know the nature of the claim, e.g. is it an unfair dismissal or a redundancy claim. It is then possible to make an assessment of:

— the grounds of the claim;

— the strengths and weaknesses of your case;

— the likelihood of the claim succeeding.

This preliminary appraisal will help you take a rational and objective decision as to whether to bring a claim. A vexatious, frivolous or otherwise unreasonable case should get nowhere, and may be penalised by an award of costs under Rule 11 (1)(*a*) (*see* Chapter 40). You must be careful that the recommended investigation does not risk a potential claim being out of time (*see* Chapter 4). If there is a danger of the claim not being in time, make it anyway and continue the investigation with all practicable speed. The claim can always be withdrawn at a later stage but if there is unreasonable delay this could be penalised. (*TVR v Johnson* [*1978*] *IRLR 555*).

Keep your objectives in mind

1.15   It is important to keep your objectives in mind throughout the preparation of the case, as this will tend to determine how the case is prepared. It is advisable to write these down lest you forget what your priorities are in bringing the claim.

Chapter 2

Commencing a Claim

Written application to an industrial tribunal

2.1   IT procedure is commenced ('originated') by complying with Rule 1(1) of the Regulations. This is achieved by making a written application to an IT, usually on a specially prepared form known as an 'IT 1' (*see* figure 3 on pages 18–19). This form, which is revised from time to time, can be obtained from any local Employment Office, Jobcentre or Unemployment Benefit Office. It is not strictly necessary to use the IT 1 form provided the requirements of Rule 1(1) are complied with. (*Burns International Security Services Ltd v Butt [1983] IRLR 438*, and for redundancy cases, see *Price v Smithfield Group [1978] IRLR 80*). A letter incorporating the details specified in the rule (i.e. the claimant's and his opponent's name and address, and particulars of the grounds of the application) will be a sufficient originating application. However, for the purposes of this book it will be assumed that an IT 1 is used.

Receipt starts the claim

2.2   A claim will be started as soon as the completed IT 1 is received by the Secretary of the tribunals at the:

— Central Office of the Industrial Tribunals (England and Wales), 93 Ebury Bridge Road, London SW1W 8RE.
   Tel: 01-730 9161; or the

— Central Office of the Industrial Tribunals (Scotland), Saint Andrew House, 141 West Nile Street, Glasgow G1 2RU.
   Tel: 041-331 1601.

Chapter 3

Completing the Originating Application (IT 1)

Introduction

3.1   Some of the paragraphs of the IT 1 require amplification. This is best achieved by taking the reader through the various paragraphs of figure 3 on pages 18 and 19.

Paragraph 1: Question(s) for the tribunal to decide

3.2   In this paragraph the nature of the claim is stated. There may be more than one claim and therefore several questions for the tribunal to decide upon. Even if the right questions are not referred to, the IT has discretion to amend this paragraph on its own initiative and to incorporate the right questions to be decided upon even as late as the hearing. (*Sherringham Development Co Ltd v Browne [1977] ICR 20*). If you are unsure as to the correct questions you should include everything that can possibly be relevant and always keep the questions simple. The following are examples of the words which can be used:

redundancy payment: whether I have a right to a redundancy payment or the amount of the redundancy payment to which I am entitled.

sex or race discrimination: whether the respondent has committed an act of discrimination against me which is unlawful.

time off work: whether my employer has failed to permit me to perform the duties of my office as a JP.

equal pay (by employer): to make an order declaring rights in relation to the effect of an equality clause on the pay of Z, who is an employee of ours.

maternity pay: whether my employer has failed to pay maternity pay to which I am entitled.

Remember that the tribunal has power to amend this paragraph of your application and it is not essential to get it correct at this stage.

Paragraph 2: Identity of the applicant

3.3   The person or organisation making the application now becomes known as the 'applicant'. Although usually an employee or former

ORIGINATING APPLICATION TO AN INDUSTRIAL TRIBUNAL

IMPORTANT: DO NOT FILL IN THIS FORM UNTIL YOU
HAVE READ THE NOTES FOR GUIDANCE.
THEN COMPLETE ITEMS 1, 2, 4 AND 12
AND ALL OTHER ITEMS RELEVANT TO YOUR CASE,
AND SEND THE FORM TO THE FOLLOWING ADDRESS

For Official Use Only	
Case Number	

To: THE SECRETARY OF THE TRIBUNALS
CENTRAL OFFICE OF THE INDUSTRIAL TRIBUNALS (ENGLAND AND WALES)
93 EBURY BRIDGE ROAD, LONDON SW1W 8RE   Telephone: 01 730 9161

1 I hereby apply for a decision of a Tribunal on the following question. (STATE HERE THE QUESTION TO BE DECIDED BY A TRIBUNAL. EXPLAIN THE GROUNDS OVERLEAF. *Whether I was unfairly dismissed and whether my employer unreasonably refused to provide reasons for my dismissal.*

2 My name is (Mr/~~Mrs/Miss~~ Surname in block capitals first):—
RIDER   JOHN
My address is *34 WESTMOUNT ROAD*
LONDON NW11 9 DX
.... Telephone No. *01 822 4321*
My date of birth is *19.8.47*

3 If a representative has agreed to act for you in this case please give his or her name and address below and note that further communications will be sent to your representative and not to you *(See Note 4)*

Name of Representative:— *FRANK HITCHCOCK (DISTRICT SECRETARY)*
Address:— *WAREHOUSEMEN'S TRADE UNION (W.T.U.) 128 FURLONG ROAD LONDON EC1 2JA* Telephone No. *01 222 8361*

4 (a) Name of respondent(s) (in block capitals) ie the employer, person or body against whom a decision is sought *(See Note 3)*
MASON (UK) LIMITED
Address(es) *UNITS 10-14, HUMBER TRADING ESTATE, EDGWARE MIDDLESEX MS2 8SL* Telephone No. *01 987 5638*

5 Place of employment to which this application relates, or place where act complained about took place.
AS IN 4

6 My occupation or position held/applied for, or other relationship to the respondent named above (eg user of a service supplied in relation to employment).
WAREHOUSE SUPERVISOR

7 My employment began on *SEPTEMBER 1970* and *(if appropriate)* ended on *13.1.84*

8 (a) Basic wages/salary *£155 p.w*
    (b) Average take home pay *£119 p.w.*

9 Other remuneration or benefits *PENSION*

10 Normal basic weekly hours of work *37½*

11 (In an application under the Sex Discrimination Act or the Race Relations Act)
Date on which action complained of took place or first came to my knowledge ....

Please continue overleaf

IT I (Revised September 1981)

Reproduced by permission of HMSO

Figure 3: Originating application (IT 1)

12   You are required to set out the grounds for your application below, giving full particulars of them.

I have been with Masons for 14 years and after 7 years became supervisor of the Warehouse. Warehouse Managers came and went and it was always left to me to show them the job. Brian Rogers only started last June and thought he knew everything about the job. I tried to explain how we did things but he insisted on his way. About the beginning of October he told me to use a forklift truck to move some containers through a restricted area. This was against the law so I refused. After that he made my life impossible and used every excuse to get the personnel department involved. It was obvious he wanted me out and after I returned from the Christmas break I was sacked with three months money.

I consider I have been unfairly treated.

I asked for written reasons for my dismissal but these have not been given.

13   If you wish to state what in your opinion was the reason for your dismissal, please do so here.

14   If the Tribunal decides that you were unfairly dismissed, what remedy would you prefer? (Before answering this question please consult the leaflet "Unfairly dismissed?" for the remedies available and then write one of the following in answer to this question: reinstatement, re-engagement or compensation)

Reinstatement and compensation

Signature ...John Rider...   Date ...2.2.84...

FOR OFFICIAL USE ONLY	Received at COIT	Code	ROIT	Inits

Reproduced by permission of HMSO

Figure 3 (continued)

employee, the applicant may be an employer where for example the Secretary of State has failed to pay him the correct redundancy rebate [*EPCA s 101*], or a TU where there has been no notification or consultation relating to impending redundancies. [*EPA s 101*].

The date of birth is required for several purposes including:

— the establishment that the applicant is under the upper age limit;

— the calculation of a redundancy payment;

— the calculation of a basic award (*see* Chapter 39).

Paragraph 3: Applicant's representative

3.4   Applicants are entitled to bring their own claims without formal representation. However, if an applicant is represented, for example by his TU or a solicitor or a local CAB, the name, address and telephone number of the representative should be stated. This is because all communications with the IT will be through the representative. If you are advised on an informal basis but intend taking the case personally to the tribunal, leave the paragraph blank so that all correspondence is conducted with you direct.

Paragraph 4(a): Identity of the respondent

3.5   The applicant's opponent in a case is referred to by the tribunal as the 'respondent'. In the vast majority of actions the respondent will be an employer, but his exact identity may not be straightforward. For those with written statements of their terms of employment or computerised pay slips there may be little difficulty. However, many employers have trade names or sub-contract their workforce to others, and this could result in identification difficulties. A perusal of the yellow pages of the telephone directory or contacting a local chamber of commerce or searching the Companies Registry may provide the answer. This research may also prove useful in finding out the size and other details of the organisation if, for example, questions of alternative employment should arise. Even if an error is made the tribunal has extensive powers to put the matter right under Rule 14.

Why does the IT want to know the telephone number of the applicant, the respondent and their representatives? There are two basic reasons. The first is obvious; the tribunal finds this is the easiest and quickest way to contact the parties. Secondly, in most tribunal cases a conciliation officer is involved and he will usually contact the parties by telephone. More will be said of the conciliation officer's functions in Chapter 20.

Paragraph 4(b): Respondent's relationship to the applicant

3.6   The respondent's relationship to the applicant is usually straightforward. But in some cases there will be a very distant relationship, e.g. the Secretary of State for Employment or the EOC or CRE.

Paragraph 5: Place of work

3.7   The place of work could be important where there is a dismissal because of a refusal to transfer. Note that even a homeworker can bring a claim provided there is an employment relationship governed by a contract of employment. (*Nethermere v Gardiner [1983] IRLR 103*).

Paragraph 6: Applicant's position

3.8   In most cases the applicant will be an employee or ex-employee, and it should not be difficult to know or find the correct job title, espccially as this should be contained in the written statement of terms and conditions of employment. [*EPCA s 1*]. However, if in doubt insert 'employee'. If the applicant is a recognised TU the name of the union should be stated. In some cases there will be no relationship to the respondent e.g. the Health and Safety Inspector.

The job title can be important, particularly where the claim arises from the alleged failure of the employee to obey a lawful order.

Paragraph 7: Period of employment

3.9   In most IT actions it is necessary to show a continuous service qualification as shown in column 5 of Appendix A. Therefore, it is important to determine accurately when employment began and ended. The commencement date may be known from memory or contained in the written statement. However, the date employment ends can cause difficulty. It is necessary to define the 'effective date of termination' (EDT) to know what to insert for unfair dismissal cases, and the 'relevant date' for redundancy cases (see Chapter 4).

The EDT will be one of the following:

(*a*)   Where the contract of employment *is terminated by notice* (whether given by the employer or employee) it is the date on which the notice expires. [*EPCA s 55(4)(a)*]. For example, if an employee was given two weeks' notice on Wednesday 25 January 1984, employment ended on Tuesday 7 February 1984.

(*b*)   Where an employee gives *counter notice* and resigns while under notice from the employer, it is the date he leaves. For example, an employee is given four weeks' notice on 25 January 1984 to expire on 21 February, but he does not wish to remain that long so he serves counter notice on 27 January that he will leave on 3 February and does so, then employment will end on that day. (*Note: EPCA s 55(5)* which for certain purposes extends the EDT to the date on which the minimum statutory notice would have expired.)

(*c*)   Where *pay in lieu of notice* is given, it is the date of that notice (*Dixon v Stenor Ltd [1973] IRLR 28*), provided it is made clear employment is to end on that date (*Dedman v British Building and Engineering Appliances* [*1973*] *IRLR 379*). For example, if an employee was given two weeks' notice on 25 January 1984, and told he would not be required to work any more but would be paid wages in lieu of notice, employment will end on 25 January.

(*d*)   Where the contract is terminated *without notice* by the employer, it will be the date on which the termination takes effect. [*EPCA s 55(4)(b)*]. For example, if an employee was summarily dismissed on 25 January 1984, employment will end on that day.

(*e*)   Where an employee *resigns*, as say in a constructive dismissal case, it is the date he leaves whether or not he gives notice.

(*f*)   Where an employee is employed under a *fixed term* contract (cf a specific job contract which is discharged by performance — *Wiltshire County Council v National Association of Teachers in Further & Higher Education* [*1980*] *IRLR 198*), it is the date when the term expires and the contract is not renewed. [*EPCA s 55(4)(c)*].

(*g*)   Where a woman exercises her right to *return to work following maternity leave* and the employer refuses to take her back, it will be the notified date of return. [*EPCA s 56*].

If the dismissal is by letter the EDT will not be when the letter is sent but when it is received by the employee or when he might reasonably have expected to receive it. (*Brown v Southall & Knight* [*1980*] *IRLR 130*).

These definitions establish the date when employment would end for the purposes of setting down a 'base' date from which the specified period in column 6 of Appendix A can be calculated where a dismissal is involved. For example, Appendix A indicates that an unfair dismissal claim must be brought within three calendar months of the 'base' date. In practice the 'base' date is likely to be the last day on which the employee worked. If it is not possible to fit the termination date into any of the above categories then insert the date of the last day worked.

Note that complications can arise, however, because the EDT for the purposes of calculating the continuous service qualification (in column 5 of the Tribunal Table in Appendix A) in unfair dismissal and redundancy claims, is extended from this base date. So where neither the employee [*EPCA s 55(6)*] nor the employer gives the statutory minimum notice required under EPCA s 49, then the EDT will be when the statutory notice would have expired if it had been given. [*EPCA s 55(5)*]. For example, if notice in lieu is given on 18 January 1984, and the employee has been continuously employed for 18 months, his employment terminates on 24 January (as he is statutorily entitled to one week's notice).

Many employers have disciplinary procedures entitling a dismissed employee to *appeal* against the decision internally and this could affect the EDT. If the dismissed employee is treated as suspended without pay pending the determination of the internal appeal, the dismissal still takes effect from the original date of dismissal (assuming the internal appeal fails) although the provisions of the appeal procedure are still in operation. (*Savage v J Sainsbury Ltd* [*1980*] *IRLR 109*). On the other hand where the employee is suspended with pay pending an appeal the effective date of termination may not be until the appeal is resolved. (*Duffy v Northampton Area Health Authority, EAT 650/78;* but see *The Board of Governors, The National Heart and Chest Hospitals v Nambiar* [*1981*] *IRLR 196*).

This means that a dismissed employee cannot afford to await the outcome of an internal appeal before bringing an IT claim; delay may cause it to be out of time (see Chapter 4).

Paragraph 8: Gross and take-home pay

3.10   The basic wage or salary refers to gross pay in a particular period, say per week, month or year. Where the amount varies because piece work is involved for example, the average gross pay over something like a 12 week period should suffice to establish a week's basic pay. In many lower paid industries wages are controlled by statutory joint industrial councils or wage councils. If the actual gross pay is less than the statutory entitlement the latter should be the figure inserted. The local Wages Inspectorate will provide details of statutory entitlements. Average take-home pay is basic pay after deducting income tax, national insurance contributions, etc. However, where trade union dues, club membership contributions etc. are also deducted these should be added back, and therefore paragraph 8(a) of IT 1 is somewhat misleading.

Paragraph 9: Other remuneration or benefit

3.11   Basic wages are usually the principal payment under the contract of employment, which will be either a piece or time rate. Any other pay or remuneration entitlement of a permanent or regular nature is relevant to this paragraph including:

— overtime;

— incentive payments (e.g. commissions and bonuses for increased productivity);

— fringe benefits (e.g. luncheon vouchers, company cars, subsidised meals, free accommodation etc.);

— pension schemes.

Paragraph 10: Normal hours of work

3.12   This paragraph can be misleading: the information required is the normal hours actually worked each week or those which may be required to be worked each week (whichever is the greater). For example, in *Merseyside County Council v Bullock [1978] ICR 419* (but see *Nottingham Area Health Authority v Gray, EAT 163/81*), a part-time fireman was on call for $102\frac{1}{2}$ hours per week, though on average he was only on duty for $10\frac{1}{2}$ hours a week. He was regarded as being employed under a contract to be available to work for $102\frac{1}{2}$ hours per week so this was the figure to be inserted in this paragraph. However, hours of voluntary work are not included. (*Lake v Essex County Council [1979] IRLR 241*).

Where an employee works different hours every other week, then both sets of hours should be inserted. For example, where a person works $20\frac{1}{4}$ hours one week and $13\frac{1}{2}$ hours the next, turn and turn about, then both sets of hours should be referred to. In this example it will mean the applicant is not qualified to bring a claim which requires regular working of at least 16 hours a week. (*Opie v John Gubbins (Insurance Brokers) Ltd [1978] IRLR 540;* but see *Secretary of State for Employment v (1) Deary (2) Cambridgeshire County Council, EAT 186/83, IRLIB 251.10*). Compulsory overtime, however, should always be included. [*EPCA Sch 14 Part I*].

Paragraph 11: Date of discrimination

3.13   This paragraph relates to unfair discrimination cases. Either put down the date of the incident which occurred, or if it was going on for some time, when it was first realised that discrimination was taking place.

Paragraph 12: Grounds for application

3.14   This paragraph is the most important and most difficult to complete. It is not sufficient to simply write 'I have been unfairly dismissed'. If you are unaware of the reasons for your dismissal, because, say, the employer has not complied with a Section 53 request for written reasons, the paragraph should be completed along the following lines:

> I have not yet been given any reasons for my dismissal despite making a *EPCA s 53* request and, therefore, would like to reserve the particulars of my grounds for this application until after receiving this information. In the meantime, I maintain I have been unfairly dismissed.

If the reasons are known, sufficient particulars of the grounds must be given as illustrated in the unfair dismissal case in the example in figure 3, hence the need to carry out the pre-commencement investigation referred to in Chapter 1. Other examples of how this paragraph can be completed are set out below.

Constructive unfair dismissal: On 15 February I gave my employer two weeks' notice in writing terminating my contract of employment with effect from 28 February. I did so by reason of the following conduct of my employers which entitled me to terminate my contract. It was a term of my contract that I was entitled to receive a cost-of-living increase on 1 January 1984. My employer has refused to pay the increase, etc.

Indirect discrimination on grounds of sex: I am a married woman aged 33. On 26 March 1984 I applied for employment with the respondents as a trainee personnel officer. I was informed by Garry Stokes, on behalf of the company, that I was not eligible for employment because of a requirement that applicants should be at least 18 and under 30 years of age. I was unable to comply with this requirement which was to my detriment. The proportion of women who can comply with this requirement is considerably less than the proportion of men who can comply with it. Accordingly I claim:

(i) a declaration that I was entitled to be considered for the job of trainee personnel officer

(ii) a recommendation that the company withdraw the requirement

(iii) compensation.

Paragraph 13: Applicant anticipating the respondent's reason

3.15 This paragraph is only relevant to applications involving a dismissal. The onus of proof is still on the employer to show the reason for the dismissal [*EPCA s 57(1)*] , so it is somewhat unfair to ask an applicant something which it was the employer's obligation to show. This paragraph is therefore best left blank, except perhaps where the burden of proof is clearly on the applicant as it is in constructive dismissal, discrimination and unfair selection for redundancy cases.

Paragraph 14: Remedy

3.16 To some extent the reason for bringing the action discussed in Chapter 1 will help decide which remedy is sought.

This paragraph, which only applies to unfair dismissals, can also be misleading, since it gives the impression that once completed, the applicant is stuck with that remedy. This is not correct. By choosing one sort of remedy rather than another you are not excluding the right of the tribunal to make any order which it has power to make. For details of remedies, see Chapter 39.

Summary

3.17 Some of the paragraphs will only be relevant to some claims. Therefore irrelevant paragraphs should be left blank. Despite many years of experience and several revisions of the form, COIT has still not produced a wholly satisfactory originating application. Perhaps the adoption of several specially designed forms for different categories of action would be better.

Chapter 4

Claiming in Time

Introduction

4.1 Once the IT 1 has been completed and the applicant (or his representative) has signed his name where indicated at the bottom of the second side of the form it should be sent by ordinary post (preferably with a certificate of posting) or delivered personally to the Secretary of the Tribunals at the appropriate address given in 2.2. A copy of the IT 1 should be retained. Both COITs have secretaries who are responsible for the *administration* side of their respective offices. Connected with each COIT are Regional Offices (ROIT) which are administered by assistant secretaries and their staff. A list of ROITs can be found in Appendix D. Secretaries and assistant secretaries have similar powers and functions (except as mentioned in Chapter 5).

The *judicial* side of each COIT is presided over by its President. Each ROIT also has a president who is known as a Regional Chairman.

Time of receipt of IT 1

4.2 The IT 1 should arrive at COIT not later than the end of the period indicated in column 6 of Appendix A. In an unfair dismissal case, for example, it must arrive within three calendar months of the effective date of termination (EDT, see 3.9). The three month period will run out at midnight on the day before the equivalent date three calendar months ahead. (*Post Office v Moore* [1981] ICR 623). So where employment is terminated on 29 June, the last day for presentation to COIT will be 28 September assuming that this is a working day. If 28 September is a Saturday, Sunday or a Bank Holiday, in other words a non-working day, the IT 1 must be presented no later than that day and the time limit cannot be treated as expiring on the next working day. (*Hetton Victory Club Ltd v Swainston* [1983] ICR 341).

It is possible for an IT 1 to be lodged before the EDT provided notice of termination has been given. [*EPCA s 67(4)*]. For example, where the applicant resigns and four weeks' notice of resignation is given on 3 January to expire on 2 February, he can lodge the application claiming constructive dismissal at any time between 3 January and 2 May. (*Presley v Llanelli Borough Council* [1979] IRLR 381).

Actual receipt of IT 1

4.3   The date of actual receipt of the IT 1 by COIT in unfair dismissal cases is relevant, not the date on which it is posted. (*Hammond v Haigh Castle & Co Ltd [1973] ICR 148*). In redundancy cases, by contrast, it is the date the claim is actually *sent* to COIT. It is sufficient in redundancy cases, therefore, to post the application in time. (*McCutcheon v Sykes Macfarlane Ltd (1967) 2 ITR 621*). Sometimes the application is mistakenly sent to the applicant's local ROIT who then have a practice of forwarding it to COIT. What happens if the application is received in time by ROIT but is out of time by the time it is received by COIT? As the assistant secretaries have power to accept applications under Rule 12(6) the claim will be good (*Bengley v North Devon District Council [1977] ICR 15*), but the practice is not recommended.

These time limits can be extended in certain circumstances. To illustrate when this can happen we shall look at the more frequent claims.

Most frequent claims

Unfair dismissal claims

4.4   These paragraphs consider unfair dismissal claims under EPCA s 67(2). Where the application is not submitted within three calendar months, it will be rejected by COIT unless it was 'not reasonably practicable' to present it in time. In *Dedman v British Building and Engineering Appliances [1973] IRLR 379*, the Court of Appeal (CA) said that if an employee does not know about the time limit and there is nothing to make him aware of it then it is not practicable to present the claim in time. In other words if the employee or his adviser is not at fault then the time limit can be extended by a tribunal. In *Wall's Meat Co Ltd v Khan [1978] IRLR 499*, the CA emphasised that what is not reasonably practicable is essentially something for a tribunal to determine. It involves no legal concept but a common-sense approach by a tribunal. This sort of empirical approach, which was recently confirmed by the CA in *Palmer & Saunders v Southend-on-Sea Borough Council [1984] IRLR 119*, can be seen from the following examples of out of time applications in 4.5 below.

Out of time applications accepted

4.5   In these cases it was found *not* reasonably practicable to present the application within three months:

(*a*)   Where an IT 1 is sent by first class recorded delivery post the day before the expiration of the three month period but arrives three days out of time at COIT. (*Burton v Field Sons & Co Ltd [1977] ICR 106*). However, in 1980 the EAT commented in *Beanstalk Shelving Ltd v Horn [1980] ICR 273*: 'it seems to us an extremely dangerous practice for applicants to industrial tribunals to leave the posting of their applications until the last day . . . it will be open to tribunals to hear evidence as to what is now the reasonable expectation as to delivery, even of first class mail, which is posted at a particular time and on a particular day'. (See also *Ali v Acre Produce Ltd EAT 588/82 IRLIB 234.13*).

(*b*)   Where an applicant presents a claim within three months to a Social Security Appeal Tribunal (formerly the National Insurance Local Appeal Tribunal), appealing against disqualification from unemployment benefit which he genuinely thought would also deal with his unfair dismissal claim. (*Wall's Meat Co Ltd v Khan* [*1978*] *IRLR 499*).

(*c*)   Where a former employee is suffering from depression and is on prescribed drugs and as a result is not in a fit state during the time limit to understand its significance. (*Tesco Stores Ltd v McKeown EAT 719/78*).

(*d*)   Where the employer expressly requests the employee and his TU representative not to pursue his claim until negotiations with a view to settlement have been completed. (*Owen v Crown House Engineering Ltd* [*1973*] *IRLR 233*).

(*e*)   Where the employee was told he was dismissed on redundancy grounds but several months later discovered that someone else was doing his job. (*Churchill v Yeates & Son Ltd* [*1983*] *IRLR 187*).

(*f*)   Where soon after dismissal the employee's father was taken ill and died, and he was preoccupied with family responsibilities and the problems of the funeral. (*Pesticcio v British Steel Corporation NIRC 2934/73*).

In the *Dedman* case in 4.4 above, the court considered that 'illness or absence or . . . some physical obstacle, or . . . some untoward and unexpected turn of events' were the sort of matters which would make it impracticable to comply with the time limit.

The main argument put forward by workers with out of time claims has been ignorance of the law or its details. As Lord Denning said in the *Dedman* case:

'If in the circumstances the man knew or was put on inquiry as to his rights and as to the time limit then it was "practicable" for him to have presented his complaint within the time limit and he ought to have done so but if he did not know and there was nothing to put him on inquiry then it was not practicable and he should be excused.'

You are 'put on inquiry' where you are in possession of literature about unfair dismissal or if you are aware that there is a time limit but do not find out how long it is.

Out of time applications not accepted

4.6   So where the employee is at fault and there is no good reason or excuse, as illustrated by the following examples, the claims will be out of time:

(i) Where the applicant employs a skilled adviser who makes a mistake, such as a solicitor (*Norgett v Luton Industrial Co-operative Society* [*1976*] *ICR 442*), TU official (*Syed v Ford Motor Co Ltd* [*1979*] *IRLR 335*), or a CAB worker (*Riley v Tesco Stores Ltd* [*1980*] *IRLR 103 CA*), but it would be a reasonable excuse where the adviser was not specifically asked for advice about unfair dismissal (*Associated Tunnelling Co Ltd v Wasilewski* [*1973*] *IRLR 346*) — unless the adviser should still have brought the matter to the applicant's attention (*Luckings v May & Baker Ltd* [*1974*] *IRLR 151*) or where advice was sought from a person or body which does not exist for that purpose, e.g. an employment exchange (*Ruff v Smith* [*1975*] *IRLR 275*).

(ii) Where the employee awaits the outcome of other court proceedings. (*Porter v Bandridge Ltd* [*1978*] *IRLR 271*).

(iii) Where the employee awaits the outcome of a domestic disciplinary or grievance hearing, unless the employer has actively encouraged the employee not to pursue his claim. (*Times Newspapers v O'Regan* [*1977*] *IRLR 101*).

(iv) Where the employee awaits the outcome of negotiations with a view to settlement, unless the employer actively encouraged the employee not to pursue his claim. (*Times Newspapers v O'Regan*).

'Further reasonable period'

4.7 Even where a tribunal is satisfied that it was not reasonably practicable to present a claim within the three month period, it is still necessary for the claim to be made within a 'further reasonable period'. Again the test is the same and will be based on the facts of each case. For example, in *Wall's Meat v Khan* the three month period expired on 22 November 1976. It was not until 9 December that Mr Khan found he had gone to the wrong tribunal and was advised to consult a solicitor. He started to look for one after going to a community centre and eventually saw a solicitor on 7 January 1977. On 7 January his solicitor sent off the claim. The tribunal found this further period of approximately 47 days reasonable.

From looking at past cases on this point it appears that as a rough guide two to three weeks after it became practicable to present the IT 1 will be considered a further reasonable time. But there are exceptions, like the *Khan* case.

Duty to check receipt in 'last moment' claims

4.8 *Note* that, where you have left the application to the last moment in an unfair dismissal case and do not receive an acknowledgement from COIT within a week or 10 days, then you have a duty to check that the application arrived safely, otherwise you risk the IT 1 being out of time. (*Harris v Associated Heat Services Ltd EAT 47/83 IRLIB 240.13*).

4.9   *Claiming in Time*

Redundancy payment claims

4.9   In redundancy payment cases under EPCA s 101 (*see* claim 14 in Appendix A), a claim can be made at any time provided one of the following events takes place within six months of the date of dismissal (the 'relevant date'). This may be extended where there is a 'trial' period. [*EPCA s 84*].

(*a*) The payment has been agreed and paid;

(*b*) A written notice claiming payment has been given to the employer (*Price v Smithfield Group Ltd [1978] IRLR 80*);

(*c*) A claim has already been made to an IT (whether about the right to the payment or unfair dismissal).

If none of these events has occurred within the six month period then the time limit can be extended by a further six months (i.e. 12 months from the relevant date where a tribunal considers it 'just and equitable . . . having regard to the reason shown by the employee for the delay) and to all other relevant circumstances'. Unfortunately, just to complicate matters, this is a different test to the 'reasonably practicable' test, but appears to be less restrictive and enables an IT to take into account anything which it judges to be relevant.

Sex and racial discrimination claims

4.10   Cases of sex and racial discrimination are dealt with under SDA s 76(5) and RRA s 68(6). In individual sex and race cases (*see* claims 7(*a*) and 8(*a*) in Appendix A) the time limits are three months from the date the act of discrimination took place or, where there are a number of discriminatory acts over a period, then three months from the date of the last act. Where a dismissal is involved then the three month period is from the date of dismissal not when notice was given. (*Lupetti v Wrens Old House Ltd [1984] ICR 348*). Again these time limits can be extended where 'in all the circumstances of the case . . . it is just and equitable to do so'. This test is similar to the redundancy test and may give the tribunal a wider discretion than in unfair dismissal cases (but see *Hutchinson v Westward Television [1977] IRLR 69*).

Chapter 5

Lodging the IT 1

Applicant 'qualified' to bring the claim

5.1   When the IT 1 is received by COIT the lodged application is 'vetted' to ensure that a tribunal has jurisdiction to deal with the claim; that is to say that the applicant is 'qualified' to bring proceedings. If the secretary is of the opinion that the claimant is not qualified he will return the application indicating why in his opinion the tribunal has no power to give relief (Rule 1(2)). An example is where the applicant is over the upper age limit. This does not mean that the claim cannot proceed. If the applicant replies in writing to the secretary to the effect he wishes to proceed, the secretary has no alternative but to register the application. He will automatically register applications he considers valid.

Action by COIT

5.2   Registered applications will be allotted a case number, which should be quoted in all future correspondence between the IT and the parties and between the parties themselves.

The secretary will then forward the IT 1 to the applicant's local ROIT (*see* Appendix D for a list of addresses). From then on the assistant secretaries have all the powers of the secretary except in relation to vetting (Rule 12(6)).

Figure 4 on page 32 represents the sort of letter which will be sent to the applicant at this stage. In Scotland, the ROIT will send a copy of the IT 1 back to the applicant. A surprisingly large number of applicants do not retain a copy of their own applications and this practice would be welcome in England and Wales. It should be noted that the applicant is informed that the services of a conciliation officer are available to him (*see* Chapter 20).

Where paragraph 12 of the IT 1 does not contain sufficient particulars, a letter may be sent to the applicant requesting more particulars of the claim. If the reply is still unsatisfactory the tribunal can either insist on a 'pre-hearing assessment' or dismiss, strike out or amend the IT 1 under Rule 4(4) or both. These powers are really further extensions of the tribunal's vetting powers, and both are considered in later chapters. The power to hold a pre-hearing assessment was introduced by the 1980 Regulations in order to help sift out meritless claims.

31

Regional Office of the Industrial Tribunals
19-29 Woburn Place
London
WC1H 0LU

Telephone: 01 632 4921

Mr F Hitchcock   Your Reference
District Secretary
W.T.U.   Case No 269/84
128 Furlong Road
London   Date: 4 February 1984
EC1 2JA

THE INDUSTRIAL TRIBUNALS (RULES OF PROCEDURE)
REGULATIONS 1980
NOTICE

1 The application for a decision of a tribunal under the above Regulations
has been received. It has been entered in the Register and allotted
the case number shown above. This number should be quoted in any
further communications which should be sent to the address at the
head of this notice.

2 A copy of the application has been sent to the respondent and a
copy of any reply will be sent to you.

3 A notice of hearing will be sent to you not less than 14 days before
the dated fixed for the hearing of the application.

4 In all cases where the Act under which the application is made
provides for conciliation the services of a conciliation officer are
available to the parties. In such cases a copy of the application
is sent to the Advisory Conciliation and Arbitration Service
accordingly.

Signed.. ....
for Assistant Secretary of the Tribunals

IT5

Reproduced by permission of HMSO

Figure 4: ROIT acknowledgement of IT 1 (IT 5)

Statistics on industrial tribunal applications

(Taken from the COIT Fact Sheet published in February 1984.)

5.3   The Table below shows that the number of applications registered in England and Wales have more than trebled between 1972 and 1976, as the number and scope of tribunal jurisdictions increased. Then the intake declined until 1981 when there was an increase of 10.5 per cent over the previous year, no doubt caused by the recession. However, the figure for 1982 is 2.4 per cent lower than that for 1981 and the figure for 1983 is 8.1 per cent lower than *that* for 1982.

Applications	1972	1976	1977	1978	1979	1980	1981	1982	1983
registered	13,555	43,066	41,995	38,601	36,476	36,250	40,042	39,073	35,890

In 1983 some 1,365 applications received by the Secretary were not registered in accordance with the procedure referred to above. The applications which were registered fell into the following categories and approximate percentages:

Unfair dismissal	72.9%
Redundancy payments	9.3%
Unfair dismissal/Redundancy payments	5.5%
Employment protection	4.8%
Equal pay	3.5%
Race relations	1.5%
Sex discrimination	0.9%
Contracts of employment	0.9%
Health and safety	0.4%
Industrial training levy	0.3%
Miscellaneous	0.09%

Chapter 6

Responding to a Claim

Introduction

6.1   It is only at this stage that the respondent, usually an employer, becomes involved in the proceedings. He will receive a letter from ROIT in a form similar to figure 5 on page 35 known as an IT 2, together with a copy of the IT 1, leaflet ITL 1 (which is a booklet on procedure) and a blank form IT 3 which is technically known as a 'notice of appearance'. Note that he is now referred to as the 'respondent' and will be referred to as such throughout the rest of the proceedings. The letter enclosing the IT 1 is in effect 'serving' the IT 1 on the respondent. Where appropriate, copies will also be sent to ACAS, the Secretary of State, CRE, EOC etc.

Service

6.2   Service is normally effected by properly addressing, pre-paying and posting by ordinary first or second class post a letter or notice containing the relevant document. Until the contrary is proved, service will be deemed to be effected at the time at which the letter is delivered in the ordinary course of the post. The letter or notice will be sent to the address inserted in paragraph 4 of the IT 1. If the applicant has got it wrong the tribunal can use its discretion to find the correct address. Failing service by ordinary post, recorded delivery service is used. As a final resort the IT has power to make an order under Rule 17(6) for substituted service in any such manner as is considered fit, e.g. publication in a local newspaper, ROIT has only to send the IT 1 to the last known address or place of business or the registered office or principal office of a company under Rule 17(3)(*d*) for service to be good. It follows that simply returning documents unopened from a registered office will not make the proceedings go away!

Serving process on foreign companies

6.3   The general principle is that an industrial tribunal being a civil court can only exercise jurisdiction over those within its territorial boundaries or who are willing to submit to it. Oversea companies who establish a place of business in GB are required to deliver to the Registrar of Companies:

(*a*)   a certified copy of the memorandum and articles of association, or

INDUSTRIAL TRIBUNALS (RULES OF PROCEDURE) REGULATIONS 1980

NOTICE OF ORIGINATING APPLICATION

Case No. 269/84

Regional Office of the Industrial Tribunals
19-29 Woburn Place
London WC1H 0LU

Tel: (01) 633 4921

1.   I enclose a copy of an originating application for a decision of a tribunal in which you are named as respondent. Under the rules of procedure you are required to enter an appearance within 14 days of receiving the copy of the originating application. You can do this either by completing and sending to me the enclosed form of notice of appearance or by sending a letter giving the information called for on the form. This form and any other communications addressed to me may be sent by post or delivered to me at the above address.

2.   The proceedings on this application will be regulated by the rules of procedure contained in the above Regulations and these are explained in the enclosed leaflet. The case number of the application is indicated above and should be quoted in any communications with regard to these proceedings.

3.   If you name a representative at item 3 of the form, further communications regarding the case will be sent to him and not to you, and you should arrange to be kept informed by him of the progress of the case and of the hearing date. When the application is heard by the tribunal the parties (other than a respondent who has not entered an appearance) may appear and be heard in person or be represented by anyone they choose.

4.   If you do not send me the completed form (or other notice of appearance) you will not be entitled to take any part in the proceedings (except to apply for an extension of time to enter an appearance). If you do not take part in the proceedings a decision which may be enforceable in the county court may be given against you in your absence. Whether or not you enter an appearance you will be notified of the date of hearing and sent a copy of the tribunal's decision.

5.   In all cases where the Act under which the application is made provides for conciliation the services of a conciliation officer are available to the parties. In such cases a copy of the application is sent to the Advisory Conciliation and Arbitration Service accordingly, (see leaflet ITL1 page 6).

Signed ...... *A Norton* .... Dated ...4 February 1984................................. .
for Secretary of the Tribunals

To the Respondent(s)

Mason (UK) Limited
Units 10-14
Humber Trading Estate
Edgware
Middlesex MS2 8SL

IT2

Reproduced by permission of HMSO

Figure 5: Notice of originating application to respondent (IT 2)

some other document defining the company's constitution (with a certified translation into English); and

(*b*)   the names and addresses of one or more persons resident in GB authorised to accept service of any court or tribunal proceedings on behalf of the company.

[*Companies Act 1948, ss 406–416*]. Failure to do so may lead to a fine.

It would appear that even though a company is in breach of these provisions and there is no one on whom to serve the IT 1 in the UK, service on the company's registered office overseas will be sufficient service to comply with Rule 17(3)(*d*)(i). (*Knulty v ELOC Electro-Optiek and Communicatie BV [1981] ICR 732*). Provided the company carried on business in this country and the cause of the claim arose wholly or in part here, tribunals would seem to have jurisdiction.

Prior involvement

6.4   The respondent may have become indirectly involved prior to receiving the IT 2. For example he may have received a Section 53 request (*see* figure 1, page 7) or a discrimination questionnaire (*see* figure 2, pages 8–11). As the replies to these requests are admissible in evidence in a tribunal hearing and there are penalties for failing to comply (*see* Chapter 1), they must be treated seriously and to the extent of regarding them as part of the proceedings.

Also this is an opportunity to prevent meritless claims. These procedures are usually used where the applicant is being advised. If your replies indicate that a potential claim has no reasonable prospect of success it may never be brought: these procedures are not so much threats as opportunities to avoid proceedings altogether.

Chapter 7

The Respondent's First Steps

Introduction

7.1   It is now advisable for the respondent to take the following steps:

(*a*) peruse the IT 2 and its enclosures;

(*b*) inform ROIT if the time limits cannot be complied with;

(*c*) clarify the law involved;

(*d*) consider the evidence;

(*e*) apply for further particulars if required;

(*f*) make a preliminary assessment of the likelihood of successfully defending the claim and decide on the objectives for defending;

(*g*) complete the IT 3.

These are considered separately below.

Peruse the IT 2

7.2   You must carefully read the IT 2 and its enclosures, the most important of which is the IT 1. Figure 3 on pages 18–19 should first be examined to check that the details in paragraphs 4, 5, 6, 7, 8, 9, 10 and 11 are correct. Secondly, whether or not these details are correct, you should consider whether the applicant is qualified to bring a claim. For example, you may not agree with the date when employment ended and may be able to prove that the applicant did not have the requisite period of continuous service.

Thirdly, you should note the type of claim in paragraph 1 and decide whether you are satisfied with the grounds given under paragraph 12, and if not, seek further clarification. Finally, note the remedy sought. If this is reinstatement or re-engagement you are on notice to be prepared for these remedies (*see* Chapter 39).

Time limits

7.3   It will be noted from the IT 2 that you have only 14 days from the date of receiving a copy of the IT 1 to provide an answer or 'enter an appearance'. If the investigation is likely to take longer, you should inform ROIT as soon as possible by letter that you will be unable to comply inside the time limit, and ask for an extension of say 28 days giving reasons for the request. It is invariably granted especially if further particulars are being sought (Rule 3(2)(ii)). In fact, under Rule 3(3) a late notice of appearance automatically includes an application for an extension of time. However, it is better to send the letter suggested than rely on the application being successful, because the consequences of not succeeding are far-reaching.

If there is no response within 14 days the respondent is likely to receive a letter in the form of figure 7 on page 47 and this letter will be sent by recorded delivery under Rule 17(5)(*a*). If an extension is not granted and the notice of appearance is presented outside the time limit, or not at all, then, under Rule 3(2) the employer will not be entitled to take any further part in the proceedings. In particular, this means that the respondent cannot ask for further and better particulars (*see* Chapter 13), witness orders (*see* Chapter 16), or for discovery of documents (*see* 13.9–13.20) nor will written representations (*see* Chapter 17) be allowed to be submitted; and he will not be allowed to be represented at the hearing. The only remaining rights are to make an application or further application for an extension of time, or to give evidence as a witness if called by someone other than himself.

Clarify the law

7.4   It may be sensible to consult with a legal adviser to make sure there are no complicated legal principles involved. Legal advice for a respondent may come from an in-house lawyer, solicitor, employers' association, local chamber of commerce or even a CAB. Otherwise there are plenty of free leaflets available from the DE, ACAS, EOC, CRE and Health and Safety Executive. Any of these can give an indication of the law involved (*see* Chapter 12). This indication is necessary so that the significant matters which must be proved can be identified. It is as well to find out what the other party has to prove.

Consider the evidence

7.5   In the vast majority of cases respondents will not be taken by surprise by an application. An employer may have already sent a letter of dismissal and replied to a Department of Employment questionnaire. In order to get to the stage of dismissing and providing these written statements, the reasons for dismissing should have been investigated and documented and there may be no need to obtain any further evidence to proceed to the next step.

If not, then an investigation will be necessary at this stage to find out:

(*a*) whether the dismissal or act complained of took place;

(*b*) if it did, what was the reason for it;

(*c*) if a dismissal, the fairness of the circumstances leading to the dismissal (e.g. were procedures followed?).

This evidence can be collected in the form of statements from witnesses (*see* Chapter 15) and documents (*see* Chapter 13) and must be considered in the light of what has to be proved.

Apply for further particulars if required

7.6   If it is difficult to consider the evidence without seeking clarification of the applicant's grounds for the claim, then this should be sought. A request for further particulars is permitted at this stage and before the IT 3 is submitted. The procedures and rules relating to such a request are described in Chapter 13. Suffice it to say that an order for those particulars may be obtained from the tribunal if necessary.

Preliminary assessment

7.7   It should now be possible to assess the implications of the IT 1. You must now try to be objective and carry out a similar exercise to that suggested for applicants in Chapter 1. This will involve deciding the objectives for resisting the claim and whether there is a good defence.

If the objective is to dispose of the case without the possibility of adverse publicity, a settlement should be sought. Where there is a matter of principle involved there may be no alternative but to fight the case, despite an assessment that the chances of success are slim or that there is sympathy for the applicant.

To sum up, at this stage you, as respondent, have to consider the following questions:

(*a*) what is the claim?

(*b*) is it justified?

(*c*) what is your defence?

(*d*) what is your objective for resisting the claim?

It may not be possible to answer these questions precisely, because, for example, the applicant's claim is incoherent. There will be plenty of opportunities to clarify the claim and these will be examined in the following chapters.

In practice one of the respondent's main objectives is to dispose of the application in the cheapest and quickest way. In order to do this an attempt must be made to find out what compensation could be awarded by an IT. In unfair dismissal cases the assessment form shown in figure 32 on page 199 can be useful. Effective use of the form will require some knowledge of the methods of calculating compensation which can be found in Chapter 39. In addition, the estimated costs in terms of, say, lost management time and disruption of industrial relations etc., should be made. The time taken to prepare and eventually

<u>INDUSTRIAL TRIBUNALS</u>

NOTICE OF APPEARANCE BY RESPONDENT

To the Assistant Secretary of the Tribunals

Case Number 269/84

FOR OFFICIAL USE	
Date of receipt	Initials

1.   I*do/~~do not~~ intend to resist the claim made by Mr J Rider

2.   *~~I~~/Our name is *~~Mr~~/~~Mrs~~/~~Miss~~/Title (if a company or organisation):-

   Name: Mason (UK) Limited

   Address: Units 10-14, Humber Trading Estate,

   Edgware, Middlesex MS2 8SL   Telephone Number

   01 987 5638

3.   If a representative is acting for you, please give his/her name and address and note
   that all further communications will be sent to him/her, not to you:

   Name:

   Address:

   Telephone Number

4.   (a)   Was the applicant dismissed ?   *YES/~~NO~~

   (b)   If YES, what was the reason for dismissal?

   (c)   Are the dates given by the applicant as to the period of employment correct?
        *YES/~~NO~~

   (d)   If NO, give dates of commencement _____ and termination _____

   (e)   Are details of remuneration stated by the applicant correct? *YES/~~NO~~

   (f)   If NO, or if the applicant has not stated such details, please give the correct details:-

        Basic Wages/Salary: __£145 p.w.__

        Average take home pay £112 p.w.

        Other remuneration or benefits Pension

*Delete inappropriate items   Please continue overleaf

Reproduced by permission of HMSO

Figure 6: Notice of appearance (IT 3)

(g) (To be completed <u>only</u> when the application relates to Maternity Rights)

When the applicant's absence began were you employing more than 5 persons?
*YES/NO

(h) (To be completed in other applications)

(i) When the applicant's employment ended were you employing more than 20 persons?   *YES/N⊠X

(ii) If NO, had you at anytime during the applicant's employment with you employed more than 20 persons? *YES/NO

5. If the claim is resisted, you should give below sufficient particulars to show the grounds on which you intend to resist the application.

(Continue on a separate sheet if there is insufficient space below).

> The warehouse was running inefficiently so we recruited Brian Rogers to get things right. Unfortunately he and John Rider did not get on: John refused to carry out instructions and despite several warnings matters grew worse. On 17th December John was given a final warning, but when he returned from the Christmas break he still refused to work properly with Brian. We had no alternative but to dismiss him. At that time he was told the reason for his dismissal although he already knew.

Signature . *Janet Hawkins*.
Personnel Manager
Date ..16..February..1984...................

*Delete inappropriate items

Figure 6 (continued)

present a case may be considerable. A typical case could involve three or four other employees who may each lose a day's work. Productivity may be adversely affected. Relations with trade unions could be soured. Therefore cost-benefit analysis is a necessary part of the preliminary assessment.

Complete the IT 3

7.8   Figure 6 on pages 40–41 is an example of a completed IT 3. Guidance on completing this form is given in the following chapter (Chapter 8).

Completing the Notice of Appearance (IT 3)

Introduction

8.1   Figure 6 on pages 40–41 is an example of a completed IT 3. Some of the paragraphs require explanation.

Paragraph 1: Whether claim to be resisted

8.2   Even if it has been decided not to oppose the application, a notice of appearance should be entered and this paragraph completed accordingly. This may happen where only the amount of compensation is in dispute.

Paragraph 2: Name of respondent

8.3   As already indicated, the applicant may incorrectly state the respondent's name, or the person or organisation stated may not be the respondent. If it is the latter, still complete the IT 3 and state this fact in paragraph 5. Insert the correct name and address and telephone number together with the reference of the person dealing with the matter.

Paragraph 3: Representative

8.4.   Remember that no direct communication will be received from ROIT once this paragraph is completed.

Paragraph 4(a): Was the applicant dismissed?

8.5   If the applicant resigned then delete 'Yes' even if he is alleging constructive dismissal. If the action is not one relating to dismissal, e.g. discrimination in selection, then again delete 'Yes'.

Paragraph 4(b): Reason for dismissal

8.6   Where 'No' is deleted in paragraph 4(a) then the reason for the dismissal must be given. This will invariably be connected with one of the permissible reasons for dismissal such as redundancy, gross misconduct, ill health, unsatisfactory work performance, lack of qualifications, re-organisation for economic necessity etc. More than one reason may apply. The grounds for the reason(s) will be dealt with in paragraph 5.

Paragraph 4(c) and (d): Dates of employment

8.7   These paragraphs are particularly relevant to establish the exact period of employment for the purposes of the continuous service qualification requirement, assessment of compensation, etc. An applicant may not have inserted the correct dates in the IT 1, particularly because of the complicated way of determining the date of 'termination'. Although the onus is on the employee to show that he is qualified to bring the claim, it is important for the respondent to work out the exact date when employment commenced and ended. If the employee does not have the necessary continuous service this can be referred to in paragraph 5.

Paragraph 4(e) and (f): Remuneration

8.8   Unfortunately some employers do not provide itemised pay slips (although obliged to do so under EPCA s 8). Therefore the details in the IT 1 should be checked, particularly where there is a bonus scheme or obligatory overtime. If paragraphs 8 and 9 of the IT 1 are incorrect paragraphs 4(e) and (f) are where these details can be correctly stated.

Paragraph 4(g) and (h): Small establishments

8.9   These paragraphs are designed to deal with the small employer exemptions. [*EPCA s 64A*].

Paragraph 5: Grounds

8.10   Where it is considered the applicant is not qualified to bring the claim this paragaph should be used to convey the point. Such a qualification matter is often referred to as a 'preliminary' point of jurisdiction. However, the grounds for opposing the application should still be given in case the tribunal finds it has jurisdiction. This is called 'pleading in the alternative'. An example of the words which can be used is 'the applicant was employed for less than one year, but if you find she was qualified then the grounds for dismissal were . . .' If the respondent does not back the case both ways he may not be permitted to argue the fairness of the dismissal. (*Nelson v BBC [1977] IRLR 148*).

Where it is considered that the applicant is qualified then, under Rule 3(1), it is now necessary for the respondent to set out 'sufficient particulars to show on what grounds' he relies to resist a claim. These particulars should be consistent with any reasons given in, say, a letter of dismissal, a reply to a Section 53 request for written reasons, or the replies to a questionnaire submitted by the CRE, EOC or SSAT. If the particulars are inconsistent, there is likely to be an inference that the dismissal was unfair (although bear in mind these could be separate jurisdictions). Where a respondent is in that position, serious consideration should be given to the question of whether to oppose the claim. It is no good relying on events which were discovered after the date of dismissal as these are irrelevant except in connection with the remedy. (*Devis & Sons Ltd v Atkins [1977] IRLR 315*). There is a note of caution here: if sufficient particulars are not provided, the IT 3 can eventually be struck out by the tribunal under Rule 4(4).

Besides the example given in figure 6 the following are other examples of how this paragraph could be completed:

(*a*) *Statutory restriction:* The applicant was employed as a driver. He was found guilty of driving whilst under the influence of alcohol and was disqualified from driving for 12 months from 4 May 1984. We did everything possible to try and find him alternative work which he could perform during the disqualification period, but without success. In all the circumstances (having regard to equity and the substantial merits of the case) we acted reasonably in treating his loss of driving licence as a sufficient reason for dismissing the applicant.

(*b*) *Ill health:* Mr Z had been absent from work for 12 months and according to medical certificates produced by him this was due to a slipped disc. On 5 April 1984 we discussed with Mr Z his medical position and as a result he submitted to us a report from his own GP indicating it would be a further 12 weeks before he would be able to resume work but only on the lightest work. As a result he agreed to be examined by a doctor in our occupational health department who confirmed Mr Z's own GP's report. Mr Z was employed as a mechanical fitter and it was not practicable for us to arrange for his work to be done without taking on a permanent replacement. We had no suitable alternative vacancies.

(*c*) *Other substantial reasons:* Miss X was informed in writing on her engagement that her employment was temporary and would be terminated on the return to work of Mrs Y who was absent because of maternity confinement. Miss X was dismissed in order to make it possible to give work to Mrs Y when she returned to work. There was no alternative work available for Miss X.

Miscellaneous matters

8.11 Like the IT 1, this form is revised from time to time. It is likely, for example, that paragraph 4(h) will be revised to indicate that small employers must count the employees of 'associated' employers (definition *EPCA s 153(4)*) when replying to question 4(h)(i).

Once completed the IT 3 should be signed by the respondent, or his representative on his behalf, and sent by ordinary post to ROIT. An accompanying letter dealing with questions of preliminary hearings (*see* Chapter 19), date and length of hearing (*see* Chapter 18) may also be appropriate.

Chapter 9

Lodging the IT 3

Return of IT 3 to ROIT essential

9.1   As mentioned in the previous chapter, if the IT 3 is not returned to ROIT, the respondent will be debarred under Rule 3(2) from taking any further part in the proceedings except as indicated in that sub-rule. Where the tribunal has not heard from the respondent within 14 days, a reminder similar to figure 7 on page 47 will be sent to him. In practice, a late submission will nearly always be treated as 'in time' even as late as the start of the hearing, the tribunal exercising its power to that effect under Rule 13. In fact, a tribunal cannot refuse an extension without giving the employer an opportunity to show why the time limit should be extended. (*St Mungo Community Trust v Colleano [1980] ICR 254*). A copy will then be sent to the applicant or his representative and any others having an interest in the proceedings, such as ACAS. If sufficient particulars of the grounds for resisting the claim are not given in paragraph 5 of the IT 3, the tribunal has power to order that these particulars are given under Rule 4(1)(*a*)(i) (*see* 13.1). Where the order is not complied with, the tribunal can strike out before or at the hearing the whole or part of the IT 3 or debar the respondent from defending the proceedings under Rule 4(4).

Regional Office of the Industrial Tribunals
19-29 Woburn Place London WC1H 0LU

Telephone Direct Line 01-632
Switchboard 01-632 4921/5

Mason (UK) Limited
Units 10-14
Humber Trading Estate
Edgware
Middlesex MS2 8SL

Your reference

Our reference   269/84

Date   20 February 1984

Dear Sir

THE INDUSTRIAL TRIBUNALS (RULES OF PROCEDURE) REGULATIONS 1980

       Rider   -v-   Mason (UK) Limited

Notice of an Originating Application which has been filed against you by
Mr J Rider   was sent to you on 4 February 1984

The statutory time limit for you to enter an appearance stating whether
you intend to resist the claim and if so giving your grounds has now
expired but if you wish to take part in the proceedings you should complete
and return the Notice of Appearance to this office immediately. In
accordance with Rule 3 a Notice of Appearance sent after the time limit
is deemed to include an application for an extension of time allowed.

                Yours faithfully

                A Winton

              for Secretary of the Tribunals

cc   Mr F Hitchcock
     District Secretary
     Warehousemen's Trade Union
     128 Furlong Road
     London EC1 2JA

~~cc The Secretary of State for Employment~~

cc Conciliation Officer - Advisory Conciliation & Arbitration Service

Reproduced by permission of HMSO

Figure 7: Reminder to respondent that time limit to enter appearance has expired

Chapter 10

Representation

Introduction

10.1   Tribunals have been criticised because they are no longer seen to be as informal, speedy and cheap as was originally envisaged by the Donovan Commission. It has been suggested that one of the reasons for this has been the extent of legal representation at tribunals. As most lawyers have been trained in the use of procedures practised in ordinary courts (which are more formal, often very lengthy, and certainly not cheap) there has been a tendency to continue to use such practices, perhaps inappropriately, in industrial tribunals. Statistics, collected in 1982, show that about 36 per cent of all applicants and 49 per cent of all respondents were legally represented at the hearing.

One of the objects of this book is to encourage laymen to take their own tribunal cases in line with Donovan's justification for ITs and to avoid unnecessary legislation. However, a party should always consider whether he should be represented, and it is preferable that any representative should be involved at the earliest opportunity in a case, and therefore the decision on representation should be taken at an early stage in the proceedings.

Tribunal rules on representation

10.2   Under Rule 7(6) of the Regulations 'at any hearing of or in connection with an originating application a party and any person entitled to appear may appear before the tribunal and may be heard in person or be represented by counsel or by a solicitor or by a representative of a trade union or an employers' association or by any other person whom he desires to represent him'. So it can be seen there are no restrictions on representation as far as tribunals are concerned, and it is up to the parties to decide whether or not they should be represented, and by whom.

The need for legal representation

10.3   The starting point for any decision on representation must be to recognise that the vast majority of unfair dismissal cases heard before tribunals involve concepts of 'reasonableness' and 'fairness' in an industrial context, and by far the best person to deal with those concepts is one who has experience of industry and is familiar with its customs and practices.

Perhaps the most formidable aspect of any tribunal case for the lay person is the hearing itself. In England and Wales tribunals have tended to adopt an 'adversary' system. This means that they have considered that the prime responsibility for determining the course of the hearing and the presentation of evidence and legal argument should be taken by the representative. However, because of the system already practised in Scotland and the changing practices of chairmen in England and Wales, the system is moving towards a more 'inquisitorial' approach. This means, in practice, that tribunal members, particularly the chairman, take over the prime responsibility for determining the course of the hearing so as to ensure that all relevant matters of evidence, fact and law have been brought out and that those that are in dispute have been argued at the hearing. As a greater number of chairmen seem to be taking a more inquisitorial role there is perhaps less need for lawyers.

Whether lawyers or other representatives are used, however, will to a large extent depend on the circumstances of the party involved and the case itself. Perhaps a guide to the sort of cases which would be appropriate for legal representation would be the Royal Commission on Legal Services' recommendations as to where legal aid should be extended to representation before industrial tribunals:

— where a significant point of law is involved;

— where the evidence is very complex;

— where a test case arises;

— where the ability of an individual to follow his occupation is at stake.

With this background in mind, the decision as to whether to be represented and by whom may depend on whether we are looking at the question from the viewpoint of the employer or the employee. Therefore, we will examine these viewpoints separately.

From the point of view of the employer

10.4   There are several choices open to the employer which depend to some extent on the size and administrative resources of the particular employer involved.

   (a) *In-house representation.* The larger employer with its own personnel or industrial relations department with, say, a nominated person responsible for tribunal matters will be in a position to represent itself at a tribunal. Whether or not it chooses to do so will depend, no doubt, on company policy in this respect. However, it would seem that such a company is ideally placed to represent itself, and to reduce costs accordingly. These organisations usually have legal departments who can provide the necessary representation or simply advise on any legal points which arise. It should be noted, however, that in-house lawyers are likely to be specialists in commercial and company law rather than in employment law.

(*b*) *Representation by representative bodies.* Smaller companies, and even some larger ones, are often members of employers' associations which may provide a service to their members in this area. One such organisation is the Engineering Employers Federation. In 1983, the EEF handled 1,538 unfair dismissal and redundancy cases on behalf of its members, of which 705 involved representation at a tribunal. In 1982 approximately 10 per cent of employers were represented by such bodies.

(*c*) *Legal representation.* The statistics given above indicate that approximately 50 per cent of employers are represented by lawyers. This does not mean only lawyers in private practice, but also includes legal representation by in-company lawyers as well as lawyers employed by employers' associations, etc. It also includes lawyers who are paid for under a legal expenses insurance policy. Therefore, the costs of legal representation will vary depending on the source of that representation.

Legal costs

10.5   The vast majority of legal representation is through solicitors in private practice, and often barristers will be instructed to appear at the tribunal hearing. It is very difficult to assess accurately the cost of such legal representation because it depends on a variety of factors, from the particular firm of solicitors involved to the number of years standing of the barrister or counsel instructed. In the *Financial Times* publication 'The real cost of dismissal', the FT revealed that in one case lasting over 40 days in which they were involved, their legal fees exceeded £20,000. Although this is an extreme case, it is not unusual to find that Counsel's brief fees for a tribunal hearing of one day could be anything from £200 to £500, depending on the expertise of that counsel. Where the case goes into a second and subsequent days, the fee could be £100 to £200 per day. On top of these fees are, of course, the solicitor's own charges.

Legal expenses insurance

10.6   Over the last few years more and more small employers have been turning to insurance as a means of underwriting their legal expenses. Most insurance companies operating in this field cover a wide range of legal expenses claims. Insurance to cover employers' defences to tribunal claims is an important area of cover. Some policies not only cover the policy holder's own legal costs and expenses but also any compensation or costs awarded against the policy holder. There are a number of companies offering such insurance. The extent of their cover and premiums charged vary from one insurance company to another. Policy holders are generally entitled to instruct their own solicitors although some insurance companies can provide representation from their own staff. The effect is that policy holders, who have nothing to lose financially by claiming under their policies, are likely to instruct their own solicitors. As already mentioned, legal representation is not necessarily the best form of representation at tribunals. There is, therefore, a risk that by having such a policy employers will not give proper consideration to the most appropriate form of representation.

Non-legal specialists

10.7 There are a few independent consultants specialising in employment related matters who tend to be less expensive than lawyers. Representation in tribunals will be one of the services that such consultants offer.

Costs tax deductible

10.8 The costs of outside representation, whether by lawyers or independent consultants can usually be treated as allowable expenses for tax purposes, and legal expenses insurance premiums will also be allowable for tax purposes like other insurance premiums.

From the point of view of the employee

10.9 The employee is usually in a very different position from the employer as he is unlikely to have any expert knowledge of employment law. However, if he is a trade union member his union is likely to have the necessary expertise, either through a full-time officer or lay official. The Code of Practice dealing with 'Time Off for Trade Union Duties and Activities' specifically identifies representation of a union member at an 'IT' as a function which can be carried out by lay officials during working hours. Therefore, shop stewards, convenors, branch secretaries, fathers of chapels, etc. have a quasi-legal right to time off to appear on behalf of a member at a tribunal. It goes without saying that such representation is offered by trade unions as part of the service provided for their members. In 1982 some 16 per cent of all applicants were represented by trade union officials.

Many employees are not members of a trade union, or they may be in dispute with their union and therefore have to consider other forms of available representation. An applicant appearing in person should be given every assistance by the tribunal to present his own case, and in 1982 some 40 per cent of all applicants represented themselves at tribunals.

To be realistic, though, many applicants are extremely nervous about appearing on their own or are inarticulate and need some support. There are various bodies who are prepared to provide such assistance without charge which were outlined in Chapter 1 including the EOC, CRE, Law Centres etc. As mentioned in that chapter, limited legal aid is available for preparatory work. However, this does not prevent a lawyer, or for that matter anyone else, accompanying an applicant at the hearing in order to provide advice and guidance and take notes, although not directly participating in the hearing. Such a procedure is allowed under the so called 'McKenzie Rule'. (*McKenzie v McKenzie [1970] 3 AER 1034*).

In contrast to the position of employers, the High Court in *Warnett (Inspector of Taxes) v Jones [1980] ICR 359* found that legal costs incurred by *employees* are not tax deductible.

Statistics

10.10 Taking all forms of representation, whether by lawyer or some other person, applicants were represented in some 60 per cent and respondents in some 61 per cent of all cases in 1982. Considering that ITs were set up as lay tribunals these statistics would appear to indicate a high level of representation by both employers and employees, a large percentage of which involved lawyers.

Lay representation

10.11 One of the purposes of this book is to encourage lay representation by exposing the mystique of court procedures. The writer hopes the following chapters will make industrial tribunal procedures sufficiently comprehensible to applicants and respondents whether or not they are represented by lawyers.

Chapter 11

Tribunal Forms

Introduction

11.1 The IT 1 and IT 3 are part of what are called the 'pleadings' of the case. Pleadings are the official forms some of which are presented to the tribunal and others may originate from the tribunal in the exercise of its powers. It is important that forms completed by the parties such as the IT 1 and IT 3 are accurate, although they are not binding in the same way as other court pleadings.

Later in the proceedings it may be found necessary to amend or alter the pleadings. The tribunal will usually have power to do this even to the extent of joining another party to the case.

Joining third parties

11.2 Where there are a number of persons having the same interest in a claim the tribunal has power to authorise that one or more defend on behalf of all those interested (Rule 14(3)). Under the 1980 Regulations this joinder rule was extended to applicants.

Also under Rule 14 a trade union can be joined as a respondent. For example, the Employment Act 1982 has amended Section 76 of EPCA to provide for joinder. Briefly, where an employer claims, for instance, that he is pressurised by industrial action (or the threat of it) to dismiss an employee who is not a union member or a member of that union, then the employer can require the TU to be joined as a party to any subsequent claim.

Rule 14(1) provides the mechanisms by which ITs can join unions as respondents on the application of an employer or ex-employee or for that matter on their own initiative. However, the wording of this sub-rule is somewhat at variance with Section 76. Whereas the latter provides for an employer or ex-employee to 'require' a TU to be joined as a respondent, Rule 14(1) gives tribunals discretion on joinder. It is possible therefore to envisage a situation where a tribunal may refuse an employer's application because it lacks merit. If this happened it would be in direct conflict with what appears to be an absolute right given by Section 76.

In practice it is likely that a chairman, who will actually consider such applications, will regard himself as bound to exercise his discretion to grant the application. But if he considers the application lacks merit he can later direct (under Rule 14(2)) that the TU be dismissed from the proceedings. Alternatively a pre-hearing assessment (*see* Chapter 14) might be used to discourage the employer's contention that a union induced the dismissal. Before a chairman will exercise his discretion on joinder he will want to be satisfied that the persons are directly interested in the subject of the claim. So where a party applies to join ACAS as a party he is unlikely to succeed. (*Marshall v Alexander Sloane & Co Ltd [1980] ICR 394*).

Amending tribunal forms

11.3   An application to amend, alter or join can be made by writing a straightforward letter to ROIT requesting the change and at the same time giving reasons for the request. The application will be considered by a chairman and if granted the alteration or amendment will be made and copies of the changed forms sent to both sides.

Under Rule 12(2)(*e*) the tribunal has power to strike out anything in the IT 1 or IT 3 which is 'scandalous, frivolous or vexatious', for example, a reference to the managing director of the respondent company as 'untrustworthy and a liar', where this has no apparent relevance to the case. In Scotland only 'vexatious' matters can be struck out. However, this Rule should not be used by a respondent where the grounds of the claim are unclear. The more appropriate procedure would be to apply for further particulars (see 13.1–13.8), or a pre-hearing assessment (see Chapter 14). (*Ipswich Port Authority v Wedderburn EAT 119/84 IRLIB 258.11*).

Other pleadings

11.4   The IT 1 and IT 3 are not necessarily the only pleadings. The parties may require further and better particulars of each other's grounds or discovery of a document. If these are not voluntarily supplied then the information can be sought through ROIT and will form part of the pleadings. From now until the commencement of the hearing all matters involving the IT are referred to as 'interlocutory' matters. Compared with pleadings in other courts the IT 1 and IT 3 are less formal. Interlocutory matters are dealt with relatively informally. As will be seen in the next few chapters, applications in relation to these are made by writing straightforward letters. No special forms are necessary. The informality of the proceedings is also matched by the cost of tribunal proceedings, and in contrast to any other court, there are no tribunal fees (*see* costs which can be awarded by tribunals in Chapter 40).

Chapter 12

'Evidence' and 'Law'

Twofold role of industrial tribunal

12.1   At this stage it is perhaps necessary to consider what is evidence and what is law? This is because any judicial body including an IT has a twofold role, namely:

(*a*) it must determine what are the facts of the case; and

(*b*) it must apply the law to those facts.

For the IT to determine the facts, each side will place before it evidence in the form of written and oral representations. It may determine the facts because the parties do not dispute them, or because it prefers the evidence of one side's witnesses to that of the other, or by deducing the facts from other facts. The tribunal will decide which of two conflicting stories it accepts. (*McGuire v Jarvie Plant EAT 224/83 IRLIB 243.15*). Evidence is therefore fundamental to help establish the facts required, and these will depend on the law applicable. In other words, it is necessary to know the law involved in a case in order to know what needs to be proved. If it is known what has to be proved, it is then possible to know what facts have to be established, i.e. what evidence is required.

Finding the law

12.2   The law can be found in the words of Acts of Parliament (statutes), regulations and previous judicial decisions of higher courts (*see* Chapter 37). Which statutes and which previous decisions must be looked up? Perhaps the best starting point is to obtain a comprehensive set of free leaflets from the DE, ACAS, CRE, EOC and Health and Safety Executive. These will guide you to the relevant statutory provision. The Tribunal Table in Appendix A can also be used. Column 9 indicates the actual section of the statute relating to each claim specified in the table. Copies can be obtained from HMSO (*see* Appendix D for addresses), or you can refer to any number of reference books on employment law (*see* Appendix E). These will also refer you to previous decisions or precedents (*see* Chapter 37) which might be relevant to your case. It is not possible to review such books here and the reader must find his own sources from local libraries, universities, representative groups such as trade unions, employers' associations etc.

12.3 'Evidence' and 'Law'

The more well known publications are listed in Appendix E. If you wish to go into even more detail and read the full transcript of a previous decision then you must turn to a law report such as IRLR, ICR and AER.

From this research it should not be difficult to discover what has to be proved and then to collect the evidence necessary to show the requisite facts. It is often a worthwhile exercise when considering a case to distinguish questions of fact and law.

Let us consider the following hypothetical case. Mr A (aged 66), a garage mechanic, has worked for Rogers Motors for eight years. His hours of work are 8.30 to 16.30. At 16.10 on a Friday the garage foreman stops Mr A as he is leaving work and asks him to return to finish a job. Mr A takes no notice and leaves. The foreman shouts after him 'If you don't finish that job, don't bother to return on Monday'.

Questions of fact	Questions of law
(a) The normal retiring age for mechanics.	(a) Is Mr A qualified to bring a claim?
(b) The importance of the job left unfinished.	(b) Was he dismissed?
(c) Whether the foreman has authority to dismiss.	(c) If there was a dismissal, what was the reason for it?
(d) Whether there is a custom and practice of leaving early on Fridays?	(d) Was this reason fair in all the circumstances having regard to equity and the substantial merits of the case?

It must be remembered that a tribunal cannot be expected to know or deduce any facts which have not been put before it in evidence. Similarly, it cannot be expected to reject accounts of facts which are not queried. It is your duty and not that of the tribunals to place all relevant evidence before the tribunal. (*Craig v British Railways (Scottish Region) (1973) 8 ITR 636*).

Further preparation

12.3   This means that parties to IT actions must prepare their cases properly and the following chapters of Part I will indicate what further preparation is necessary and how best this can be achieved.

Where this further preparation involves talking to the other side it should be made clear that anything said is 'without prejudice'. This means that the details of any negotiations could not, for example, be disclosed at the hearing as admissions or undertakings of one side or the other. The whole question in dispute will remain open.

Chapter 13

Getting to Know the Other Side's Case

PART A : FURTHER PARTICULARS

Know the grounds of your opponent's case

13.1   Neither side should enter a tribunal without first having established the exact grounds of his opponent's case. A party should know what case he has to face so that there is plenty of time to prepare properly and to take the preliminary assessment further. The IT 1 or IT 3 may not provide these grounds, despite the Regulations. If the grounds of the claim or defence are insufficient or unclear, action must be taken. This action takes the form of requesting 'further and better particulars' of the information required, which can only relate to the grounds relied upon by either party and any facts and contentions relevant to these grounds. In other words a request can only relate to the substance of allegations rather than the other side's evidence. For example, if a respondent received an IT 1 where paragraph **1** and **12** were completed as follows:

1   I hereby apply for a decision of a tribunal on the following grounds: 'Unfair treatment'

12   Please explain the grounds . . .
'I told my employer I was not prepared to go to Glasgow'

then it would not be surprising to find a request for further and better particulars to discover the substance of the assertion. If we refer back to figure 3 (page 18) we can see that a request similar to figure 8(a) would be advisable. Similarly, if we refer to figure 6 (page 40) a request in the form of figure 8(b) is perhaps necessary. It will be noted that figures 8(a) and 8(b) are ordinary letters sent to the applicant or respondent or their respective representatives. It is recommended that a copy is sent to ROIT at the same time. A reasonable time limit for compliance should be inserted in the letter, and if the request is not complied with in full or adequately by that time, then an application can be made to ROIT, under Rule 4(1)(*a*)(i), for an 'order' that such further particulars be supplied.

That Rule states that: 'A tribunal may . . . on the application of a party to the proceedings . . . require a party to furnish in writing to the person specified by the tribunal further particulars of the grounds on which he or it relies of any facts and contentions relevant thereto.'

MASON (UK) LIMITED, UNITS 10-14, HUMBER TRADING ESTATE, EDGWARE
MIDDLESEX MS2 8SL

Mr Frank Hitchcock   Our Ref : JH/SN
District Secretary
W T U
128 Furlong Road
London
EC1 2JA   23 February 1984

Dear Mr Hitchcock

Re: John Rider

Would you please let me have the following further particulars of your above
member's grounds for bringing his unfair dismissal claim against us:

(1)   In relation to the alleged incident at the beginning of November

       (a)   what 'containers' does Mr Rider say were required to be moved?

       (b)   through which 'restricted area'?

       (c)   what 'law' was this against?

(2)   In what ways did Mr Rogers make life impossible for your member?
       Give details of actual incidents and their approximate dates.

Please supply these particulars within the next 14 days.

Thanking you in anticipation.

Yours sincerely

Janet Hawkins.

Janet Hawkins
Personnel Manager

cc ROIT

Figure 8a: Request for further particulars by respondent

WAREHOUSEMEN'S TRADE UNION, 128 FURLONG ROAD, LOᵢ

Ms Janet Hawkins
Personnel Manager
Mason (UK) Limited
Units 10-14
Humber Trading Estate
Edgware
Middlesex MS2 8SL

Your Ref: JH/SN

Our Ref : FH/JJ

27 February 1984

Dear Ms Hawkins

Re: Rider v Mason (UK) Limited

Thank you for your letter of 23 February upon which I am taking my member's instructions. In the meantime please supply the following further and better particulars of your grounds for resisting the application:

(1)   In what way was the warehouse running inefficiently when Brian Rogers joined the company?

(2)   Give details and dates of the instructions you say my member did not carry out.

(3)   What warnings were given to Mr Rider, in particular when were they given, by whom, and what were they about?

(4)   In what way did Mr Rider refuse to work properly after the Christmas break?

(5)   What were the reasons for his dismissal on 13 January?

Please supply the above information within 14 days of this letter.

Yours sincerely

Frank Hitchcock

Frank Hitchcock
District Secretary

cc ROIT

Figure 8b: Request for further particulars by applicant

Order for further particulars

13.2   Having sent a copy of the first letter to ROIT, the assistant secretary will already have the request on file. Therefore, when a formal request for an order is made, a letter similar to figure 9 on page 61 will suffice. It is advisable to explain why the information is required, as the tribunal will only make an order in circumstances where it is genuinely necessary so that justice between the parties may be done.

At this stage it is worth recalling that further particulars can be obtained prior to the lodging of the IT 1 or IT 3 or both. For example the questionnaire procedure in discrimination cases described in Chapter 1 which is usually used before a claim is commenced. Also an employer may request further particulars before he completes the IT 3 as described in Chapter 7.

Cases on tribunal's discretion

13.3   In *White v The University of Manchester* [*1976*] *IRLR 218*, the EAT gave some guidance to tribunals as to when they should exercise their discretion to grant an order for further particulars. In this case, the University alleged that the reasons for Miss White's dismissal as a typist were that she was unable to cope with the duties associated with her job, and that her attitude to and treatment of students and other university staff had caused ill-feeling and difficulty. She requested further particulars as to the respects in which it was alleged that she had been unable satisfactorily to cope with her duties, and the way in which her attitude was said to be defective. The EAT considered this a classic case in which an order should be made. Miss White could not possibly prepare her case unless she knew in reasonable detail the allegations the respondent would make at the hearing. The EAT said in *White*:

> 'It does not require any special forms; it does not require any special learning or knowledge. It is just a matter of straightforward sense. In one way or another the parties need to know the sort of thing which is going to be the subject of the hearing. Industrial tribunals know this very well and for the most part seek to ensure that it comes about. Of course in the end, if there is a surprise, they will ordinarily grant an adjournment to enable it to be dealt with but by and large it is much better if matters of this kind can be dealt with in advance so as to prevent adjournments taking place which are time consuming, expensive and inconvenient to all concerned.'

In *International Computers Limited v Whitley* [*1978*] *IRLR 318,* the EAT made it clear that tribunals will not always order further particulars as 'in many cases it should be either quite plain what is the real issue without particulars . . . being ordered, or, alternatively, the matter can be left until the hearing without injustice to either side'. But a party 'is entitled to such particulars as are necessary to enable them to know precisely what is the case which is going to be put up against them, and to enable them thereafter to prepare their own defence'.

MASON (UK) LTD, UNITS 10-14, HUMBER TRADING ESTATE, EDGWARE
MIDDLESEX MS2 8SL

Regional Office of the	Your Ref: Case No 269/84
Industrial Tribunals	
19-29 Woburn Place	
London	
WC1H 0LU	Our Ref : FH/JJ

12 March 1984

Dear Sir

RIDER v MASON (UK) LTD

I requested further and better particulars from the applicant's representative
by letter dated 23 February 1984 a copy of which was sent to you at that
time (and a further copy is attached), but I have not yet received a reply.
This is despite having replied on 29 February to their request for further
particulars which I received on 29 February (a copy of which I sent to you).

I would now formally apply for an order for further particulars under
rule 4(1)(a)(i) of the Tribunal Regulations. I cannot possibly prepare our case
without receiving details of the allegations made in the IT1.

Finally, I would request a postponement of the hearing set down on 23 March
as I cannot see the parties being ready to proceed by that date.

Yours faithfully

Janet Hawkins.

Janet Hawkins
Personnel Manager

cc WTU
    128 Furlong Road
    London EC1 2JA

Figure 9: Letter to ROIT applying for order for further particulars

13.3 *Getting to Know the Other Side's Case*

The case of *Lynch v Syntex Pharmaceuticals Ltd (EAT 244/80 IRLIB 190.3)* provides a good illustration of how the EAT interpreted the guidance given in the *White* and *Whitley* cases as to how a chairman should exercise his discretion in practice. In this case, the company completed paragraph 5 of the IT 3 as follows: 'The applicant was dismissed, and any claim from his dismissal will be resisted on the grounds that:

> (*a*) the applicant was guilty of gross misconduct in:
>> (i) submitting returns for work carried out by him which returns were false;
>> (ii) claiming expenses based on those records;
>> (iii) being absent from work without authority.
>
> (*b*) the applicant consistently failed to reach certain minimum and reasonable targets set by the company.'

Mr Lynch asked for particulars of the material relied upon by his former employers but his request was refused by the chairman; he appealed to the EAT who said: 'It seems to us here that the company are saying that Mr Lynch had made false returns and had claimed money on the basis of those false returns. We really do not see how he could possibly deal with those allegations, which are put forward on behalf of his former employers, unless he has some particulars of them. This is a serious charge which is made against him and in our judgment justice requires that he should have the details so that he may know what the company is going to say. Moreover it seems to us to be absolutely plain that if this matter goes to a hearing without some sort of particulars being given, the high probability is that an adjournment will have to be asked for, so that Mr Lynch may prepare his answer to what is said by the company, and in those circumstances both time and a substantial amount of money will be wasted.

'We think the same is true about the allegations that he was absent from work without authority and that he failed to achieve company targets. As we see it, there is no allegation of fraud in those; but there is an allegation of conduct apparently in breach of his obligations under the contract, and we think that he is entitled to know what it is that the company are going to allege against him.

'Accordingly we . . . order that particulars be given . . . in the following form: 1(*a*), of the allegation that the applicant submitted returns of work which were false, identifying those parts of the returns which are relied on by reference to their date, or otherwise sufficiently to identify them, which are said to be false, and the respects in which they are allegedly false; 1(*b*), of the allegation that the applicant claimed expenses based on false returns, identifying the expenses which it is alleged the applicant claimed, and stating the respects in which it is alleged that those expenses were falsely claimed or were based on false returns; 1(*c*), of the allegation that the applicant was absent from work without authority, stating the dates and times of the alleged absences and the place from which it is alleged the applicant was absent . . . Finally, (2) of the allegation that the applicant failed to achieve minimum and reasonable targets set by the company, specifying the targets and dates of achievement which are referred to, and specifying in each case the actual performance of the applicant which was known to the company at the date of his dismissal and upon which reliance is placed.' (*Lynch*).

An example of a respondent being granted an order for further particulars in a constructive dismissal case can be found in *Honeyrose Products Ltd v Joslin [1981] IRLR 80*. Mr Joslin's grounds for his claim were that his employer had committed fundamental breaches of his contract of employment. The respondent denied they had committed any breaches and applied for further particulars of the alleged breaches. The tribunal chairman only made a limited order, but on appeal the EAT extended the order.

Mr Joslin had alleged that there had been a deliberate withholding of correspondence with overseas customers about business for which he said he was responsible. The EAT ordered that he: '(i) give the periods during which such correspondence was allegedly withheld; (ii) identify the overseas customers and the business concerned.' Mr Joslin alleged that there had been a secret appointment of another person to the named position of general manager, which he himself was supposed to occupy. The EAT required him to 'identify the person concerned'. Mr Joslin claimed the employers had withdrawn from him without prior consultation the entire budgeting and financial control. The EAT ordered: 'identify the relevant functions formerly performed by the applicant in relation to the respondent company which were allegedly withdrawn, and approximately when they were withdrawn.' Finally, Mr Joslin contended he had been deliberately excluded from management meetings. The EAT ordered him to provide information to the employers as follows: '(i) give dates and locations of such meetings; (ii) give particulars of the alleged deliberate exclusion.'

Granting the order

13.4 The application will be considered by a chairman, sitting alone. Having already requested the information from the other side prior to the application there should be no delay in it being considered by the IT. This is because the chairman is unlikely to use his powers under Rule 12(3) to require notice of the application to be given to the other side, as this will already have been done.

If granted, an order will be made by ROIT in a form similar to figure 10 on page 64. This will be served by ROIT sending it ordinary post to the relevant party or his representative. It will normally contain a time limit by which the further particulars must be supplied to the other party, who will also receive a copy so that both sides will know what is happening.

As mentioned in Chapter 5, even though neither party has applied for an order, the tribunal may on its own initiative order that one party provides further particulars of some ground or fact relied upon (Rule 4(1)(*b*)(i)).

CASE NUMBER: 269/84

Regional Office of the
Industrial Tribunals
19-29 Woburn Place
London WC1H 0LU
Tel: 01 632 4921

ORDER OF THE INDUSTRIAL TRIBUNAL

FOR FURTHER PARTICULARS OF ORIGINATING APPLICATION

(Pursuant to the Rules of the Industrial Tribunals Regulations As Amended)

in the case of

Applicant   Respondent

J Rider   Mason (UK) Limited

                                v

TO: WTU
         128 Furlong Road
         London EC1 2JA

Following an application by the respondent for further particulars, a Chairman of the Tribunals ORDERS that on or before 30 March 1984 .... you furnish in writing to Mason (UK) Limited, Units 10-14, Humber Trading Estate, Edgware, Middlesex MS2 8SL ....

the following further particulars of the grounds on which you rely and send a copy to this Office.

> The particulars requested in the letter of 23 February a copy of which is attached to this Order

NOTE:

Failure to comply with this Order may result in your application being dismissed before or at the hearing.

A Rotta

cc Mason (UK) Limited
     Units 10-14
     Humber Trading Estate
     Edgware, Middlesex MS2 8SL

for Assistant Secretary of the Tribunals

Date: 16 March 1984

cc Advisory Conciliation and
     Arbitration Service

EO3A

Reproduced by permission of HMSO

Figure 10: Order for further particulars (EO 3A)

Setting aside or varying an order

13.5   A party against whom an order for further particulars is made can apply under Rule 4(2) for that order to be varied or set aside. This right must be exercised before the time limit for compliance expires, although Rule 12(2) gives tribunals power to extend this limit. A chairman will consider such an application in the light of whether the particulars are genuinely necessary in order to do justice between the parties.

Non-compliance with order

13.6   If the order is not complied with, this could adversely affect a party's case, because the tribunal under Rule 4(4) can dismiss the IT 1 or strike out the whole or part of the IT 3, and where appropriate, debar a respondent from defending altogether. However, in *Morrit v London Borough of Lambeth* (*EAT 244/79*), the EAT found that an employee should not be prevented from having his case examined on its merits, just because of a procedural failure. Mr Morrit had failed to understand what was required of him and the information he supplied was not the further particulars ordered. The tribunal did not inform him that it was unsatisfactory and when he arrived at the hearing he was quite unaware that it might be suggested that his originating application might be dismissed. The EAT went on to find that he should have been warned, before the hearing, that he would be required to meet a procedural point. This set of circumstances is unlikely to recur in practice because the 1980 Regulations have been amended to oblige tribunals to send notice to a party in default before dismissing, striking out or debarring, giving him an opportunity to object to any of these courses of action being taken. The tribunal has discretion as to whether this opportunity is determined on the basis of written representations or an oral hearing.

In another case, *Martin v London Transport Executive* (*EAT 400/79*) the EAT upheld the tribunal's decision to dismiss the IT 1 where the applicant refused to provide further particulars. Mr Martin retired from London Transport on medical grounds. In his IT 1 he stated that the 'procedure was unfair' and that the 'respondent did not act reasonably'. The respondents requested further particulars of these claims, and an order was made to that effect. Mr Martin's solicitors were informed by ROIT that failure to comply with the order could result in dismissal of the originating application, and this is what the tribunal did because Mr Martin 'declined' to provide the particulars. The EAT would not interfere with the exercise by the tribunal of its discretion because the tribunal had carefully considered all relevant facts before coming to its decision.

It was thought that a chairman's discretion was more limited in the case of a defaulting applicant than in the case of a respondent. This is because Rule 4(4) only gives a chairman the power to dismiss the IT 1 whereas his power in relation to the IT 3 is to strike out the whole or *part* of the notice of appearance. However, in *Dean v The Islamic Foundation* [*1982*] *IRLR 290*, the EAT found the tribunal has discretion (under Rule 8(1)) to dismiss part of a complaint as well. In this case Mr Dean had his allegations of discrimination on the grounds of sex and race dismissed whereas his unfair dismissal claim was allowed to proceed.

Further 'further particulars'

13.7   Where the replies to a request or order for further particulars calls for yet more elaboration, there is nothing to prevent a party from making a further request. So in practice you may find that the process of requesting particulars amounts to an exchange of letters, each letter further clarifying the grounds and arguments relied upon.

Checklist

13.8   To sum up: if either party is unclear about the grounds of the other side's case, then he should:

(*a*) request by letter the further and better particulars required;

(*b*) send a copy of this request to ROIT;

(*c*) if within a reasonable time there is an ambiguous or unclear reply, or none, make a formal application to the tribunal for an order; and

(*d*) if the order is not complied with, notify the tribunal.

PART B : DISCOVERY OF DOCUMENTS

Recommended action

13.9   When preparing your case you will also have to decide on what documents will be needed to prove the case. Documents will form part of the evidence (often a crucial part) which will be put before the tribunal. Some may be in your possession, others may be held by your opponent. Therefore the following course of action is recommended:

(1) identify all documents required;

(2) request from the other side any not in your possession;

(3) also request any other documents which the other side intends to use;

(4) prepare to disclose your documents;

(5) if you cannot get full co-operation, apply for an order for discovery or inspection of documents.

These are considered separately below.

What documents do you require?

13.10   In most cases the documents required will be obvious. The following are brief checklists for the more numerous claims:

Unfair dismissal cases

(*a*) letters of appointment or promotion

(*b*) written statement or contract of employment

(*c*) disciplinary rules and procedures

(*d*) company handbook

(*e*) grievance and other procedures

(*f*) a relevant national or local agreement

(*g*) any correspondence or memos relating to the matters in issue, especially between the parties

(*h*) written warnings

(*i*) any minutes or records of disciplinary hearings

(*j*) personal or company records

(*k*) details of the company pension scheme — contributions of employer/employee

(*l*) expert reports, e.g. medical report

(*m*) wage and fringe benefit details

(*n*) documents relating to the alleged reason for dismissal, e.g. sales records, production figures, appraisal reports

(*o*) documents showing mitigation of loss, e.g. letters requesting, and in answer to, job applications, advertisements etc.

(*p*) documents showing previous enforcement of a company rule

(*q*) letter of dismissal or resignation

(*r*) written statement of reasons for dismissal under EPCA s 53

(*s*) documents relating to unemployment benefit and any disqualification.

Redundancy cases

(i) details of company's general financial position, accounts, sales figures, productivity, etc.

(ii) documents relating to the need for redundancy selection policy, areas of redundancy and selection policy

(iii) internal memos ascertaining if suitable alternative vacancies are available or exist.

Sex or race discrimination cases

(A) criteria used in other selection decisions

(B) information on other job or promotion applications

(C) assessments of all applicants including interview notes

(D) company statistics on ratio of women/men or black/white employees.

These are not exhaustive lists but are representative of the sort of documents which may be needed to prepare the average case.

In some cases the nature of the documents required will be more difficult to ascertain. For example, under EPA s 99 employers are obliged to consult a recognised TU at the earliest opportunity where they are proposing redundancies, but there are certain minimum periods by which consultation must commence depending on the number of employees involved. If these minimum periods are not complied with the union may apply to an IT for a 'protective award' for those employees. The only defence open to an employer is that there were special circumstances making it not reasonably practicable to comply with the time limits. *[EPA s 99(8)]*. If the circumstances alleged are, say, that the employer had suddenly lost a major contract, it may be necessary to disclose documents showing a breach or frustration of contract.

Obtaining documents not in your possession

13.11   Any documents which are required but are not in your possession should be requested by letter as shown in figure 11 on page 69, a copy being sent to ROIT. Note that a time limit should be set. Be prepared to pay reasonable copying charges. If it is impracticable to photocopy a document arrange to inspect the document at, for example, your opponent's premises.

Request all documents to be used by the other side

13.12   In the same letter it is advisable to ask your opponent if there are any other documents which he will be using, and to let you have copies or an opportunity to inspect them. If possible you should get to know the full details of your opponent's case including all documentary evidence to be used against you.

Open disclosure policy

13.13   Your opponent will be more likely to co-operate if he knows you are prepared to disclose all your documentary evidence to him. In other words, there should be full disclosure on both sides. The sacrifice of disclosing your own documentary evidence is better than the risk of your opponent surprising you with new documents.

Tribunals are actively encouraging parties to get their heads together and agree on a bundle of documents before the hearing and are sending figure 12, on page 71, to the parties. In nearly all other court proceedings a document not disclosed is a document not allowed to be

WAREHOUSEMEN'S TRADE UNION, 128 FURLONG ROAD, LONDON EC1 2JA

Ms Janet Hawkins   Your Ref: JH/SN
Personnel Manager
Mason (UK) Limited   Our Ref : FH/JJ
Units 10-14
Humber Trading Estate
Edgware
Middlesex MS2 8SL   14 March 1984

Dear Ms Hawkins

Re: Rider v Mason (UK) Ltd

Further to my letter of 27 February I require disclosure of the following documents and would be grateful if you could supply copies:

(1)   Mr Rider's contract of employment

(2)   Your disciplinary procedure

(3)   Any note of disciplinary interviews held with Mr Rider or of oral warnings given to him

(4)   Any other personnel records you hold relating to Mr Rider

(5)   Written warning(s)

In view of the pending hearing, please supply copies within seven days. I am prepared to pay any reasonable copying charges involved.

If you will be relying on any other documents perhaps you would let me have copies of these, and I will reciprocate with any other documents the applicant will be relying on.

Yours sincerely

Frank Hitchcock

Frank Hitchcock
District Secretary

cc ROIT

Figure 11: Request for disclosure of documents

produced. Although IT procedure is different, the parties are now encouraged to adopt an open disclosure policy in order to minimise delays at the hearing caused by one party or the other introducing documents not yet disclosed which result in an adjournment of the proceedings. In practice, it is more likely that the employer will be required to produce documents than the employee (particularly in discrimination cases). This is for the simple reason that most relevant documents will be in the possession of the employer. The open disclosure policy helps bring this part of the evidence to light well before the hearing, and should facilitate proper preparation, and in turn reduce the length of any hearing. In addition it may encourage settlement of a case or withdrawal of the application.

Order for discovery or inspection

13.14　If the other side will not co-operate then a formal application can be made under Rule 4(1)(*a*)(ii) to ROIT for discovery or inspection of the documents required, an example of which can be found in Figure 13 on page 72. The application can again be made by letter and should include the reasons for requiring the documents. If the chairman considers that the information is material or relevant to the issues in the case or is necessary for disposing fairly with the proceedings or for saving costs, he has discretion to grant an order 'to the person making the application such discovery or inspection (including the taking of copies) of documents as might be granted by a County Court'. In other words, the chairman has discretion to order discovery of such documents as he thinks fit subject to the qualification deriving from the County Court Rules that 'discovery shall not be ordered if and so far as the court is of the opinion that it is not necessary either for disposing fairly of the proceedings or for saving costs.'

Figure 14(a) on page 73 provides an example of a typical order for discovery of documents. The tribunal will serve the order by sending it by ordinary post to the relevant party and will send a copy to the other party. It will usually specify a time limit in which, and a place where, the order must be complied with. The difference between 'discovery' and 'inspection' will be apparent from figure 14(b) on page 74. Discovery requires copies of documents to be sent to the other side, whereas 'inspection' only requires the documents to be made available at, for example, the employer's premises for the employee to inspect, and then an entitlement to take copies. The inspection option is usually exercised by the chairman where it is apparent that not all of a particular document will be relevant or it would be too bulky to photocopy.

Where inspection becomes necessary in Scotland there is a special mechanism involved known as an action in 'commission and diligence'. It involves the appointment by the tribunal of an independent commissioner. He acts for the tribunal and assesses which documents appear to be relevant to the case. He then makes certificated disclosure

PREPARATION OF DOCUMENTS FOR THE HEARING

At an Industrial Tribunal hearing parties frequently wish to refer to certain letters or documents in support of their case.

It wil be helpful, and may simplify and shorten the hearing, if each party sends to the other, well in advance of the hearing date, a list of documents which he or she intends to produce at the hearing.

It will then be open to either party to ask to see, or to receive a copy of, particular documents before the hearing. Experience has shown that compliance with such a request may be to the advantage of both parties in avoiding delays or adjournments of hearings to permit documents to be studied.

Would you please send to this office a copy of any list of documents which you send to the other party. The documents themselves or copies of them should not be sent to this office.

NOTE FOR PROFESSIONAL ADVISERS

Professional advisers should prepare a bundle containing all correspondence and other documents on which they intend to rely at the hearing arranged in correct sequence and numbered consecutively. It is desirable, whenever it is practicable, that there should be an agreed bundle.

Three sets of documents should be made available for the use of the tribunal.

Reproduced by permission of HMSO

Figure 12: Preparation of documents for the hearing

WAREHOUSEMEN'S TRADE UNION, 128 FURLONG ROAD, LONDON EC1 2JA

Regional Office of the
Industrial Tribunals
19-29 Woburn Place
London
WC1H 0LU

Your ref: CASE NO 269/84

Our ref : FH/JJ

26 March 1984

Dear Sirs

RIDER v MASON (UK) LTD

I am in receipt of the order for further particulars dated 16 March which I will endeavour to reply to before 30 March.

You will recall I sent you a copy of a request dated 14 March for disclosure of certain documents from the respondent. I have not received a reply to this letter and therefore apply for an order for their disclosure under rule 4(1)(a)(ii) of the Tribunal Regulations. Without seeing these documents it will be impossible to prepare my case properly.

Yours faithfully

Frank Hitchcock

Frank Hitchcock
District Secretary

cc Mason (UK) Ltd

Figure 13: Letter to ROIT applying for an order for disclosure of documents

CASE NUMBER: 269/84

Regional Office of the
Industrial Tribunals
19-29 Woburn Place
London WC1H 0LU

ORDER OF THE INDUSTRIAL TRIBUNALS

FOR DISCOVERY OF DOCUMENTS

(Pursuant to the Rules of the Industrial Tribunals Regulations As Amended)

in the case of

Applicant	Respondent
J Rider	Mason (UK) Ltd

.... v ....

To:

Mason (UK) Ltd
Units 10-14
Humber Trading Estate
Edgware
Middlesex MS2 8SL

Following an application by .... the applicant ....

for discovery of documents, a Chairman of the Tribunals ORDERS that on or before

.... 11 April 1984 .... you send to .... Warehousemen's Trade
.... Union of 128 Furlong Road, London EC1 2JA ....

a list of such of the documents specified in the Schedule below as are, or have

been, in your possession or power, and send a copy of the list to this Office.

THE SCHEDULE

1   The applicant's contract of employment

2   The respondent's disciplinary procedure

3   Any written warnings relating to the applicant

4   Any written notes of disciplinary proceedings or
    oral warnings relating to the applicant

NOTE:

Failure to comply with this Order may result in a fine of up to £200 being imposed
upon you under paragraph 1(7) of Schedule 9 to the Employment Protection (Consolidation) Act 1978.

cc   WTU

cc   ACAS

A Norton

for Assistant Secretary of the Tribunals

Date: 28 March 1984

E02

Figure 14a: Order for discovery of documents (EO 2)

CASE NUMBER: 269/84

Regional Office of the
Industrial Tribunals
London (North)
19-29 Woburn Place
London WCIH OLU
Telephone: 01 632 4921

ORDER OF THE INDUSTRIAL TRIBUNAL

FOR INSPECTION OF DOCUMENTS

(Pursuant to the Rules of the Industrial Tribunals Regulations As Amended)

in the case of

Applicant		Respondent
J Rider	v	Mason (UK) Limited

TO:

Mason (UK) Limited, Units 10-14, Humber Trading Estate, Edgware, Middlesex MS2 8SL

Following an application by ....

a Chairman of the Tribunals ORDERS that on reasonable notice you shall on or before ....11 April 1984................... produce for inspection at Mason (UK) Limited, Units 10-14, Humber Trading Estate, Edgware, Middlesex MS2 8SL ....

the documents referred to in the Schedule below and permit copies to be taken.

THE SCHEDULE

The relevant parts of the records of Mr Rider held by you other than those which are already the subject of the order for disclosure of documents.

NOTE:

(1) Failure to comply with this Order may result in a fine of up to £200 being imposed upon you under paragraph 1 (7) of Schedule 9 of the Employment Protection (Consolidation) Act 1978.
(2) If you wish, you may comply with this Order by supplying to the other party a photocopy of the documents.

A Newton

for Assistant Secretary of the Tribunals

Date: 28 March 1984

cc   WTU
128 Furlong Road
London EC1 2JA

cc   ACAS

EO4

Reproduced by permission of HMSO

Figure 14b: Order for inspection of documents (EO 4)

of appropriate excerpts. In practice it is seldom used but is extremely useful where there is opposition to disclosure as mentioned below, as it provides an independent assessment of what should and can be disclosed.

Defences to disclosure

13.15 Tribunals will automatically exercise their discretion to order disclosure of documents which are relevant or material to the issues in dispute. If the documents demanded are confidential or discovery would be oppressive in the sense of being burdensome physically or financially then tribunals may not exercise, or may limit the exercise, of their discretion, or not exercise it at all.

Although documents may be relevant to a case they may also be regarded, by an employer in particular, as *confidential*.

In the well-known cases of *Nassé v Science Research Council* and *Vyas v Leyland Cars [1979] IRLR 465*, the House of Lords (HL) laid down certain guidelines to be followed by ITs where employers claim that documents required to be disclosed by employees are confidential. Although these were discrimination cases, the guidance relates generally to the disclosure of confidential documents:

— ITs must decide whether the confidential material is relevant to an issue which arises in the case;

— If the material is relevant, ITs must determine whether discovery is necessary for disposing fairly with the claim;

— It should do this by inspecting the documents in question in a way which avoids delay and unnecessary applications;

— This inspection should be carried out by a chairman and will usually take place before the hearing so that, if discovery is ordered, the employee has time to consider any documents that are produced;

— The chairman may take into account the following: the fact that the material is confidential and that to order disclosure would involve a breach of confidence; the sensitivity of particular types of confidential information; the extent to which the interests of third parties such as other employees may be affected; the interest of preserving confidentiality of personal reports, and to any wider interest which may be seen to exist in preserving confidentiality of systems of personal assessment;

— If the tribunal decides discovery is necessary to fairly dispose of the claim then it must order disclosure notwithstanding confidentiality;

— However, in a case where there is a pressing need to preserve confidentiality, the tribunal must first consider whether the necessary information can be given or obtained in a way that will not involve a breach of confidence;

— It must also see where confidentiality can be preserved by special measures such as 'covering up', substituting anonymous references for specific names or, in rare cases, a hearing in private.

Confidentiality

13.16   It is worth reviewing the facts of *Nassé* and *Vyas* to illustrate the sorts of situations which could give rise to a question of confidentiality.

In the latter case, Mr Vyas was employed as a method analyst and he applied for a transfer from one division of British Leyland's Cowley Works to another. There were two vacancies for which Mr Vyas and three white employees were interviewed. He did not get the position and claimed it was because of his race. He applied to the IT for further particulars and discovery covering a wide range of information including some received in confidence about the four men and the confidential forms on which the interviewing panel had recorded their opinions of the persons interviewed.

In the former case, Mrs Nassé was employed as a clerical officer and applied for promotion to executive office grade. The promotion procedure was based on an annual confidential report on each clerical officer, containing assessments of performance and opinions as to whether employees were suitable for promotion. The next stage in the procedure involved the reports being considered by senior staff and then by a Local Review Board. On the basis of those reports, and without interviewing the person concerned, the Local Review Board recommended clerical officers for promotion and these recommendations, together with minutes of the Review Board's meetings and the reports, were sent to the Director of the relevant Senior Review Committee. From there, the matter went to the Central Review Board who put forward names for interview. Mrs Nassé was turned down for a promotion interview and claimed it was because she was a married woman and because she had taken part in trade union activities. She asked for disclosure of the annual confidential reports for 1975 and 1976 on herself and two clerical officers in her establishment who had been selected for personal interview. She also asked for the minutes of the Local Review Board relating to the decision in the three cases whether to select for interview and recommend for promotion to executive officer or not.

In both cases the HL ordered that the requests go back to the tribunal for the chairman to inspect the relevant documents and determine which, if any, should be disclosed, in order to dispose fairly of the complaints.

Another example of the discovery of confidential documents can be found in the case of the *DHSS v Sloan* [*1981*] *ICR 313*. Mrs Sloan was retired on medical grounds. The DHSS would not disclose certain medical reports to her because there was a provision in her contract of employment which disentitled her to see such documents and because they thought it might be detrimental to her mental health. On appeal against the chairman's order to disclose the medical reports to Mrs Sloan, the EAT were sensitive to the effect that such disclosure might have on her and therefore ordered that the medical reports should be disclosed to her doctor. If the doctor came to the conclusion that in his opinion disclosure would not be harmful to his patient, then the tribunal should disclose the reports giving whatever protection was possible to Mrs Sloan.

Disclosure 'oppressive'

13.17   The other defence to disclosing documents is where such disclosure would be oppressive. In *Wilcox v HGS Ltd [1975] IRLR 211*, the tribunal was faced with a request that a Gas Board should be required to disclose approximately 600,000 documents. The CA upheld the EAT's approach to recommend that the tribunal should order that a representative sample be disclosed.

Both defences considered

13.18   More recently both defences to an order for disclosure of documents were considered together in the case of *Perera v Civil Service Commission [1980] IRLR 233*, where the EAT gave further guidance to ITs to the effect that they must try to balance the applicant's need for information upon which to base his case, against the employer's interest in minimising the burden and cost of large-scale production of documents.

Mr Perera, an executive officer with the Civil Service who was born in Sri Lanka, was interviewed for the post of legal assistant in 1977. Although he was recommended for the interview he was unsuccessful. He made two subsequent applications for the same post in 1978 and 1979, and was again unsuccessful: On these occasions he even failed to get a first interview. Mr Perera felt that given his qualifications and experience the reason for his rejections could only have been because of his colour. Consequently in order to establish evidence of racial discrimination he applied to an IT for a wide range of documents relating to all the applicants for posts in 1977, 1978 and 1979, a total of almost 1600. The tribunal chairman dismissed the application as oppressive.

On appeal, the EAT accepted that such an order would be oppressive but at the same time recognised that without disclosure being ordered the proceedings could not be fairly disposed of as Mr Perera would be seriously handicapped in establishing his case. As a result the EAT felt that limited discovery should be ordered which was fair to Mr Perera and convenient to the Civil Service Commission. Accordingly the EAT ordered that certain information should be provided in relation to 78 applicants who had been interviewed by the same board which interviewed Mr Perera in 1977, in so far as this information was available. Such information was to include date and place of birth, nationality at birth of the applicants and their fathers. In addition he was to be shown copies of the final report and assessment of the board, but in order to preserve confidentiality, the names of candidates were to be blanked out.

Non-compliance with order

13.19   Even if the parties do not apply for an order the tribunal can on its own initiative order the parties to bring documents to the hearing, or dislcose them to the other side (Rule 4(1)(*b*)(ii)). The party receiving the order may, for various reasons, not wish to comply with it because, for instance, the documents requested are confidential or the order is oppressive. In such cases the party should write to ROIT, within the time limit set for compliance, giving the reasons why he objects to the order. The chairman may then invite the parties (or their representatives) to ROIT to make oral representations about the order before a chairman in his private rooms. The chairman can vary or set aside the order under Rule 4(2).

Remember that if you wish to rely on a document the onus is on you to provide it. So, if you are relying on the terms of a disciplinary procedure and at the hearing there is a conflict of evidence as to the substance of that procedure and you have forgotten to make a copy of it available, you are likely to be at a disadvantage. If an order is made and not complied with and there has been no application to vary or set aside, the likely inference will be detrimental to the party failing to comply. The tribunal has similar powers to those relating to failure to comply with an order for further particulars: under Rule 4(4) it can strike out a notice of appearance or dismiss an application, provided it has first given the party concerned an opportunity to show why such action should not be taken. Also a non-complying party will be liable on summary conviction to a fine not exceeding £200.

Documents held by third parties

13.20   Where a relevant document is held by a third party, who is not involved in the proceedings, then it would appear the tribunal has *no* power to order that third party to disclose the document. However, the tribunal does have power under Rule 4(1)(iii) to order that that third party attend the hearing and produce the document at the hearing.

Chapter 14

Pre-hearing Assessments

Introduction

14.1   The objective of the pre-hearing assessment (PHA) is to provide a means of discouraging meritless claims. The procedure also applies to meritless defences, but in practical terms this part of the PHA procedure has not proved very important.

The Rules

14.2   The Tribunal Rules relating to PHAs are set out in Rule 6. Rule 6(1) reads: 'A Tribunal may at any time before the hearing . . . consider, by way of pre-hearing assessment, the contents of the originating application and entry of appearance, any representations in writing which have been submitted and any oral argument advanced by or on behalf of the party'. Sub-rule (2) continues: 'If upon a pre-hearing assessment, the Tribunal considers that the originating application is unlikely to succeed or that the contentions or a particular contention of a party appear to have no reasonable prospect of success, it may indicate that in its opinion, if the originating application shall not be withdrawn or the contentions or contention of the party shall be persisted in up to or at the hearing, the party in question may have an order for costs made against him at the hearing under the provisions of Rule 11'.

It is immediately apparent that PHAs cannot prevent claims proceeding, but can only act as a warning that if claims or defences are proceeded with then costs may be awarded against the applicant or respondent. So the net effect is that of deterrent rather than prevention.

The procedure

14.3   The procedure for PHAs is designed to be as straightforward as possible. Either party can apply under Rule 6(1) for a PHA. Although the Rule does not require such an application to be in writing it is better to send a letter to the assistant secretary at ROIT requesting a PHA. The letter does not have to be in any particular form but, should give reasons for the application.

On receipt of such a letter a chairman will determine on the face of the written representations before him whether there is any useful purpose

Table: Pre-hearing assessments

Applications approved or initiated by tribunals

Central Office of the Industrial Tribunals
(England and Wales)

Period	Number of cases	PHA at request of			Party with weak cases		Withdrawn/ settled before PHA		Legal representation at PHA		Costs warning given against	
		A	R	C	A	R	W	S	A	R	A	R
1 Oct '80– 25 Sept '81	1,778	19^a	776^a	984	—	—	199	87	256	435	699	12
28 Sept '81– 24 Sept '82	2,349	22^b	1,005^b	1324	2308	41	505	234	347	519	894^c	18
27 Sept '82– 30 Sept '83	3,479	27^a	1,639^a	1814	3356	123	898	282	481	737	1202	34

A   = Applicant
R   = Respondent
C   = COIT
W   = Withdrawn
S   = Settled
Suc = Succeeded
D   = Dismissed

Cases where warning given against applicant			Cases where *no* warning given against applicant				
Withdrawn/ settled after PHA before hearing	Case succeeded/ dismissed	Costs awarded against applicant	Withdrawn/ settled after PHA before hearing	Case succeeded/ dismissed	Costs awarded against applicant	Average time of PHA (mins)	
W	S	Suc	D		W	S	Suc	D		
	30	12	107	37	177	127	90	377	11	34
5	42	10	116	51	132	207	98	279	5	30
7	56	20	249	74	170	277	186	464	13	27

Includes one case where PHA requested by both applicant and respondent.

Includes two cases where PHA requested by both parties.

Includes one case where applicant warned.

in holding a PHA. Where there are triable issues of both fact and law which are unlikely to be resolved without hearing evidence then the chairman is unlikely to grant a PHA. Where this is not the case, a PHA may be ordered.

If the tribunal grants a PHA it will send a notice to both parties in a form similar to figure 15 on pages 83 and 84. It should also be appreciated that the tribunal itself can require a PHA on its own initiative although one has not been requested by either party. In fact the Table on pages 80 and 81 shows that over half the PHAs ordered originate from the tribunals rather than the parties and the vast majority of these are aimed at sifting out meritless claims. The Table gives details of PHAs for the first three years of their operation. Of the 7,606 PHAs to October 1982, 2,205 were withdrawn (8 per cent) or settled (21 per cent) after the notice but before the actual assessment was held. The notice itself therefore seems to have the effect of encouraging a determination on average of some 29 per cent of the cases where a PHA was ordered.

Where cases proceed to an assessment, both parties are entitled to attend with or without representatives. Neither party, however, has to attend. In fact, in Scotland, the respondents are to some extent discouraged from attending, the rationale being that where the merits of the claim are being questioned it is for the applicant to show that he can succeed.

Written representations

14.4   Figure 15 indicates that the tribunal will, at the assessment, consider the contents of the IT 1, IT 3 and any other written representations. This means that parties who prepare written representations before the assessment to be submitted at this stage or at the actual PHA will have such representations taken into account. There is no requirement that written representations be submitted because both parties have an opportunity to appear at the assessment. Also the IT 1 and IT 3 in their own right may contain all the representations required for the purposes of the assessment.

There are circumstances, however, where the opportunity might be important. For example, if the respondent chooses not to attend the assessment he may wish to submit further representations in addition to those contained in the IT 3.

It should be borne in mind that a letter of request for a PHA will itself be a written representation which the tribunal will take into account.

Witnesses

14.5   What is clear from Rule 6 is that parties cannot give oral evidence at the assessment. In other words, they cannot call witnesses. Another important part of the evidence is likely to be contained in documents. Often IT 1s and IT 3s have such documents attached and therefore the tribunal at a PHA must consider them. Similarly if documents are

Regional Office of the Industrial Tribunals
London (South)
93 Ebury Bridge Road London SW1W 8RE

Telephone 01-730 9161 ext

Mr M Fortune 23 Armorial Road London SW17	Your reference JA/SM Our reference 1589/84 Date 19 March 1984

THE INDUSTRIAL TRIBUNALS

NOTICE OF PRE-HEARING ASSESSMENT

in the case of

Applicant		Respondent
Mr M Fortune	–v–	Perman Ltd

Notice is Hereby Given that pursuant to Rule 6 of the Industrial Tribunals Rules of Procedure 1980 a tribunal will hold a pre-hearing assessment at 93 Ebury Bridge Road, London, SWI, at   10   am/pm on   Wednesday, the   4   day of   April   19 84. .

1   The parties (other than a respondent who has not entered an appearance) are entitled to attend and to be heard at this pre-hearing assessment and to submit representations in writing. A party may bring a representative if he or she so wishes. Attendance should be at the above time and place.

2   No oral evidence will be taken. The tribunal will consider the contents of the originating application and entry of appearance, any representations in writing which have been submitted and any oral argument advanced by or on behalf of a party.

3   If the tribunal considers that the originating application is unlikely to succeed or that any particular contention of the applicant appears to have no reasonable prospect of success, it may indicate that in its opinion, if the application shall not be withdrawn or the contention shall be persisted in up to or at the hearing, the applicant may have an order for costs made against him or her at the hearing under the provisions of Rule 11 of the above Rules.

4   If at the pre-hearing assessment the Tribunal gives an indication of its opinion pursuant to Rule 6 written notice to that effect will be sent to the parties.

Reproduced by permission of HMSO

Figure 15: Notice of pre-hearing assessment

5   It is not considered necessary for the respondent to be present on this occasion though
he/she is at liberty to attend if he /she so wishes.

Signed.........*A Norton*............................

for Assistant Secretary of the Tribunals

Date: 19 March 1984

To the Applicant

Note: Representatives who receive this notice
must inform the party they represent of the
date, time and place of the hearing. The party
will not be notified direct.

and the Respondent

Perman Ltd
36 Westway Road
London SE9
~~and the Secretary of State for Employment.~~

and the Conciliation Officer, Advisory Conciliation and Arbitration Service

SL8A

Reproduced by permission of HMSO

Figure 15 (continued)

attached to other written representations the tribunal will be obliged at least to consider them. The right to submit written representations, therefore, at PHAs may be a means of strengthening a party's argument, without actually being able to call witnesses.

At an assessment, witnesses cannot be called to introduce documents, but nevertheless the tribunal will be obliged to consider the contents of, for example, a job description at an assessment because it is attached to a written representation.

Tribunals tend to discourage lengthy representations, otherwise there is the danger the procedure will not retain its present simplicity. Nor will they permit such a procedure to be used to introduce evidence 'by the back door'. For example, it is unlikely they would consider proofs of evidence (*see* Chapter 15).

The assessment

14.6   Up until October 1983, 5,401 PHAs had been held. The average length of time taken at the assessments so far recorded is approximately 30 minutes. The assessment is held before a full tribunal in the same way as a hearing (Rule 12(4)), with a clerk in attendance, but it is much less formal.

The informality can also be seen in the way the PHA is conducted. There is no order of proceedings. In fact, it is very much up to the individual chairman how he conducts the assessment. However, a pattern has emerged where the party who is being called upon to show that his claim or defence is not meritless is asked to argue first. This is quite logical as the chairman will invariably open the assessment by explaining to the applicant that the reason for the PHA is that there is, prima facie, a weak claim. He will then seek to find out from the applicant whether the facts are in dispute and, if not, will wish to know why the applicant considers he has an arguable claim. Only then will he give the respondent, if present, an opportunity to argue why the claim has no reasonable prospect of success.

Again it must be emphasised that neither party will be entitled to give oral evidence, and there is no point in taking witnesses to the assessment. This may account for the fact that PHAs are sometimes held in private. Only 'hearings' have to be held in public, subject to some exceptions (Rule 7(1)). Regulation 2 of the 1980 Regulations defines a hearing in terms of a tribunal receiving oral evidence to enable it to reach a decision. A PHA's purpose is different in that the tribunal is being asked to give an opinion rather than make a decison.

The opinion

14.7   After hearing the arguments, the tribunal will ask the parties to retire so that they can consider whether or not a warning should be issued. The tribunal members will consider the contents of the IT 1, IT 3, any written representations and the oral argument. If, as a result, they are of the unanimous opinion that the originating application is unlikely to succeed or that any particular contention or contentions of either party appear to have no reasonable prospect of success, they will indicate this by giving a warning. The parties will return, and the applicant, will be told, for example, that if the application is not withdrawn or if the contention is persisted with up to or at the hearing then the applicant may have an order for costs made against him at the hearing. (The question of costs will be considered in detail in Chapter 40.)

Alternatively, where the tribunal is not of such an opinion, then the chairman will say as much and then the case will proceed normally to a hearing. A party who does not attend will not be aware of this and tribunals consider that such a party need not be told the result of the PHA. Where a warning is given to an applicant a letter will be sent to him together with an opinion in a form similar to figure 16. A copy of the letter will be sent to the respondent. So where a non-attending respondent receives no copy of a document recording a warning on costs he can assume no warning was given. Where the warning is given to the respondent the opinion will be in a slightly different form.

It is apparent from these opinions that neither the applicant nor the respondent are prevented from continuing with their claims or defences but rather discouraged from doing so.

The hearing

14.8   A PHA should not, in theory, affect the hearing. In other words, the case should be set down for a hearing and a notice of hearing issued in the usual way despite the fact a PHA is pending. So it may well be that a notice of hearing has already been sent to the parties before the assessment. This means that an application for postponement of a hearing because of a pending PHA will not be received very sympathetically.

Tribunal members on the PHA cannot be members of the tribunal which hears the full case (Rule 6(4)). If an opinion is given, this will not be made available to the next tribunal until after a decision has been made as to whether or not the claim succeeds or fails. This is so that the second tribunal is not influenced by the opinion of the first tribunal. In order to ensure this happens most ROITs have adopted a system where every case file where there has been a PHA contains a sealed envelope marked 'PHA'. The envelope either contains nothing or an opinion plus the chairman's notes. The tribunal will decide at the end of the hearing whether or not to open the envelope. There is nothing in the Tribunal Regulations which requires the tribunal to take note of an opinion.

The effect of warnings

14.9   From the Table on pages 80 and 81 it can be seen that of the 5,401 cases which proceeded to an assessment, where a warning had been given

Regional Office of the Industrial Tribunals
London (South)

Case No: 1589/84

93 Ebury Bridge Road, London SW1W 8RE

Telephone : 01 730 9161

THE INDUSTRIAL TRIBUNALS

OPINION OF THE TRIBUNAL FOLLOWING A PRE-HEARING ASSESSMENT
(Pursuant to Rule 6 of the Industrial Tribunals Rules of Procedure 1980)

in the case of

Applicant		Respondent
Mr M Fortune	-v-	Perman Ltd

Pre-hearing assessment held at London (South)

on 4 April 1984

Chairman Mr J H Engel   Members Mrs F Star

Mr C Rattle

THE TRIBUNAL considers that the originating application herein is unlikely
to succeed.

In its opinion if the originating application shall not be withdrawn the applicant
may at the hearing of the originating application have an order for costs made
against him under the provisions of Rule 11 of the Industrial Tribunals Rules
of Procedure 1980.

JH Engel

Chairman

Date 4 April 1984

Reproduced by permission of HMSO

Figure 16: Opinion of a tribunal following a pre-hearing assessment

some 42 per cent were withdrawn (40 per cent) or settled (2.4 per cent) before a hearing. Where no warning was given some 20 per cent of cases were withdrawn (8.8 per cent) or settled (11.3 per cent).

The combined effect of the whole PHA procedure was to settle or withdraw some 73 per cent of the 7,606 PHAs ordered between 1 October 1980 and 30 September 1983. This compares in a slightly different period with some 68 per cent of all cases which are settled or withdrawn before the hearing.

Appeals

14.10　It is worth noting that except on procedural matters it is not possible to appeal against a PHA as an opinion does not constitute a decision. (*Mackie v John Holt Vintners Ltd [1982] IRLR 236*).

Chapter 15

Taking Statements from Witnesses

Introduction

15.1 A statement or proof of evidence is a typed or written account in the first person of the evidence which a witness is able to adduce or impart in relation to the issues arising in the case. The most important witnesses are often the parties themselves. The statement forms the basis of the evidence which that particular witness will give to the tribunal at the hearing. It will only be used by the witness in the preparatory stages and not at the hearing.

Oral evidence and previously prepared statements

15.2 Tribunals usually require oral evidence to be given without reference to a previously prepared statement, because among other things evidence given from memory is regarded as the more credible. The major exception is where a party is presenting the case in person and obviously has no experience of a tribunal hearing. In this situation the chairman is usually happy for a person to read out a previously prepared statement.

Miss Watson-Smith represented herself in a three day case before a tribunal hearing her complaint of unfair dismissal. The chairman refused to allow her to give evidence by reading a prepared statement and said she must give evidence by word of mouth. She was found not to have been unfairly dismissed. On appeal the EAT said, (allowing the appeal and remitting the case for re-hearing):

'When a party who is represented gives evidence, the advocate asks the questions on the basis of the party's proof. The advocate asks his questions so as to elicit the relevant evidence fully and in proper order. All the witness has to do is answer the questions and produce any exhibits which he is called on to produce. The witness is properly not allowed to answer by reading from his proof. If he has made a contemporary note he will be allowed to refresh his memory from that note: see for example the universal practice in the examination of police officers.

'The case is utterly different where there is no representation. The party may have a complex story to tell, complex evidence to give. That was the situation here, in a case which lasted three days, of which Day 1 had been occupied by the company's case.

'The effect of the chairman's ruling was to deprive Miss Watson-Smith of the props which are necessary to enable even the professional advocate to elicit evidence properly. She was left to remember what she meant to deal with, without a note of any kind. In our judgment this necessarily put her at the gravest possible disadvantage in the presentation of her case, as the chairman would we are sure have realised had he thought through the inevitable effect of his ruling.'

(*Watson-Smith v Tagol Ltd t/a Alangate Personnel EAT 611/81 IRLIB 213.9*).

Tribunals will prefer copies of the statement to be made available so that they can follow the evidence more clearly.

Proofs: Recording evidence to be given before tribunal

15.3   A properly prepared proof is essential because the evidence must be recorded in some convenient form so that the representative or party in person knows exactly what evidence is available to him, and can then decide which evidence to use. From the witness' point of view, the proof is important as an exercise to record the facts and familiarise himself with his evidence for the hearing, perhaps months after the incident. Also, a witness seeing his proof of evidence in writing, especially one he is required to sign, will tend to recognise any omissions of relevant facts. Therefore the exercise is useful in helping to complete the evidence.

Some witnesses give evidence on background information only. Such as explaining the workings of a collective agreement. Others give evidence relating to particular incidents. Some give both. There are no strict rules, it is for you to decide. Tribunals will prefer copies of the statement to be made available so that they can follow the evidence more clearly.

Interviewing witnesses

15.4   It is advisable to interview witnesses as early as possible before recollections begin to fade. During the interview with a witness you should let him tell his story in his own way, only interrupting where some matter is unclear. Meanwhile make brief notes sufficient to keep the main facts in your head. Where he refers to anything which is or may be contained in a document, if you do not already have it, make sure you get it.

When he has completed his story, question him closely on any parts of it which strike you as being still unclear or unlikely. Basically satisfy yourself as far as possible of the accuracy of what he has told you. This done, write out a statement of his evidence.

What form should the proof take? Figure 17 on page 91 provides an example of a proof of evidence. Points to note are considered below.

STATEMENT of ARTHUR DAVID CAMPKIN of 72 Maxwell Drive, Harpenden

I have been a personnel officer at Masons for the last three years. Among other things I am responsible for seeing that the company's disciplinary procedure is applied properly and consistently by our line managers. I personally drafted our present procedure which basically follows the Code of Practice and provides for a number of steps to be taken before an employee can be disciplined and ultimately dismissed. These include a series of oral and written warnings, a disciplinary hearing and a right of appeal against any disciplinary action taken (exhibit employee handbook).

I do not have authority to take disciplinary action. My function is purely advisory. Disciplinary procedures may be used by line managers. However, the decision to dismiss can only be taken after consultation with our personnel manager and my immediate boss, Ms Hawkins.

Towards the end of August, I recollect Brian Rogers, the warehouse manager, asking me for advice on how to handle John Rider. Brian informed me that John was being obstructive towards changes Brian was proposing in order to make his department more efficient. We discussed ways of improving the relationship between the two men and of getting John to be more receptive to change.

I recall Brian next contacting me about John early in October; I met him on 6 October (diary) and was told John had refused to move some containers and was continuing to be difficult. I explained the company's disciplinary procedure to Brian and suggested that he should talk to Janet Hawkins about the problem. Later that day I told Janet about my meeting with Brian, and she then took over the case.

On 6 January Janet asked me to arrange a disciplinary hearing, which she would chair, to consider John Rider's case. I contacted Mr Atkins, John's shop steward, Brian Rogers and several witnesses, and arranged the hearing for 11 am on Friday 13 January. I attended that hearing as an observer but also with the job of taking full notes.

At the end of the hearing, John Rider was informed by Janet that he would be dismissed with three months' notice in lieu of pay. Janet then explained that he had a right of appeal against this decision and that if he wished to appeal he or his shop steward should let me know in writing within seven days. The meeting finished at 12.45 pm. Immediately after lunch my notes were typed and copies distributed to all parties who were present. I have never received a written notice of appeal.

17 March 1984

Figure 17: Statement of a witness

15.5   *Taking Statements from Witnesses*

Statement checklist

15.5   The following is a checklist for taking statements from witnesses:

(*a*) The witness' name and private address are given.

(*b*) The witness' job title or position is given, and if necessary his type of work explained.

(*c*) The background to the witness' involvement or that of his company or his trade union is described.

(*d*) The nature of any relevant collective agreements, procedures, contracts of employment etc. are explained.

(*e*) Only then are the facts of the particular case referred to in chronological order which should include when events happened, where they happened, what exactly happened, who was involved and why things happened as they did.

(*f*) These facts are restricted to those relevant to this case.

(*g*) Expression of opinions should be avoided.

(*h*) What someone else heard or saw should not be referred to unless first-hand evidence is unavailable.

(*i*) Documents are best introduced into the proceedings through witnesses, and this procedure also helps witnesses to remember facts which otherwise are being given from memory in the witness box. References to such documents should be contained in the proof.

(*j*) The proof should cover evidence which it is anticipated will be dealt with in cross-examination by the other side (*see* Chapter 35).

Finalising the statement

15.6   Before finalising the proof you may have to see the witness again for two purposes:

— to enable him to assist you in filling any gaps which have become apparent as a result of further preparation;

— to give the witness an opportunity of reconciling any variation between his evidence and that given by another witness or disclosed by documents which you have now received.

At the hearing, you will use the proof of evidence as the basis for your examination of the witness and also to enable you to prepare points in cross-examination of the other side's witnesses. The tribunal will not require to see the statement, only to hear the evidence. A well prepared proof will mean a well prepared witness, which should enable you to present evidence with little or no advocacy skills. All that will be necessary is the well directed question prompting the witness to give the evidence in his proof.

It should be emphasised that the evidence given by a witness must be the truth and not what would best serve your case regardless of the truth.

Chapter 16

Selecting Witnesses

Introduction

16.1   During the earlier stages of the preparation some witnesses will already have been identified and statements taken from them in order to decide whether to bring or oppose the claim in the first place. It is now necessary to decide which of those or any other witnesses will be required to give evidence at the hearing and to make sure you have full statements from each.

First, it must be appreciated that tribunals give *more weight to oral evidence* than to written representations (which will be discussed more fully in Chapter 17). Documents are usually introduced or exhibited to the tribunal through witnesses. Therefore, the calling of witnesses in a case is essential. Secondly, you must decide which witnesses will be needed to *prove* your case and *rebut* the other side's allegations. Thirdly, you must be prepared to call evidence to prove every material point however obvious it seems to you.

The difficulty is deciding whom to call as witnesses at the hearing. If there is no conflict in the evidence the decision may be easy. It will only be necessary to bring along the persons on both sides who can clearly state the facts from which the tribunal must come to a decision. It may be possible to agree with the other side which witnesses will be called and what evidence they will give. For example, both parties may accept that there has been continuous employment for 15 years for the purposes of a redundancy payment calculation, but the Secretary of State believes there was a break in the employment and will not provide the employer with the appropriate rebate.

Such cases are rare and usually there will be a conflict in the evidence and, therefore, the choice of witnesses will be the responsibility of each side. The following are some of the factors to bear in mind when selecting witnesses.

Witness checklist

16.2   The following provides a checklist to help with the selection of witnesses:

(*a*)   Your evidence must be clearly given to the tribunal.

(*b*)   The best way of doing this is through witnesses.

(*c*)   You must assess the strength of potential witnesses in terms of their likely performance in 'the witness box' bearing in mind that their testimony will usually be given on oath.

(*d*)   The assessment of the strength of a witness is extremely difficult and comes as a matter of experience. However, certain matters can be identified to help assess your witness:

— does he tell the truth?

— is his evidence consistent?

— does he answer questions precisely or ramble on into irrelevancies?

— how does he react when you cross-examine him? Is he easily led into saying something suggested to him?

— to what extent will the unfamiliarity of the tribunal proceedings unnerve the witness and make him unpredictable?

— will the evidence embarrass the witness, e.g. because it is against a friend or employer: therefore can he be relied upon?

— is he over emotional and will he get angry?

— the other side is not restricted to cross-examining on the evidence given by the witness. Cross-examination can cover any relevant matters. Is this dangerous to your case?

— is his manner presentable? Is he a shifty character . . .! The demeanour of a witness is highly relevant, particularly because the EAT in *Paterson v Barratt Developments (Aberdeen) Ltd [1977] IRLR 214* recognised that a tribunal can take this into account when assessing the credibility of that witness.

(*e*)   Only witnesses who are essential should be called. Remember that every witness could contradict himself under cross-examination.

(*f*)   There is no reason why non-essential or second line witnesses should not be brought along to the tribunal as the decision to call them does not need to be made until after the hearing has commenced. Maybe one of these second liners will be able to clarify or add extra weight to certain evidence, although you must remember that cross-examination will not be restricted to that evidence. However, bringing along such non-essential or second line witnesses may be rather costly.

Warnings to selected witnesses

16.3   On the whole the worst witnesses are those who have something to hide. Also those who have worked out how the case should go and try to give their answers along those lines are potentially dangerous to your case. It is important that the witness tells the truth and not what he thinks you want him to say. You are well advised to warn the selected witnesses:

— to be courteous and tell the truth;

— to stick to what they know;

— to give specific answers and not to ramble;

— never to be misleading by, for example, concealing material evidence;

— never to try to score off the other side's representative by, for example, asking him questions.

How to ensure witnesses attend the hearing

16.4   It may become apparent when preparing a list of witnesses you would like to call that some are uneasy about attending for reasons other than 'natural nerves'. This may be because a witness finds the prospect of giving evidence against his boss or a brother trade unionist extremely difficult or embarrassing. So, once the list is established, the witnesses should be requested to undertake that they will attend. If they refuse to give such an undertaking or equivocate or reply in such a way as to leave you in reasonable doubt that they will attend then you have to consider whether to apply for a 'witness order'.

A witness order or 'subpoena' is an order of the IT requiring a witness to attend at the hearing. Under Rule 4(1)

'A Tribunal may—
(*a*) subject to Rule 3(2), on the application of a party to the proceedings made either by notice to the Secretary of the Tribunals or at the hearing of the originating application, . . .
(*b*) (iii) require the attendance of any person (including a party to the proceedings) as a witness wherever such witness may be within Great Britain;
and may appoint the time at or within which or the place at which any act required in pursuant of this Rule is to be done.'

It is clear from this Rule that the tribunal has discretion to grant such an order. Guidance as to how this discretion should be used was given by the NIRC in *Dada v The Metal Box Co Ltd [1974] IRLR 251.* In this case the industrial tribunal refused to issue witness orders on the grounds that Mr Dada had not shown that the witnesses in question would not attend the hearing voluntarily. The court said that they thought there were only two matters on which a tribunal must be satisfied before issuing a witness order. First, that the witness can give *relevant* evidence; secondly, that it is *necessary* to issue a witness order. The court considered the necessity for an order in some detail, which can be summarised as follows. The witness should always be *invited* to attend before a witness order is applied for. If the witness does not reply, or refuses to attend, or equivocates in some way, then a witness order should be considered and the issue of the order will be a matter for the judgment of the tribunal. There is also the case of the willing witness who finds it easier to attend under a witness order because, for example,

MASON (UK) LTD

Units 10-14
Humber Trading Estate
Edgware
Middlesex MS2 8SL

Tel: 01 987 5638

To :   Regional Office of the Industrial Tribunals   Your ref: case no 269/84
       19-29 Woburn Place   Our   ref: JHS/IL
       London WC1H 0LU
                                                          26 March 1984

Dear Sirs,

Re: Rider v Mason (UK) Ltd

I wish to apply for a witness order to be issued against:

Mr P. Atkins
27 Church Street
London EC3 4JA

Mr Atkins is the shop steward of the WTU at Masons.   Unfortunately, he
is unable to give me an undertaking that he will attend the hearing.   He
was present on two occasions when the applicant was warned as well as
at the disciplinary hearing, and his attendance is required at the tribunal
hearing.

Yours faithfully

Janet Hawkins.

Janet Hawkins
Personnel Manager

Figure 18: Letter to ROIT applying for a witness order

his employer does not wish to release him. This may also be a reason for an order.

This guidance similarly applies to respondents applying for witness orders.

How to apply for a witness order

16.5   An order can be applied for by simply sending a straightforward letter to ROIT requesting an order, such as the example given by figure 18 on page 96. Note that the letter indicates:

(*a*)   briefly what evidence can be given by the proposed witness – you do not need to go into detail as to his evidence;

(*b*)   the subject-matter of his evidence;

(*c*)   the extent to which it is relevant;

(*d*)   why he is unwilling to attend voluntarily.

The application will be considered by a chairman alone. If he decides to exercise his discretion to grant the order, ROIT will send to the party requesting the order, a letter similar to figure 19(a) on page 98, which will contain several enclosures. One enclosure will be the witness order itself which will be similar to figure 19(b) on page 99. It is then up to the party requesting the order to 'serve' it on the witness to ensure that the witness receives the notice. There are two principal methods of doing this under Rule 17. The first is by personal service. This can be achieved by handing the order to the witness personally or leaving it at the address contained in the order. The second method is to send the order by recorded delivery post to the witness.

It may be necessary to 'prove' service at the hearing if the witness does not attend. Therefore, either the server or an affidavit of service or the recorded delivery slip should be available for the hearing.

Can a witness object to the order?

16.6   It will be noted from figure 19(b) that any witness who fails to attend a hearing after a witness order has been served on him makes himself liable on summary conviction to a fine not exceeding £200. The only exception to this contained in Rule 4(3) is where the witness has a 'reasonable excuse', such as being taken ill at the last moment.

A witness can, however, object to an order under Rule 4(2). Thus,

'. . . a person on whom a requirement has been made under paragraph (1)(iii) may apply to the Tribunal by notice to the Secretary of the Tribunals before the appointed time at or within which the requirement is to be complied with to vary or set aside the requirement'.

One could imagine a situation where a witness will be away on holiday

Regional Office of the Industrial Tribunals
19-29 Woburn Place London WC1H 0LU

Telephone Direct Line 01-632
Switchboard 01-632 4921/5

Masons (UK) Ltd Units 10-14 Humber Trading Estate Edgware Middlesex MS2 8SL	Your reference Our reference 269/84 Date 29 March 1984

Dear Sir(s)

J. Rider

-v-

Masons (UK) Ltd

In response to the request in your letter of
please find enclosed the following:

    a.   Witness Order(s) to be served by you;

    b.   A copy of the Witness Order(s) for your retention;

    c.   Map(s) which may be of assistance to the witness(es) and

    d.   Leaflet ITL1 (When orders are served on witness(es) their
attention should be drawn to the allowances they may be able
to claim as given in this leaflet).

Would you note that it is your responsibility to notify the witness(es) immediately
of any change of date, time or place of the hearing, or if his/her presence is no
longer required (e.g. if there is a postponement, settlement or withdrawal of the
case). Also note that if service on the witness is by post, this should be done
by recorded delivery.

Yours faithfully

A Nixon

for Assistant Secretary
of the Tribunals

ENCS

Reproduced by permission of HMSO

Figure 19a: Letter enclosing witness order

98

CASE NUMBER

269/84

Regional Office of the
Industrial Tribunals
19-29 Woburn Place
London WC1H 0LU

....

ORDER OF THE INDUSTRIAL TRIBUNAL

FOR ATTENDANCE AS WITNESS

(Pursuant to the Rules of the Industrial Tribunals Regulations As Amended.)

in the case of

Applicant		Respondent
John Rider	v	Mason (UK) Ltd

TO: Mr P Atkins
27 Church Street
London EC3 4JA

1.   You are hereby required by ORDER of a Chairman of the Tribunals to attend at
19 - 29 Woburn Place, London WC1

.... on . Thursday.......day, the .19......
day of .. April.................... 19 84 at ... 10.00 .... am/pm and at any postponed
or adjourned hearing of the proceedings to give evidence.

2.   The Tribunal has power to vary or set aside this Order on the application of
the person to whom it is directed but can only do so for good cause. No such
application can be entertained unless made before the date specified in paragraph
1 of this Order.

NOTE:

Failure to comply with this Order may result in a fine of up to £200 being imposed
upon you under paragraph 1(7) of Schedule 9 to the Employment Protection
(Consolidation)Act 1978.

A Norton

_____
for Assistant Secretary of the Tribunals

Date: 29 March 1984

E01

Reproduced by permission of HMSO

Figure 19b: Witness Order (EO 1)

on the date of the hearing and applies to vary the order so that the hearing is postponed to a more convenient date. In *(1) Eagle Star Insurance Co Ltd, (2) Dunbar v Hayward (EAT 418/81)* Mr Dunbar applied for the witness order against him to be set aside. Mr Dunbar was the Assistant General Manager of the Cheltenham office of the Eagle Star Insurance Company. The applicant, Mr Hayward, was a Senior Systems Analyst at Eagle Star's computer centre at Cheltenham. He was dismissed for alleged misconduct involving the misuse of the company's computer facilities. Some weeks later another employee, a Mr Laine was given a final written warning for a similar offence. Not surprisingly, Mr Hayward applied for a witness order requiring Mr Dunbar to give evidence at the tribunal hearing as to the consistency of the respondents' disciplinary action, and this was granted. Subsequently, Mr Dunbar applied for the order to be set aside and this application was refused. The EAT upheld the tribunal's decision following the principles laid down in the *Dada* case (see 16.4 above): not only was Mr Dunbar's attendance required to give evidence as to the consistency of the application of the respondents' disciplinary procedure, but also because Mr Dunbar had indicated he would not attend unless ordered to do so.

Hostile witnesses

16.7   Witness orders should be treated with caution because an involuntary witness may be a hostile witness. Their use should be restricted in the most part to those witnesses who, although willing to give evidence, wish to appear to be compelled to do so. An example is a trade union official who does not wish to be seen to be giving evidence voluntarily against a brother trade unionist.

If you are unable to interview a witness and know that he will not come voluntarily, it is dangerous to require him to attend simply because you or another witness think that he could give vital evidence for your case. It is too great a risk to have a potentially hostile witness whose exact evidence you do not know.

Victimisation

16.8   It has unfortunately happened that witnesses are victimised or intimidated once it is known they will be giving evidence for one side or the other. This may involve the threat of dismissal or withdrawal of a union card. It is usually very difficult to prove victimisation or intimidation. However, a letter to the employer or trade union concerned indicating that any adverse action taken will be appropriately dealt with is usually enough. Appropriate action would involve making a complaint to the Divisional Court of the Queen's Bench Division of the High Court which has the power to issue an injunction to prevent an act calculated to interfere with the administration of justice in an industrial tribunal. (*Attorney General v BBC [1978] 1 WLR 477*).

If adverse action is taken, the witness himself may for example have to resign and claim constructive dismissal. A threat of violence should be immediately reported to the police. Even if no prosecution takes place a visit from the police will be sufficient to deter most offenders.

Exchange of information on witnesses

16.9   The Tribunal Regulations do not provide any machinery to enable you to find out whom the other side will call as witnesses and what evidence they will give. The only way of finding out is to ask the other side, who may, quite naturally, be reluctant to provide you with this information, unless you are prepared to reciprocate. The advantage of knowing who will give evidence is that it can help you to further prepare your own case and to select the witnesses who can, for example, deal with any conflicting evidence to be given by the other side's witnesses.

Chapter 17

Written Representations

When written representations should be used

17.1 It has already been indicated (see 16.1) that much greater weight is given to oral than to written evidence. Therefore, if the other side present conflicting oral evidence to your written evidence, the former is more likely to be believed. There are, however, some situations where written representations can and should be used, for instance:

— where there is no conflict in the evidence, e.g. a company's annual accounts as filed at the Companies Registry;

— where specialist or expert evidence is required which is unlikely to be challenged, e.g. a medical or consultant engineer's report;

— where the evidence could not be given in any other way e.g. if your witness is an MP who cannot afford the time to appear and you are not prepared to subpoena him, but it is still important that his evidence is given in some form.

Affidavits

17.2 In such a situation a written representation can be used, preferably in the form of an affidavit. An affidavit is a sworn statement or proof of evidence which is signed by the witness, who swears to its truthfulness before a person who is empowered to administer oaths such as a solicitor. The format is different to that of the proof of evidence described in 15.3. It takes a form similar to that of figure 20 opposite. The reason for having the proof in this form is that tribunals may give more weight to a sworn statement than an unsworn representation.

'The seven day rule'

17.3 Under Rule 7(3) a copy of the written representation must be sent to the other side and to ROIT *at least seven days* before the tribunal hearing. If there is a sworn statement the original should be sent to ROIT or be available at the hearing. The tribunal then has a discretion whether or not to admit the written representation. However, it does not have this discretion unless the 'seven day rule' is complied with if the other party insists on adherence to the rule. It is best to discover, from ROIT, on the phone if necessary, whether the evidence is acceptable in this form. If not, you still have the option of calling a suitable witness. ROIT may tell

Case no. 269/84

Rider v Mason (UK) Ltd

I DANIEL JACOBS of 29 Spring Road, London NW3 make oath and say as follows :

1   I am financial director of Mason (UK) Ltd.

2   In January 1983 the Distribution Division of the company was running at a cost of £2.3m p.a. compared with a budgeted cost of £1.75m p.a. The operation of the Warehouse accounted for 65% of the deficit.

3   I recommended to the Board at that time that steps be taken to cut these costs and improve the efficiency of the Division and the Warehouse in particular.

Daniel Jacobs

Sworn at 23 Chancery Lane, London WC1
this 3rd day of April 1984
Before me

J. Thomas

A Solicitor

Figure 20: Sworn statement

you the matter will be left in abeyance until the hearing; you should try to insist on knowing whether it will be accepted before the hearing otherwise you may be forced to bring along an unnecessary witness.

Pleadings as written representations

17.4   By now the pleadings should be complete. They are themselves treated as written representations. The applicant could ask the tribunal to rely on these representations and not attend the hearing himself (Rule 7(4)). Obviously this would be extremely risky if the case was opposed by other than similar written representations.

In some cases the parties, or the tribunal itself, may suggest or desire the case to be dealt with by means of written representations only. For example, if the tribunal has already given its decision and only the question of costs remains (*see* Chapter 40), it may suit those involved not to have to return to the tribunal but deal with this outstanding matter by way of written representations.

Chapter 18

Notice of the Hearing

The length of the hearing

18.1   Industrial tribunals hear cases on five days a week, Monday to Friday inclusive. A tribunal usually sits between 10 a.m. and 4 p.m., with approximately one hour's break for lunch. Different regional tribunals have different customs. Some have coffee breaks in the morning, some tea breaks in the afternoon, some start at 9.45 a.m., others at 10.30 a.m. There are some 60 tribunals sitting in England and Wales on each working day.

Regional offices

18.2   It is necessary to get to know the practices of your regional office. Although the tribunal will sit from say 10 a.m., that does not mean that your case will start at that time. The ROIT listing officer lists 'floaters' for a particular day. These are cases which will be heard by a tribunal as soon as it has disposed of a '10 a.m. case' and can sometimes be identified in the notice of hearing (IT 4) by a later hearing time such as 11 a.m. or 12 midday. The listing officer usually has little idea of how long a case will take as the parties rarely advise him of the likely time, so a floater may only be part-heard or not even started on the listed hearing day. Therefore it is important at this stage of the preparation to consider how long the hearing will take. An accurate assessment comes with experience. However, it is not difficult to realise that if you have at least three witnesses whose evidence will take approximately 30 minutes to give, with cross-examination and other delays, your case will take a minimum of half a day. A telephone call to the other side can establish the approximate length of their case. You should then inquire with the listing officer where your case stands in the list. Then if necessary this can be followed by a joint application in writing to ROIT asking that the case be set down for at least one full day, giving the reasons, e.g. at least six witnesses are being called. If the other side will not co-operate, your own application will usually be sufficient. In fact some regional offices now take the initiative and ask the parties how long the hearing will take.

Cases exceeding one day in length

18.3   If both parties feel the case will take more than one full day, a special hearing can be requested identifying the number of days required. Remember, if a case is not completed on the day for which it is listed it

THE INDUSTRIAL TRIBUNALS

NOTICE OF HEARING

Regional Office of the
Industrial Tribunals
19-29 Woburn Place
London WC1H 0LU

Case No ....269/84...

NOTICE IS HEREBY GIVEN THAT THE application of   Mr J Rider
has been listed for hearing by an Industrial Tribunal at:-

19 - 29 Woburn Place
London WC1H 0LU

on   Thursday,   19 April   19 84   at   10 am/pᵐᵐ

1.   Attendance should be at the above time and place. The parties (other than a respondent who has not entered an appearance) are entitled to appear at the hearing and to state their case in person or be represented by anyone they wish. A party can choose not to appear and can rely on written representations (which if additional to any already submitted must be sent to the Tribunal and copied to the other party not less than 7 days before the hearing). However, experience shows that it is normally advisable for a party and any witnesses to attend in person even if they have made statements or representations in writing.

2.   It is very important that each party should bring to the hearing any documents that may be relevant, eg a letter of appointment, contract of employment, Working Rule Agreement, pay slips, income tax forms, evidence of unemployment and other social security benefits, wages book, details of benefits and contributions under any pension or superannuation scheme, etc.

3   If the complaint is one of unfair dismissal or refusal of permission for a woman employee to return to work after a pregnancy the tribunal may wish to consider whether to make an order for reinstatement or re-engagement. In these cases the respondent should be prepared to give evidence at the hearing as to the availability of the job from which the applicant was dismissed, or held before absence due to pregnancy, or of comparable or suitable employment and generally as to the practicability of reinstatement or re-engagement of the applicant by the respondent.

4   If for any reason a party (other than a respondent who has not entered an appearance) does not propose to appear at the hearing, either personally or by representative, he should inform me immediately, in writing, giving the reason and the case number. He should also state whether he wishes the hearing to proceed in his absence, relying on any written representations he may have made. If an applicant fails to appear at the hearing the tribunal may dismiss or dispose of the application in his absence.

5   The hearing of this case will take place at the time stated above or as soon thereafter as the tribunal can hear it.

To the Applicant(s) (Ref Mr F Hitchcock   )

Warehousemen's Trade Union
128 Furlong Road
London EC1 2JA

Signed ....*A Norton*.................................
for Assistant Secretary of the Tribunals

Date ..2 April 1984..

> NOTE Representatives who receive this
> notice must inform the party they
> represent of the date, time and place of
> the hearing. The party will not be notified
> direct.

and the Respondent(s) (Ref Ms J Hawkins   )

Mason (UK) Ltd
Units 10-14
Humber Trading Estate
Edgware
Middlesex MS2 8SL

~~and the Secretary of State for Employment~~
and the Conciliation Officer, Advisory Conciliation and Arbitration Service

IT4

Reproduced by permission of HMSO

Figure 21: Notice of hearing (IT 4)

will be adjourned to another day. This could be several weeks or even months later and is unsatisfactory because:

(*a*) it increases the time and expense of the case;

(*b*) an undecided case can result in unnecessary stress and strain for those still involved;

(*c*) an unemployed applicant may be unable to obtain work or finalise his appeal against a refusal to pay unemployment benefit;

(*d*) it is difficult to get all the witnesses together yet again;

(*e*) the loss of continuity in presenting and hearing a case is not very satisfactory for representatives or the tribunal.

Date of the hearing

18.4   Soon after the IT 3 has been returned to ROIT both parties will receive a notice of hearing (IT 4): for example, see figure 21 opposite. Under Rule 5(1) tribunals must give at least 14 days notice of the hearing. The reason for the speed in setting down the case is to achieve the tribunal's objective of dispensing 'quick' justice. Obviously, such expeditious justice is not necessarily good justice if the parties are not ready. If you are not prepared and you require a guarantee of at least a full day's hearing or more, a postponement should immediately be requested in writing. It is also a good idea to inform the other side, and see if there is any possibility of agreeing a suitable date, as well as the length of the case. Then a mutually convenient date can be discussed with the listing officer on the phone, and hopefully the next notice of hearing you receive should be for a suitable date and an appropriate period of time. In the meantime you should hear from ROIT granting the postponement in the terms of figure 22 on page 108.

Postponing the hearing

18.5   Under Rule 12(2)(*b*) the tribunal has extensive powers to postpone or fix a time for or adjourn a hearing. You may have noted that figure 10 on page 64 requested such a postponement on the grounds that one of the representatives would be on holiday on the date the case was originally listed for hearing. However, this power must not be taken for granted, particularly by an applicant. This is because under Rule 12(2)(*f*) the tribunal, on a respondent's application or on its own initiative, can strike out the IT 1 for excessive delay in proceeding with the application, provided the applicant has had the opportunity of showing why such action should not be taken.

Tribunals in Scotland

18.6   A much better system exists in Scotland. A Scottish ROIT does not set a firm date in the peremptory fashion employed in England and Wales. Notice is sent to all parties, proposing that a hearing take place between two specified dates covering as a rule a period of two or three weeks. The

Regional Office of the Industrial Tribunals
19-29 Woburn Place   London   WC1H 0LU

Telephone Direct Line 01-632
Switchboard 01-632 4921/5

Ms J Hawkins Mason (UK) Ltd Units 10-14 Humber Trading Estate Edgware Middlesex MS2 8SL	Your reference JH/SN Our reference 269/84 Date 16 March 1984

Dear S̶i̶r̶s̶/Madam

John Rider

-v-

Mason (UK) Ltd

Your letter/t̶e̶l̶e̶p̶h̶o̶n̶e̶ ̶c̶o̶n̶v̶e̶r̶s̶a̶t̶i̶o̶n̶ of .....12 March.....................1984
has been referred to a Chairman of the Tribunals who has granted your application
for the hearing, listed to take place on ....23rd......... day ...March.......1984,
to be postponed. Please accept this letter as formal notification of the postponement pending settlement. I would be grateful if you would keep us informed
of the progress of the negotiations.

Yours faithfully

A Norr

cc WTU
128 Furlong Road
London EC1 2JA

for Assistant Secretary
of the Tribunals

c̶c̶   S̶e̶c̶r̶e̶t̶a̶r̶y̶ ̶o̶f̶ ̶S̶t̶a̶t̶e̶ ̶f̶o̶r̶ ̶E̶m̶p̶l̶o̶y̶m̶e̶n̶t̶

cc   Industrial Relations Officer, Advisory Conciliation & Arbitration Service

Figure 22: Letter from ROIT granting a postponement

parties are asked to identify days within that period which are not convenient. They are told that, in the absence of any such information, all days within the period will be regarded as suitable. This simple and courteous approach is most effective in terms of cost savings and smooth administration. It is already being adopted by some ROITs in England and Wales.

Venue

18.7   The hearing often takes place at the offices of the ROIT with which the parties have been corresponding. Usually the administrative and judicial functions of a ROIT are in the same building. There are now 24 permanent centres for hearing applications in England and Wales. The actual address of the place of hearing will be indicated on the IT 4 as shown in figure 21 on page 106. The tribunals will not sit elsewhere unless the ROIT covers a large geographical area which would make access difficult for the parties; as a result some sub-offices have been set up.

However, if these are clearly inconvenient for the parties you can make an application to ROIT for a more convenient venue. Such applications sometimes succeed because ITs are conscious of providing easily accessible justice. For example, a Birmingham tribunal has heard a case in the smoke room of a public house. This spirit of accessibility even extends to conducting hearings in Welsh. It is also possible to ask for a transfer of venue from one office to another. Under Rule 16 the president or regional chairman has power either on his own initiative or on the request of a party to transfer venues across jurisdictions (i.e. from England to Scotland or vice versa) where he takes the view that the proceedings would more conveniently be determined by a tribunal, say, in Scotland.

Before giving a direction transferring venues the tribunal must send a notice to the parties concerned giving them an opportunity to show why such a direction should not be made. For example a North Sea oil worker may present his IT 1 at the Exeter ROIT which is the nearest to his home. If the respondent is an oil company based in Aberdeen application may be made for a change of venue to Aberdeen. The applicant may resist as he no longer works in Scotland, is unemployed, and finds Exeter more convenient.

Chapter 19

Preliminary Hearings

Introduction

19.1   The 'preliminary hearing' is a hearing specifically designed to deal with qualification questions. Tribunals only have jurisdiction to hear claims where applicants have fulfilled the qualification requirement of the particular claim. So it is not surprising to find a procedure where ITs can decide whether they have jurisdiction to hear the claim. If they decide they do not have jurisdiction this in effect prevents the claim going any further and means the tribunal will not have to go into the substantive issues of the claim, for example, whether the applicant was unfairly dismissed, at a full hearing. This in turn could result in considerable savings of time and expense.

When would you use a preliminary hearing?

19.2   A preliminary hearing could be used where for example, in an unfair dismissal claim it is *not* considered that the applicant:

(*a*)   has one year's continuous employment; or

(*b*)   is contractually obliged to work for 16 hours or more per week; or

(*c*)   is below the upper age limit; or

(*d*)   ordinarily works inside GB;

or for any other areas where a tribunal's jurisdiction may be in doubt.

Such preliminary issues will usually only be suitable for a preliminary hearing where they involve questions of fact. For example, where there is a dispute as to the date when someone was dismissed, this will affect the preliminary issue of whether the claim was brought within the three months time limit. However, legal issues may also be involved. For example in *Thompsons Soft Drinks Limited v Quayle EAT 12/81*, the preliminary issue related to what was then the 26 weeks' service qualification in an unfair dismissal case which also involved a service continuity problem to which the statutory legal rules on continuity applied and these were argued at the preliminary hearing.

Preliminary hearings on issues of law are however rare. In *Turley v Allders Department Stores [1980] IRLR 4* the EAT gave the following guidance to tribunals:

'It is common and sensible that where questions arise going to jurisdiction which usually involve the decision of questions of fact (for example, whether an originating application has been made in time) such questions should be decided as preliminary issues. But it is in our judgment undesirable that issues of law should be dealt with in this way, which can only be argued upon assumptions if the facts to found the argument have not been decided . . . In truth, the effect of the course taken here was that this court is asked to come to a conclusion of law on a hypothetical situation, something against which the courts normally set their face. There is a provision in the Rules of the Supreme Court for the trial of preliminary issues of law on the basis that the facts pleaded are correct, whether traversed or not. It is a provision only used in exceptional circumstances. The industrial tribunal's power to do what has been done in this case should in our judgment never be used where, as here, there is a fundamental issue of fact. Once the facts are found, then is the time to see whether the legal problem arises, and what the answer is. It may well be found to have gone away.'

In this case Mrs Turley complained that she had been dismissed by Allders Department Stores because she was pregnant. As she lacked the necessary continuous service to bring a claim for unfair dismissal she brought her complaint under the SDA. The company denied that the reason for dismissal was Mrs Turley's pregnancy. The tribunal decided, however, to try as a preliminary issue the question whether

'if there was a dismissal on the ground of pregnancy, was that unlawful discrimination within the meaning of s 1(1)(*a*) and/or s 1(1)(*b*) of the Sex Discrimination Act?'

without having first established whether or not she was dismissed by reason of her pregnancy. The tribunal concluded that a pregnancy dismissal was not unlawful discrimination and the EAT upheld that decision, despite criticising the way the tribunal had dealt with the matter as a preliminary issue.

Some preliminary questions cannot really be dealt with properly without going into the merits of the case, for example, whether the applicant is an 'employee', whether the applicant has been constructively dismissed and whether the contract under which the applicant has been employed is illegal. These are issues which will invariably tend to involve issues of law as well as facts. Therefore it is most unlikely that a tribunal will exercise its discretion to hear such matters at a preliminary hearing.

How to apply for a preliminary hearing

19.3   Either party can apply for a preliminary hearing, but in practice the respondent will probably do so because he will wish to challenge the applicant's qualifications to bring the claim. A respondent may request a preliminary hearing simply by writing to ROIT pointing out that there

Regional Office of the Industrial Tribunals
London (South)
93 Ebury Bridge Road London SW1W 8RE

Telephone 01-730 9161 ext

Brownsilk Plc	Your reference LV/RW/1001
24-36 Fleet Road	Our reference 606/84
London W1	
	Date 24 April 1984

THE INDUSTRIAL TRIBUNALS

NOTICE OF PRELIMINARY HEARING

Applicant   Respondent

J Partridge   -v-   Brownsilk Plc

Mr Partridge
NOTICE IS HEREBY GIVEN that the Originating Application of/   has been listed for
a preliminary hearing by an Industrial Tribunal at 93 Ebury Bridge Road, London SW1, at
10 am/pxx on   Thurs day, the 17 day of May 19 84

1   Attendance should be at the above place and time. The hearing will be limited on
this occasion to consideration of the following preliminary issue(s):

Whether the applicant is disqualified from the right not to be unfairly dismissed by
the provisions of section 64(1)(a) of the Employment Protection (Consolidation)
Act 1978 (as amended) regarding a minimum period of continuous employment (one year).

2   The parties (other than a respondent who has not entered an appearance) are entitled
to appear at the hearing and to state their case in person or be represented by anyone they
wish. They may adduce oral evidence which is relevant to the preliminary issue(s) to be
decided. They may also make written representations, provided that such representations
are sent to the Tribunal and copied to the other party not less than 7 days before the date
of the hearing.

2A   In the circumstances, the respondent need not attend the preliminary hearing, though
he is, of course, at liberty to do so. If he elects not to attend no decision on the preliminary
issue(s) which is adverse to his interests will be made at this hearing.

3   If / Mr Partridge does not intend to appear in person or by a representative he should inform
me immediately, in writing, giving the reason and the case number. He should also state
whether he wishes the hearing of the preliminary issue to proceed in his absence. If he
does not attend the Tribunal may dispose of the preliminary issue(s) in his absence.

4   A party attending the hearing should bring with him any documents that may be relevant
to the preliminary issue(s).

5   The parties will be informed in due course in writing of the decision of the Tribunal
on the preliminary issue(s) and of the date and time of any further hearing.

Reproduced by permission of HMSO

Figure 23: Notice of hearing on preliminary point of jurisdiction only

112

6   The hearing of the preliminary issue(s) will take place at the time stated above or as soon thereafter as the Tribunal can hear it.

Signed.......A Norton.....................................

for Assistant Secretary of the Tribunals

Date.......24 April 1984......................

To the Applicant

    J Partridge Esq
    203 Hyde Park Corner
    London W1

NOTE: Representatives who receive this notice must inform the party they represent of the date, time and place of the hearing. The party will not be notified direct.

To the Respondent

and the Secretary of State for Employment

and the Conciliation Officer, Advisory Conciliation and Arbitration Service

Reproduced by permission of HMSO

Figure 23 (continued)

is a preliminary point of jurisdiction and asking that it should be dealt with at a preliminary hearing only. Under Rule 5 a chairman can grant an application if he considers such an issue could be dealt with at a preliminary hearing. This request could be made at the time the IT 3 is submitted or soon after as the respondent should be aware from his knowledge of the applicant's terms of employment whether he is qualified to bring the claim.

If the application is granted, a notice of hearing will be served on the parties in a form similar to figure 23 on pages 112–113. The first paragraph of this notice differs from the usual and indicates that only the preliminary issue will be dealt with.

Ordered by IT. The tribunal may on its own initiative order that a preliminary hearing be held to consider a jurisdictional matter. The tribunal derives this power from Rule 12 which enables it to regulate its own procedure. Therefore it sometimes happens that even the respondent is taken by surprise when he receives a notice of hearing in a form similar to figure 23, which has not been requested by him. In these circumstances the respondent might consider not attending the hearing and should make further inquiries with ROIT as to whether he need attend or whether he could just submit written representations, or neither. He should attend, however, unless advised by the Regional Office that it is unnecessary.

The procedure

19.4   The procedure for preliminary hearings is basically the same as for full hearings. However, as indicated in paragraph 1 of figure 23, only evidence and argument relevant to the question of jurisdiction will be admitted at the hearing. If the tribunal decides that the applicant is not qualified to bring the claim, this puts an end to the application (subject to appeal). If the tribunal decides that he is qualified, the decision is an interim one which will be followed by a full hearing on the merits of the claim. A fresh notice of hearing will be issued, without any reference to a preliminary question of jurisdiction; often the full claim will be heard by the same tribunal.

Preliminary hearings can increase costs

19.5   If the tribunal finds that the applicant is qualified to bring the claim then such a finding could increase costs because a full hearing will usually follow. In *Meghani v Career Care Group Limited (EAT 772/78)*, the EAT sounded a cautionary note for chairmen faced with making an order for a preliminary hearing:

'These are cases, obviously, in which it is of advantage and results in a saving of costs if a preliminary hearing is held before the merits of the case are investigated. That kind of order has to be made with care because sometimes it duplicates the time of the hearing and indeed increases the cost . . . We repeat that orders of this kind should be made with caution, to avoid prejudice and duplication.'

Therefore respondents should determine that they have a reasonable prospect of success before applying for an order for a preliminary hearing.

There is no doubt that tribunals have the power to order preliminary hearings in any claim that may come before them. For example in the race relations case of *Ghaffar v The Council of Legal Education (EAT 772/80)*, the EAT said:

'It is clearly right to say that under this legislation, care has to be exercised to ensure that the case is a proper one for a preliminary question of law to be decided. Sometimes the taking of a preliminary question of law can in the long run lead to even more protracted proceedings than otherwise, and because of the difficulties inherent in bringing a claim can lead to unfairness. But, subject to that, clearly it is open to an industrial tribunal, in a proper case, to decide these questions in whichever order is felt, in the particular circumstances of the case, to be appropriate.'

The distinction between a preliminary hearing and a pre-hearing assessment

19.6   The objective of a preliminary hearing is to ensure that tribunals do not hear the substantive issues of claims for which they have no jurisdiction. In contrast the main objective of a pre-hearing assessment is to discourage meritless claims. However, because of the wording of Rule 6 it is possible for qualification issues to be considered at PHAs. An applicant is 'unlikely to succeed' where he is unqualified to bring his claim. Therefore such an issue could be raised at a PHA. Because such assessments are usually set down for hearing more quickly than a preliminary hearing and the hearing itself is much shorter, it might seem more sensible to apply for a PHA rather than a preliminary hearing.

Therefore it is worth examining the differences between the two procedures. The reason why PHAs are shorter is because frequently respondents are not required to attend and in any case evidence is not permitted. In contrast, at preliminary hearings both parties will normally attend with witnesses and provide oral and written evidence. Only an opinion can be given at a PHA whereas a tribunal at a preliminary hearing will make a decision upon which the rest of the case depends. An appeal can be made against a decision, but there is no appeal against an opinion. Finally, the decision of a tribunal at a preliminary hearing can end the case whereas an opinion at a PHA cannot do so although it might result in the application being withdrawn or case settled.

Which procedure should be used?

19.7   There seems to be no evidence of any regular practice of using PHAs to deal with qualification points. However, because they are a quicker procedure they might be used as a more expeditious way of bringing to the applicant's attention the fact that he is unqualified to bring the particular claim. If this is not successful then it would be necessary to apply for a preliminary hearing and such a dual procedure would increase not only costs but also the length of the proceedings. It is therefore advisable to use PHAs for the purpose for which they were designed, namely to sift out meritless claims, and preliminary hearings to deal with qualification points.

A PHA, however, cannot be turned into a preliminary hearing. In *Raisbeck v Hambro Life Assurance Limited (EAT 424/81)*, an industrial tribunal, having fixed a date for the full hearing, on its own initiative postponed that hearing and directed there should be a PHA. A formal notice, similar to the notice in figure 15 on page 83, was sent to the parties, indicating among other things, that this would be a PHA where no oral evidence could be given and that the tribunal would consider the contents of the IT 1 and IT 3 and any representations in writing that the parties might submit. The notice also indicated that if the tribunal considered that the applicant had no reasonable prospects of success, then that tribunal could indicate that fact and that if the application was persisted in up to or at the hearing there might be an order for costs made against the applicant under Rule 11 of the Regulations.

Neither of the parties appeared in response to that notice, but they lodged written representations with the tribunal. At the PHA the tribunal took a most unusual course. Notwithstanding the fact that they quite rightly recorded that it was a PHA as to the chances of success of the applicant, they gave a decision dismissing the whole application on the grounds that they had no jurisdiction, heading their decision and reasons 'Preliminary hearing'.

On appeal, the EAT found 'the sole jurisdiction and function of a tribunal holding a pre-hearing assessment under Rule 6 is to seek to put in order the proceedings and clarify the issues and, if it thinks fit, to express an opinion. It has no right on a pre-hearing assessment, to make any "decision".'

Chapter 20

Settling and Withdrawing Cases

Introduction

20.1   A settlement can take a variety of forms from the withdrawal of the originating application to the reinstatement of the employee. The importance of settling can be seen from the statistics disclosed by ACAS in their latest Annual Report. Of the 46,996 cases (England, Wales and Scotland) the Service received in 1982, 68 per cent were settled or withdrawn, although not all through conciliation. (This figure includes 6,132 cases where no formal complaint was made to an IT but ACAS assistance was sought under EPCA s 133(3) or s 134(3).)

One of the main reasons for such a large proportion of settlements is no doubt the success of ACAS as a conciliator. However, the desire of most parties to avoid additional costs when the same or a similar result could be achieved through a settlement must also be an important factor in determining the number of settlements.

The parties who are most likely to reach a satisfactory settlement are those familiar with their own cases and that of their opponents. These parties are in a position to assess the strengths and weaknesses of a case so that they are in a proper position to negotiate a settlement. Settlements are frequently not reached because of inadequate preparation which results in one side holding out for unreasonable terms.

Monetary compensation

20.2   Most settlements are for money. This is because applicants are mainly interested in monetary compensation and this lends itself more easily to settlement. Therefore, one of the exercises which should be carried out in order to facilitate the possibility of a settlement is an assessment of the compensation which might be awarded by a tribunal. Obviously such an assessment can only be carried out satisfactorily where preliminary preparation of a case has been undertaken, and that is why this chapter is placed at a later point in Part I of this book.

It is possible for parties to work out the likely monetary award if the case were to proceed further and the applicant were to succeed. Chapter 39 explains how such an award would be worked out in an unfair dismissal case. That chapter refers to the recoupment provisions (EPCA s 132) which allow the DHSS or the DE to recoup from the respondent a sum equivalent to any unemployment and supplementary benefit paid to a successful applicant between the date of dismissal and the hearing. They only apply where compensation is awarded by a tribunal following a hearing. They do not apply to settlements. Therefore, where there is a settlement the parties can discount such sums in arriving at an agreed figure. The fact that the recoupment provisions can be ignored is a factor contributing to lower settlement figures compared with tribunal monetary awards. This can be an incentive for some employers to settle.

Settlement not always possible

20.3   Some 32 per cent of claims reach a tribunal hearing, which indicates that settlements cannot always be achieved. There can be a variety of reasons for this. It may simply be that, although there is a desire to settle, terms cannot be agreed. There are some cases however, where settlement is not even attempted, for example, where a matter of principle is involved or where there are wider implications which could set an undesired precedent. Whether a settlement is possible will often depend on your objective for bringing or defending a claim.

Methods of settling

20.4   Parties can negotiate settlements themselves. In fact, in 1982, 3 per cent of all cases received by ACAS in England, Wales and Scotland were settled privately. But this is not a very important method of settling and there would appear to be two main reasons for this. First, ACAS tends to become involved in nearly all tribunal cases and is obliged to help the parties reach a settlement. Secondly, any settlement reached outside the auspices of ACAS will not be effective in preventing an applicant proceeding with his claim. Therefore, the most satisfactory method of settling is through ACAS.

How does ACAS become involved?

20.5   From the commencement of most claims (as will be apparent from previous chapters and illustrations), copies of all correspondence passing between ROIT and the parties will be sent to the local regional office of ACAS (*see* Appendix D). These, in turn, are sent to a particular conciliation officer who has been allocated to the case. There is only one major exception to this rule, and that relates to claims for redundancy payments. [*EPCA s 133*].

The conciliation officer

Duties

20.6   From the moment a conciliation officer is involved in this way he is given certain statutory responsibilities and duties depending on the claim. In relation to dismissals, these are set out in Section 134 of EPCA and in relation to unlawful discrimination his duties are set out in Section 55 of the Race Relations Act 1976 and Section 64 of the Sex

Discrimination Act 1975. Briefly, a conciliation officer must endeavour to promote a settlement of any complaint by an employee that he has been unfairly dismissed or discriminated against without the dispute having to go to an industrial tribunal. He can step into the dispute either at the request of both parties or on his own initiative if he thinks he has a reasonable prospect of success. Section 134(2) then goes on to provide that for the purposes of promoting a settlement:

> '(*a*) The conciliation officer shall in particular seek to promote the reinstatement or re-engagement of the complainant by the employer, or by a successor of the employer or by an associated employer, on terms appearing to the conciliation officer to be equitable; but
> (*b*) where the complainant does not wish to be reinstated or re-engaged, or where reinstatement or re-engagement is not practicable or cannot be agreed between the parties to the complaint, and the parties desire the conciliation officer to act under this section, he shall seek to promote agreement between them as to a sum by way of compensation to be paid by the employer to the complainant.'

In discrimination cases where there is no dismissal, the conciliation officer will endeavour to promote a settlement by encouraging the use of grievance procedures.

Although the conciliation officer will usually only become involved *after* the commencement of a claim, Section 134(3) of EPCA (which was added by Schedule 1, paragraph 18 to EA 1980) enables either party to request his assistance prior to a claim being lodged. He then has the same duties as already outlined.

The conciliation officer's role

20.7   Conciliation officers have very firm instructions, both during training and in their handbook, not to take sides by commenting on the merits of cases, which of course is the role of the tribunal. Official policy makes clear that it is not their job, for example, to advise the employee on the fairness or otherwise of a re-engagement proposal or a particular sum of money offered by an employer. They are not negotiators or devil's advocates; they are rather a channel of communication through whom the parties can do their bargaining. In *Duport Furniture Products Ltd v Moore and ACAS [1978] IRLR 545*, the EAT commented:

> 'There has been built up over the years a clear understanding by conciliation officers of the inherent difficulties imposed upon them by the very nature of the job which they carry out. For many years, it has been fully understood by all those involved in this most admirable process, that the role of conciliation involves the creation of an appearance of impartiality. If either side takes the view that the conciliation officer is the representative of, or the advocate for, the other side, conciliation may in fact become well nigh impossible.'

In ACAS's booklet 'Conciliation by ACAS in complaints by individuals to Industrial Tribunals' it states: 'The purpose and direction of the conciliation officer's efforts are to assist the parties to arrive at balanced judgments and to take informed decisions on the particular issues which confront them. It follows that an important part of the conciliation officer's work in trying to promote a settlement is to ensure that both sides are adequately informed, and fully understand the range of options open to them and the consequences of the different decisions they may take'. (But *see Slack v Greenham (Plant Hire) Ltd [1983] IRLR 271.*)

Privileged communications

20.8   In order to encourage parties to use the conciliation service, Sections 133(6) and 134(5) of EPCA provide that anything communicated to a conciliation officer orally or in writing in connection with the conciliation process cannot be disclosed in evidence at a tribunal hearing unless the person who communicated it to that officer consents.

These provisions do not mean that parties can make evidence inadmissible at a tribunal hearing simply by communicating it to an officer. As the NIRC said in *Grazebrook v Wallens [1973] IRLR 139*:

'It is not intended to render evidence inadmissible which could have been given if there had been no communication to the conciliation officer . . . The test is whether evidence exists in an admissible form apart from evidence based upon such communication to the conciliation officer.'

Conciliation in practice

20.9   Once the conciliation officer receives a copy of the IT 1 and the IT 3 he will usually contact the employer first to find out if he would like to discuss the case. If he expresses no interest in conciliation the officer will usually inform the other party of the position, and at the same time offer his continued assistance to either party should they wish to call on him. If on contacting the applicant information emerges which the officer thinks may revive the possibility of settling the complaint, he will seek a further contact with the respondent in order to discuss it.

Where the employer (or his representative) are willing to discuss the case in the first place then the conciliation officer will arrange to meet the respondent (or his representative), or if this is not possible at least speak to one of them on the telephone in order to find out about the facts of the case. The officer will then usually do the same with the applicant. After this, in accordance with his duties in unfair dismissal cases, he will explore the possibilities of reinstatement or re-engagement with both parties before going on to explore compensation as a more likely means of settlement. Only when it becomes quite clear that there is no prospect of conciliation will the officer withdraw and the case proceed to the tribunal for a hearing.

Confidence in the conciliation process

20.10   Occasionally you hear allegations from one side or the other that the conciliation officer was biased. As a result some parties have been reluctant to confide in them or use their services. The facts simply do not support this allegation. There is no reported case of a conciliation officer not acting impartially.

A distinction must be drawn, however, between conciliation officers acting impartially and pressure placed on one party or the other by the conciliation officer. Understandably, conciliation officers to a considerable extent will measure their success by the number of cases they settle. They cannot be expected to take a merely passive role. This may lead them to point out weaknesses in their respective cases to both the applicant and the respondent, which inevitably points them in the direction of settling their claim outside the tribunal. (See Linda Dickens 'Unfair Dismissal Applications and the Industrial Tribunal System', Department of Employment Gazette, March 1979.)

Postponements of hearings

20.11 Often during the conciliation process a notice of hearing is received by the parties. There is no easier way of obtaining a postponement of the hearing than where there is a chance of the case being settled by conciliation. The tribunal has discretion under Rule 12(2)(*b*) of the Regulations to grant a postponement in these circumstances, and generally tribunals will be only too glad to encourage conciliation if this will avoid a tribunal hearing.

Binding settlements

20.12 As indicated earlier, unless a conciliation officer is involved in the settlement process, there is no bar to the applicant proceeding. For example, in *Council of Engineering Institutions v Maddison* [*1976*] *IRLR 389*, Mr Maddison was dismissed on the alleged grounds of redundancy. He was handed an envelope containing a letter and cheque for £1,600. The letter said the cheque constituted a 'lump sum payment for severance (including redundancy payment), the acceptance of which is final settlement leaving you with no outstanding claim against the Council'. Neither the IT nor the EAT were satisfied this was a binding agreement, but found that even if it was it would have been rendered void.

This is because Section 140 of EPCA (and its predecessor Schedule 1, paragraph 32 to TULRA which was referred to in the *Maddison* case) makes any settlement between the parties void in relation to an industrial tribunal claim except where a conciliation officer 'has taken action' in accordance with the duties already described. This means that if parties enter into private settlements which attempt to exclude an applicant from taking further proceedings, such contracting out provisions will not prevent an IT from hearing the claim.

It is therefore worth examining what action a conciliation officer has to take to be sufficient to bar an applicant from proceeding further. This whole question was examined by the Court of Appeal in *Moore v Duport Furniture Products Ltd and ACAS* [*1980*] *IRLR 158*. Briefly, the facts of the case were that Mr Moore was suspended by the company following his arrest on suspicion of his having stolen property from them. The company called in a conciliation officer to advise them on the matter. During a meeting between the parties at which the conciliation officer was not present, it was made clear to Mr Moore that there was no prospect of his being given back his job. He then agreed to accept the sum of £300 and resign. The conciliation officer was then asked to come in and he recorded details of this settlement on a COT 3 form. (This is a form used by officers to record the terms of a settlement, an illustration of which can be found in figure 24a opposite.) He then took the parties through the form, explaining its meaning and implications. The form was signed by both parties. Mr Moore was subsequently informed by the police that he was not going to be prosecuted and he made a complaint of unfair dismissal.

The Court of Appeal in *Moore* found that, notwithstanding that the agreement was reached between the parties themselves, the presence of the conciliation officer in the room, his recording of the terms of the settlement on the COT 3 form, his ensuring that the parties understood and agreed to the terms and his explanation of their finality and the advantages to each side of having a settlement, was sufficient to amount to action in an endeavour to promote a settlement of the matter without it being determined by an IT within the meaning of Section 134. Therefore, the conciliation officer had taken action under Section 140 which barred Mr Moore from bringing his unfair dismissal complaint. The decision was confirmed by the House of Lords ([*1982*] *IRLR 31*).

In practice, it is unnecessary to reach a settlement in the presence of a conciliation officer or for the officer to record the terms of settlement in the presence of the parties. Often, after agreeing terms, parties will simply telephone ACAS and ask an officer to record the terms on a COT 3 form and send the form to them by post.

In *Gilbert v Kembridge Fibres Ltd* [*1984*] *IRLR 52*, the conciliation officer satisfied himself that a settlement had been reached orally between the parties and then set out the terms of settlement in writing on a COT 3. When the form was sent to Mr Gilbert for his signature, he was in two minds whether or not to sign it. Mr Gilbert did sign it but changed his mind and sent the form back to ACAS with his signature crossed out. The IT found that an offer to settle had been accepted with the assistance of the officer and that Mr Gilbert was therefore barred from having his unfair dismissal complaint heard. The EAT agreed with this decision confirming that *oral* settlements can be binding.

The whole object of settling cases is to avoid the need for a tribunal hearing and therefore it is essential, particularly from the employer's point of view, that any settlement reached is binding so as to bar the claim; hence the need to have the conciliation officer take action at least to the extent just described.

ADVISORY CONCILIATION AND ARBITRATION SERVICE

* ~~Equal Pay Act 1970~~
* ~~Sex Discrimination Act 1975~~
* ~~Race Relations Act 1976~~
* ~~Employment Protection Act 1975~~
* Employment Protection (Consolidation) Act 1978
* ~~Employment Act 1980~~
* ~~Employment Act 1982~~

* AGREEMENT IN RESPECT OF AN APPLICATION MADE TO THE INDUSTRIAL TRIBUNAL

* ~~AGREEMENT IN RESPECT OF A REQUEST FOR CONCILIATION MADE TO THE ADVISORY CONCILIATION & ARBITRATION SERVICE (NO APPLICATION MADE TO TRIBUNAL AT TIME OF AGREEMENT)~~

Tribunal case number
269/84

Applicant	Respondent
Name JOHN RIDER	Name MASON (UK) LIMITED
Address 34 WESTMOUNT ROAD LONDON NW11 9DX	Address UNITS 10-14, HUMBER TRADING ESTATE, EDGWARE MIDDLESEX MS2 8SL

Settlement reached as a result of conciliation action.

We the undersigned have agreed:

The applicant shall accept the sum of £1250 (one thousand two hundred and fifty pounds) offered by the respondent in full and final settlement of these proceedings and all other claims (if any) which the applicant could have brought against the respondent arising under the terms of his contract of employment or out of his dismissal.

Applicant *John Rider*   date 10·4·84

Respondent *Janet Hawkins*.   date 13·4·84

* Delete inappropriate item

COT3

Reproduced by permission of HMSO

Figure 24a: Conciliated settlement form (COT 3)

Terms of settlement

20.13 Under Section 134 of EPCA, the conciliation officer has to ensure that the terms of any settlement resulting in the re-engagement or reinstatement of the employee are equitable. However, according to the HL and CA in the *Moore* case (see 20.12 above), he is not under any statutory obligation to ensure that the terms of a monetary settlement are equitable. This means that the officer is not concerned with the 'rightness or wrongness' of the agreement as his main obligation is to seek to promote settlement, rather than help the parties determine the terms of agreement. Despite this finding, in practice conciliation officers do tend to help the parties reach an equitable monetary settlement by discussing with both how monetary awards would be calculated if the tribunal found the complaint justified. In *Slack v Greenham (Plant Hire) Ltd*, although the officer only discussed heads of compensation with one side, the settlement was still found to be valid. However, the better a party's preparation of his case, the more likely that he will achieve an equitable settlement.

Wording of settlement

20.14 The conciliation officer will help both parties to word the terms of the settlement reached and, as already mentioned, uses special forms for this. The COT 3 shown in figure 24a is used to record the terms of a monetary settlement. The tribunal is prepared to include terms of settlement which do not relate to its own jurisdiction. This means that the terms of a settlement could include words which would prevent employees having a cause of action in other courts. For example, the words 'in full and final settlement of any claims whatsoever the applicant may have against the respondent' may have the effect of preventing an employee bringing a claim for personal injuries in the High Court. The employee, on the other hand, may wish to incorporate in the terms the provision of a suitable job and character reference by the employer.

A typical example of the sort of wording used in monetary settlements can be found in figure 24a (page 123). Respondents who do not wish to admit any liability in relation to the claim may insist on the following words being added: 'The respondent's offer is made without any admission as to liability'. Very occasionally, the respondent is prepared to admit liability provided the applicant does not claim any compensation and you may find the following words used: 'The respondent admits that he unfairly dismissed the applicant; the applicant agrees not to seek any compensation.'

Not all settlements are based on monetary terms as above. The following are examples of the wording which could be used for other types of settlement:

Reinstatement: 'The respondents will reinstate the applicant in this position as a toolmaker in their factory at Coventry, and treat him in all respects as if he had not been dismissed, and

(i) Pay to the applicant his arrears of pay that is £95 per week (after deducting PAYE and national insurance contributions) from 12 December 1983 to 5 September 1984; and

(ii) restore to the applicant all his rights and privileges including his seniority and pension rights.'

Sex and race discrimination: 'The respondent will promote the applicant to foreman of the packing department from 5 October 1984 on the terms and conditions of employment applicable to a grade 4 manual worker. The applicant will accept the sum of £450 in full and final settlement of these proceedings and of all other claims (if any) which he could have against the respondent for compensation or damages.'

Reference: 'The respondent withdraws all allegations of misconduct against the applicant and undertakes to provide the applicant by 6 October 1984 with an open reference stating:

(i) when he commenced and terminated employment;

(ii) the nature of his employment;

(iii) the satisfactory performance of his job;

(iv) his good time keeping.'

Where a settlement is reached involving the re-engagement, reinstatement or engagement of an employee then the terms of such a settlement will be recorded on a COT 2 form, an illustration of which can be found in figure 25 on page 127.

Putting the settlement into effect

20.15   Once the terms of the settlement have been recorded on the relevant COT form, the conciliation officer will obtain the signatures of both parties to two copies of the form. He will then submit one of the signed forms to the appropriate ROIT. The tribunal has power under Rule 12(2)(*d*) to make a decision along the terms of the settlement. Within a period of usually no more than two weeks both parties will receive a decision of the tribunal in a form similar to figure 24b.

Reneging on the settlement

20.16   If the respondent does not comply with the decision then the applicant will be able to enforce any monetary award in the County Court or High Court, whichever is appropriate (*see* Chapter 41). However, where the tribunal records a decision including the words 'all further proceedings on the claim be adjourned generally until further order', as in figure 24b (page 126), the tribunal continues to have jurisdiction to deal with the claim. (*The Milestone School of English v Leakey [1982] IRLR 3*). So if the terms of the settlement are not complied with, an applicant could ask the IT to hear the complaint.

Case Number 269/84

THE INDUSTRIAL TRIBUNALS

BETWEEN

Applicant   Respondent

J Rider   **AND**   Mason (UK) Ltd

DECISION OF THE INDUSTRIAL TRIBUNAL

The applicant and respondent have agreed to settle this claim on the terms set out in the Schedule below. The tribunal therefore orders that all further proceedings on the claim be adjourned generally until further order.

SCHEDULE

That the Applicant shall accept the sum of £1250 (one thousand two hundred and fifty pounds) offered by the Respondent in full and final settlement of these proceedings and of all other claims (if any) which the Applicant could have brought against the Respondent arising under the terms of his contract of employment or out of his dismissal.

Decision sent to the parties on ———— *JH Engel* ————————
4 May 1984 and entered in the
Register

S. Herbert.

Secretary of Tribunals   16 April 1984,   London North
                                                    Date and place of decision

IT 59 B

Reproduced by permission of HMSO

Figure 24b: Decision of IT incorporating terms of settlement (IT 59B)

ADVISORY CONCILIATION AND ARBITRATION SERVICE

* ~~Equal Pay Act 1970~~
* ~~Sex Discrimination Act 1975~~
* ~~Race Relations Act 1976~~
* ~~Employment Protection Act 1975~~
* ~~Employment Protection (Consolidation) Act 1978~~
* ~~Employment Act 1980~~
* ~~EMPLOYMENT ACT 1982~~

* ~~AGREEMENT IN RESPECT OF AN APPLICATION MADE TO THE INDUSTRIAL TRIBUNAL~~

Tribunal case number
1394/84

* AGREEMENT IN RESPECT OF A REQUEST FOR CONCILIATION MADE TO THE ADVISORY CONCILIATION & ARBITRATION SERVICE (NO APPLICATION MADE TO TRIBUNAL AT TIME OF AGREEMENT)

Applicant	Respondent
Name PETER JENKIN	Name MILESTONE WEIGHTS LTD
Address 1198 EDGWARE ROAD	Address 375 MILK AVE
LONDON N4 6	LONDON N 10

Settlement reached as a result of conciliation action.

We the undersigned have agreed:

* 1   that the applicant shall be *~~engaged/re-engaged~~/reinstated in employment by

MILESTONE WEIGHTS LTD with effect from 25 MAY 1984 (date):

\#   (a)   on the terms and conditions under which he/~~she~~ was employed prior to dismissal

\#   (b) ~~on the following terms and conditions~~

* 2   that the applicant shall be paid £ 315 by the respondent.

Applicant P. Jenkin   date 18 MAY 1984
Respondent B. Graham   date 21 MAY 1984

*   Delete or complete as appropriate
\#   Complete (a) and/or (b) as appropriate

COT2

Reproduced by permission of HMSO

Figure 25: Conciliated settlement form (COT 2)

Amount of settlements

20.17   In 1982 some 38 per cent of all cases referred to ACAS were settled through conciliation. The statistics revealed in the October 1983 edition of the *Employment Gazette* indicate that compensation agreed at conciliation is on average well below that awarded by tribunals (*see* Chapter 39). For example, in 1982 82.4 per cent of conciliated settlements were below £1,000 compared with 44.9 per cent of tribunal awards, and only 2.2 per cent of conciliated settlements were over £5,000 compared with 5.7 per cent of tribunal awards.

Withdrawal

20.18   There may be a stage where the applicant realises he is not qualified to bring a claim or the merits of his case are insufficient for him to succeed. In such a situation, a letter sent to ROIT withdrawing the IT 1 or leaving it in the hands of ACAS (who will use a special form COT 4) will result in the tribunal dismissing the proceedings under Rule 12(2)(*c*), and a notice in the form of figure 26 opposite will be sent to both parties. In 1982 some 27 per cent of all cases referred to ACAS were withdrawn.

An applicant should ensure that the respondent will not make an application for costs under Rule 12(5) before agreeing to withdraw.

It should be remembered that until the decision has been made the applicant can withdraw his withdrawal. Also where there is a withdrawal a second application can still be made provided it is in time (although it could be struck out under Rule 11(2)(*e*) as being vexatious or frivolous: *Mulvaney v London Transport Executive [1981] ICR 351*). However, once the conciliation officer has taken action the applicant will be barred from proceeding.

Case Number 269/84 ....

THE INDUSTRIAL TRIBUNALS

BETWEEN

Applicant/Appellant   Respondent

J Rider   **AND**   Mason (UK) Ltd

DECISION OF THE INDUSTRIAL TRIBUNAL

The application is dismissed on withdrawal by the applicant

A J Hickson

Decision sent to the parties on
4 May 1984 and entered in the   Chairman
Register

JHSmith

for Secretary of Tribunals

16 April 1984, Birmingham
Date and place of decision

IT 59W   *Reproduced by permission of HMSO*

Figure 26: Decision of IT – applicant's withdrawal before hearing (IT 59W)

Chapter 21

Safeguards for Confidential Information

Introduction

21.1 There are three legal safeguards available to prevent confidential information from being disclosed. These are considered separately below.

Private hearings

21.2 As a general rule all tribunal hearings are in public and therefore the Press can be present. Under Rule 7(1) there are four circumstances where a party can apply for the hearing to be heard in private, where only the parties, their representatives and witnesses are permitted to attend. These are:

(*a*) where it is in the interests of national security;

(*b*) the information to be disclosed would be in contravention of an Act of Parliament;

(*c*) the information to be disclosed would be in breach of confidence;

(*d*) the information to be disclosed would 'cause substantial injury to' the respondent or another employer where the applicant works, for reasons other than its effect on collective bargaining.

The power to allow a private hearing is discretionary and is very rarely granted. It is most likely to arise in circumstances (*c*) and (*d*). Information which could be a breach of confidence may include a medical report or school report (for an example *see Cahm v Ward and Goldstone Ltd [1979] ICR 574*). Information which could cause substantial injury to a company may include information which, if in the hands of a competitor, would be financially disastrous such as early disclosure of the launching of a new product.

The procedure usually followed by tribunals on receiving a request for a private hearing is to hear the application immediately before the hearing of the complaint. (*Milne & Lyall v Waldren [1980] ICR 138*).

Privileged information

21.3   Information prepared or given to a conciliation officer or to a legal or other adviser for the express purpose of conciliation or advice on the case is 'privileged' and an IT will not order it's disclosure. But, as mentioned in the previous chapters, if the information is generally available, whether or not used for conciliation or advice, it may not be privileged.

Variation or setting aside of Rule 4 orders

21.4   As already discussed in Chapters 13 and 16, a party who has been ordered to provide further information, to disclose or allow inspection of certain documents or is required to attend as a witness, may apply under Rule 4(2) for that order to be varied or set aside.

Chapter 22

Interim Relief

Special protection for certain rights

22.1 Employment legislation has particularly protected the right of employees not to be dismissed for their membership or proposed membership of an independent trade union (TU) or for participating in the affairs of such a union. [*EPCA s 58(1)*]. Recent legislation extends this protection to cases where employees allege they have been unfairly dismissed for refusing to belong to a, or any particular, TU. [*EA 1982, s 8*]. The legislation protects these rights in three ways:

(*a*) by removing the age limit referred to in Chapters 1 and 3;

(*b*) by removing the continuous service qualification referred to in column 5 of Appendix A;

(*c*) by making available an interim procedure for dealing with such cases.

This interim procedure enables a person who considers the principal reason for his dismissal relates to trade union membership to bring a claim before an IT within a very short time of his dismissal. At this hearing the tribunal has to decide whether it is 'likely' that at a full hearing another tribunal would find that the dismissal was for this reason. (*Taplin v Shippam Ltd [1978] IRLR 450*; and for analysis of how to approach an interim relief case see *Forsyth v Fry's Metals Ltd [1977] IRLR 243*).

'Interim claims'

22.2 This claim is treated as an 'interim claim' in the sense that it does not take place at the same time as a full hearing nor instead of it but is in addition to the full hearing and occurs before it. The objective of this quick procedure is that where the tribunal finds for the applicant, it can order his reinstatement or re-engagement on terms not less favourable than if he had continued in employment; if the employer refuses those remedies, a monetary penalty may be imposed. These remedies are known as 'interim relief'.

By these powers the tribunal has the opportunity of successfully convincing an employer to take the employee back pending a full hearing or hopeful settlement of the case. In an appropriate case this will have the same effect as a 'status quo' clause in a procedure agreement, and could avoid industrial action.

Interim procedure

22.3   How does the procedure differ from that of other cases? The claim is brought in the same way by the employee completing an IT 1. However, this must be received by COIT within seven days of the effective date of dismissal (*see* Chapter 3). In addition where appropriate (not for non-membership dismissals — EA 1982 Schedule 3 paragraph 24), it must be accompanied by a certificate in writing signed by an authorised official of the independent TU involved, stating that the official has reasonable grounds for supposing that the principal reason for dismissal was the one alleged in the IT 1. [*EPCA s 77(2)(b)*]. An authorised official is one whose union has expressly given him authority under its rules to sign certificates for the purpose of supporting the interim procedure. Written evidence of the authority should be available at the hearing in case it is challenged. (*Bradley v Edward Ryde & Son [1979] ICR 488*).

In relation to non-membership dismissals, a trade union may be joined as a party 'as soon as reasonably practicable' [*EPCA s 77(3A)*] which may be outside the seven days' period, but the request must be made at least 3 days before the date of the hearing.

The procedure which then follows is similar to that already described except that everything is speeded up. The respondent is sent a copy of the IT 1, the certificate and figures 27 and 28 on pages 134 and 135. The applicant is sent figure 28 and an acknowledgement of his application. What is particularly special is that the notice of hearing (figure 27) is sent to both parties at this stage.

The IT does not have power to postpone this hearing date unless there are 'special circumstances'. [*EPCA s 77(4)*]. In other words, that date is usually adhered to. If postponements were easily allowed, the interim nature of the procedure would be lost. On average the hearing takes place two to three weeks after the dismissal.

All other interlocutory rights are available provided they are achieved quickly. In practice an application for further and better particulars, for example, will be dealt with at the hearing because of the time factor.

The interim hearing

22.4   The hearing differs from that involved in the determination of a complaint in the normal course of events described in Part II of this book. The evidence produced may be only partial in character, for the employer may not even be present. The onus of proving that the dismissal was likely to have been for, say, union membership is on the employee. Therefore he starts first. Although the standard of proof is less than that required at a full hearing (*see* Chapter 36), the applicant

22.4   *Interim Relief*

THE INDUSTRIAL TRIBUNALS (RULES OF PROCEDURE) REGULATIONS 1980

NOTICE OF APPLICATION FOR INTERIM RELIEF

UNDER SECTIONS 77-79 OF THE EMPLOYMENT PROTECTION (CONSOLIDATION) ACT 1978

Case No. 1301/84 ....

1.   I enclose a copy of an application for interim relief, to which you are named as respondent, and of the certificate supporting it, in connection with a complaint of unfair dismissal.

2.   The proceedings in this application for interim relief will be regulated by the Rules of Procedure contained in The Industrial Tribunals (Rules of Procedure) Regulations 1980 subject to the special provisions of Sections 77-79 of the Employment Protection (Consolidation) Act 1978. The case number indicated above should be quoted in any correspondence relating to these proceedings.

3.   The main complaint of unfair dismissal will be dealt with separately under the Rules of Procedure and separate communications will be sent to you regarding that complaint.

4.   The Act requires that an application for interim relief must be determined by an Industrial Tribunal as soon as practicable but that at least seven days before the date of the hearing the employer shall be given a copy of the application and certificate, together with notice of the date, time and place of the hearing.

5.   A notice of hearing is attached.

Signed *B. Williams* ....
for Assistant Secretary of the Tribunals

Date 9 April 1984 ....

Padiwack Ltd
Brass Road
Ystrad Mynach
Hengoed
Mid Glam CF8 7XW

IT14

Reproduced by permission of HMSO

Figure 27: Notice of application for interim relief (IT 14)

Regional Office of the
Industrial Tribunals

Caradog House
1-6 St Andrew's Place
Cardiff CF1 3BE
Telephone: 0222 372693/7

THE INDUSTRIAL TRIBUNALS

NOTICE OF HEARING

Case No.   1301/84
....

Tribunal   ...... 6(1) ....

NOTICE IS HEREBY GIVEN that the application for interim relief of

has been listed for hearing at

on   18   day,   April 1984   at   10 am

1.   Attendance should be at the above time and place. The parties are entitled to state their case in person or be represented by anyone they choose.

2.   The Act provides that if an application for interim relief is to succeed it must appear likely to the tribunal hearing the interim relief application that the tribunal hearing the complaint of unfair dismissal will find that the complainant was unfairly dismissed. The parties should be prepared to give evidence at the interim relief hearing accordingly and to bring to that hearing any documents that may be required.

3.   An Industrial Tribunal hearing an application for interim relief may consist of a duly authorised chairman of industrial tribunals (sitting alone).

4.   The Act requires that a tribunal shall not postpone a hearing under section 77(4) unless it is satisfied that special circumstances exist which justify it in so doing. If a party is unable to appear at the hearing at the appointed time, either personally or by representative, he should inform me immediately in writing giving the reason and the case number.

5.   Sub-section (9) of Section 77 of the Employment Protection (Consolidation) Act 1978 provides that if on the hearing of an application for interim relief under that Section the employer fails to attend before the tribunal or states that he is unwilling either to reinstate the employee or re-engage him as mentioned in sub-section (5) of Section 77, the tribunal shall make an order for the continuation of the employee's contract of employment. The relevant Section of the Act is set out in the document enclosed herewith.

Signed .... *B. Williams* ....

for Assistant Secretary of the Tribunals

To the Applicant(s)

Mrs R Davies
By her solicitor
Merryname & Co
19 High Street
Cheltenham, Glos.

and the Respondent(s)

Padiwack Ltd
Brass Road
Ystrad Mynach
Hengoed
Mid Glam CF8 7XW

IT15

9 April 1984

NOTE

Representatives who receive this notice must inform the party they represent of the date, time and place of the hearing. The party will not be notified direct.

Reproduced by permission of HMSO

Figure 28: Notice of interim hearing (IT 15)

still has to establish that he had a 'pretty good' chance of succeeding at the final hearing. (*Taplin v Shippam Ltd*).

Whether or not interim relief is granted, a full hearing will still take place unless the claim is withdrawn or settled. In practice cases tend not to proceed further than an interim hearing as a tribunal has already given its view on how the next tribunal is likely to decide. As a result, the case is often withdrawn or settled after the interim hearing.

Interim remedies

22.5   Interim relief will only be given in the form of a monetary penalty where the employer has refused to consent to an order of reinstatement or re-engagement or fails to attend the hearing. In this situation, the tribunal will order that the contract of employment continues for the purpose of ensuring the benefits under that contract continue to accrue to the employee. In practice, this will mean the employee will be paid his net wages plus other benefits without having to work until the case is settled or determined at the full hearing, whichever is the earlier. If during this interim period the employer were to change his mind and decide to reinstate the applicant, he could insist that the employee resumes work. In this situation it would be unnecessary to return to the tribunal to ask for a variation of the order. If the employer discovered that the employee was working elsewhere during the interim period, he could apply for a revocation or variation of the order on the grounds that there had been a 'relevant change of circumstances'. [*EPCA s 79(1)*].

However, whatever the situation, it is advisable from the respondent's point of view, to have the full hearing set down quickly to determine the matter.

Unfortunately from the respondent's point of view, the full hearing may not be the end of the matter. In *Zucker v Astrid Jewels Ltd* [*1978*] *IRLR 385*, Miss Zucker succeeded at an interim hearing and the tribunal ordered the contract to be continued. It took four and a half months before the full hearing was held, mainly through the fault of the respondent. At that hearing Miss Zucker failed. She appealed successfully to the EAT who sent the case back to be reheard by another IT, with the effect that the matter remained undetermined. The EAT ordered the contract to continue until Miss Zucker obtained new employment, which was not for a further six months. This meant she had received ten and a half months' wages although not working.

Chapter 23

Test Cases

Representative actions

23.1   It may happen that there are several applications relating to one or two similar issues, particularly where equal pay, sex and race discrimination cases are involved. For example, where 50 women in a factory consider they are carrying out like work to men in the same factory, but are being paid less, then all may apply to an IT for equal pay. The facts of each case may be identical. It would be ridiculous to have 50 similar hearings as the costs for both sides would be prohibitive. Also, once one decision has been made, it is very likely that all the others would be similarly decided. Therefore, tribunals have encouraged the procedure of bringing a 'representative action', i.e. taking only one case, the decision of which both parties then regard as being the decision for them all. In other words the one application is treated as a 'test case'.

Consolidation of proceedings

23.2   Under Rule 15 the tribunal has power to consider all the applications together or consolidate proceedings where:

(*a*) some common question of law or fact arises in all the originating applications; or

(*b*) the relief claimed in the IT 1 is in respect of or arises out of the same set of facts; or

(*c*) it is desirable to have a test case for some other reason.

An order consolidating proceedings may be made on the application of one or all of the parties or on the tribunal's own initiative. Therefore the tribunal can insist on taking a test case against the wishes of the parties. However, before doing this, it must notify all parties concerned to give them an opportunity to object to such an order being made. They should still consider cases separately where the facts are different. (*Paine & Moore v Grundy* [*1981*] *IRLR 267*).

Rule 15 should cover most cases where a test case is desirable. Where it does not, then it is only possible to take a test case by agreement between all the parties. (*Green v Southampton Corporation* [*1973*] *ICR 153*). It should be noted that all claimants must still submit originating applications, as the tribunal cannot consolidate actions which have not been commenced.

23.2 *Test Cases*

This procedure must not be confused with the tribunal's powers under Rule 14(3). Under that Rule, where there are several persons having the same interest in defending an action, the tribunal may authorise one or more to defend on behalf of the others (*see* 11.2).

Chapter 24

Defamation

The meaning of defamation

24.1 What is defamation? Defamation is where one person makes a false statement which damages the reputation of another person. It can be either oral or written. In the former case it is known as 'slander' and in the latter as 'libel'. Therefore, one can see many situations before and during the preparation of a case, and at the hearing itself, where a party can be defamed. Luckily, there are many defences and restrictions to an action for defamation which means that, in practice a party need not worry unduly about defaming an opponent. These are as follows:

(a) It is well established that witnesses giving testimony in ordinary courts are not subject to legal action in slander. Also, newspapers reporting slanderous testimony are not subject to legal action in libel. It has been assumed that the same privilege extends to tribunal proceedings.

(b) From the commencement of proceedings in ordinary courts the pleadings will also be privileged and it has been assumed that this privilege extends to tribunal pleadings including documents disclosed in accordance with an order. (*Riddick v Thames Board Mills [1977] 3 AER 677*). However, the tribunal has power under Rule 12(2)(*e*) at any stage in the proceedings to strike out or amend anything in the IT 1 or IT 3 which is 'scandalous, frivolous or vexatious' (in Scotland this power only relates to 'vexatious' matters).

(c) Anything communicated to a conciliation officer or an adviser is also privileged.

(d) A question of defamation could arise in written documents such as references. One of the defences to libel or slander is that a person, such as an employer, in making a statement relating to a former employee is acting under some social, moral or legal duty to another who has an interest in receiving it, such as another prospective employer (but note the effect of Section 8(3) and (5) of the Rehabilitation of Offenders Act 1974).

Defence of privilege

24.2 In the first situation 24.1(*a*) above, the defence (or 'privilege') will be absolute, i.e. there is no liability, because in the words of the Court of Appeal in *Roy v Prior* [*1970*] *2 AER 729*:

> 'The reasons why immunity is traditionally conferred upon witnesses in respect of evidence given in court are in order that they may give their evidence fearlessly and to avoid multiplicity of actions in which the value or truth of their evidence would be tried over again. Moreover, the trial process contains in itself, in the subjection to cross-examination and confrontation with other evidence, some safeguard against careless, malicious or untruthful evidence.'

Although these words refer to 'courts', the same court in *Royal Aquarium and Summer and Winter Garden Society Ltd v Parkinson* [*1892*] *1 QB 431* said that such absolute privilege attached 'wherever there was an authorised inquiry which, though not before a court of justice, is before a tribunal which has similar attributes'. It has always been assumed that ITs have similar attributes.

In the latter three situations (24.1(*b*)–(*d*) above), the defence will be 'qualified'. In other words there is no liability unless it can be shown that the oral or written statement was inspired by 'malice', i.e. it was made knowing it to be false and deliberately with a view to injuring, say, the former employee.

Legal aid not available

24.3   There is no legal aid available for defamatory actions. As the case must be brought in the High Court and the expense will be prohibitive, such actions are very unlikely in practice.

Chapter 25

Pre-Hearing Checklist

Original and final objectives

25.1 It is interesting to reflect at this stage to what extent your preparation has kept your original objectives in mind (see Chapter 1). Have they changed or been modified? If so, is there a need for further preparation? Do you have sufficient evidence to deal with matters that have to be proved? If not, is there anything further you can do? These are fundamental questions which must be asked prior to the hearing and a statement of the final objectives and the significant matters to be proved should be prepared in order to keep them in mind throughout the rest of the proceedings.

Alterations and amendments

25.2 This is also the time to go back and check that the grounds and defences inserted in the IT 1 and IT 3 are correct. If there are further matters which should be pleaded, write to ROIT requesting the necessary alterations or amendments. Because this may happen at the last moment, inform the other side in hopeful anticipation that your action will not delay the hearing. However, it is better this should happen than risk the tribunal exercising its discretion not to allow further grounds or defences once the hearing has started.

Final checklist

25.3 There are various other matters to be considered before the hearing. The following is a final checklist:

(a) Know your case thoroughly so that it can be conducted without notes if necessary.

(b) Ensure all witnesses have been informed of the time, place and date of the hearing, including second liners.

(c) Prepare witnesses properly by providing them with a copy of their proof of evidence and any documents to which they may be referred. Make your witnesses practise how to give evidence and subject them to cross-examination to ensure they know their case and are prepared to answer questions about it. Outline the nature of the hearing to give them a feeling of what is to come.

(*d*) Prepare a bundle of documents (agreed with your opponent if possible). In addition to the documents referred to in 13.10 think about what other kind of documentation can help get your case across to the tribunal: for example, a visual diagram of the workplace, photographs of a piece of equipment or even the implement itself. Arrange documents in the order to which they will be referred. Then index and number each page of the bundle as shown in figure 29 opposite. Make up six sets of copies; three for the tribunal, one for the witnesses, one for yourself and a spare copy. Mark all passages in your own copy to which you wish to make particular reference, especially in cross-examination (*see* Chapter 35).

(*e*) Know what is contained in these documents and in those which you know will be referred to by the other side.

(*f*) Prepare points in cross-examination of your opponent's witnesses (*see* Chapter 35).

(*g*) Make sure you are familiar with any 'law' involved, including precedents (*see* Chapter 37). If you are referring to the latter, know the whole judgment, not just the headnote. Prepare a list of authorities and their citations.

(*h*) Be prepared to deal with remedies (*see* Chapter 39).

(*i*) If considered necessary prepare an opening speech (*see* Chapter 34).

(*j*) Prepare a fact sheet with significant times, dates, names, and facts in chronological order for easy reference.

Having complied with all these stages you will be well equipped to proceed to the next step – the hearing.

Rider   v   Mason (UK) Ltd   Case no. 269/84

LIST OF DOCUMENTS

Date	Nature of Document	Page no
3.8.80	Rider's written statement of terms and conditions of employment	1-4
2.12.80	Disciplinary rules and procedure	5-11
	Rider's personal record card	12
9.11.83	Warning letter	13
13.1.84	Notes of disciplinary interview	14-17
16.1.84	Letter of dismissal	18

[Author's note: each page in bundle should be numbered.]

Figure 29: Index of documents

Part II

Presenting Your Case

Introduction

Eventually the date of the hearing arrives and you are faced with presenting the case you have researched and prepared.

There are several basic conventions to be noted at this stage:

(a) *Dress in a presentable manner.* Common sense should dictate a neat and tidy appearance for the representatives, the parties and the witnesses. Appearance in a tribunal is important. Neat, conventional dress is unlikely to offend anyone.

(b) *Punctuality.* One of the most inappropriate ways of starting a case is to arrive late. This will irritate the tribunal. Also, numerous steps have to be taken before the hearing commences as set out in Chapter 28 which necessitate arriving early.

(c) *Good manners.* The courteous party and representative can only benefit his case.

(d) *Never waste time.* Brevity is the keynote. Tribunals are designed for speedy, inexpensive and informal justice. Do not destroy these concepts.

Sadly, people are predisposed to accept the opinions of those they like and to reject those put forward by people they dislike. Thus, your integrity, amiability and reasonableness must, and do, play a significant part in your success in presenting a case. If you cannot be the sort of person people easily like, then at least try to be the sort of person whom people respect. You must keep your emotions under control. Never lose your temper or you are likely to lose your dignity and your case.

Chapter 26

Tribunal Composition

How the tribunal is made up

26.1   Each tribunal is made up of three members: a barrister or solicitor of at least seven years' standing who is the chairman, together with two lay members. The chairman is appointed by the Lord Chancellor and may be either full-time or part-time. The lay members are appointed by the Secretary of State for Employment after consultation with employers' organisations and trades councils, who nominate suitable persons for selection. The object is to provide members from both sides of industry. The Regional Chairman has power under Rule 5(3) to appoint to the tribunal someone having special experience in an appropriate case. For instance, often in race discrimination cases an assessor is appointed with special knowledge of race relations, although not necessarily of the same ethnic group as the applicant. (*Habib v Elkington & Co Ltd [1981] IRLR 344*). In October 1983 there were in post 64 full-time and 129 part-time chairmen and 1,816 lay members in England and Wales: (Source: COIT Fact Sheet, published February 1984.) In 1972 there were only 19 full-time and 32 part-time chairmen and 600 lay members.

It needs to be emphasised that the three members are equal members, all participating in the decision-making process, although the tribunal's written decision is signed by the chairman only. Each of the tribunal members has the opportunity to express his or her view not only as to the decision, but also as to the reasons on which the decision is based. Therefore, in theory, it is possible for the lay members to outvote the lawyer chairman on points of law. This very rarely happens in practice, and the vast majority of all decisions are unanimous. Although cases are generally heard by all three members, in the absence of one lay member, the application may still be heard but only with the consent of the parties.

Attached to each tribunal is a clerk who is not legally qualified. He advises the parties on points of procedure before the hearing begins and generally assists the parties and the tribunal.

Chapter 27

Other Proceedings Pending

Simultaneous court proceedings

27.1   What happens when proceedings in other courts are taking place simultaneously with IT proceedings and are in some way connected? It is possible in unfair dismissal cases that a matter of serious misconduct also amounts to a criminal act such as theft or a claim in the High Court for forgery and fraud. Should the tribunal case be postponed until after the other proceedings? Under Rule 12(2)(*b*) 'A tribunal may, if it thinks fit, . . . (*b*) postpone the day or time fixed for, or adjourn any hearing . . .'. The Court of Appeal in *Carter v Credit Change Ltd [1979] IRLR 361* found that this rule confers complete discretion on an IT chairman, provided he exercises that discretion judicially and there are good reasonable grounds for exercising it in that way.

Where criminal proceedings are pending and it is felt that IT proceedings may prejudice the Crown Court hearing for fear that the applicant could incriminate himself, an application should be made to the chairman to postpone the tribunal case. It would not be proper to allow cross-examination of a witness who is the subject of criminal proceedings about alleged past criminal offences committed by him. (*Wagstaff v The Trade and Industrial Press Ltd (1968) 3 ITR 1*). However, the CA in the *Carter* case would not interfere where a tribunal refused to postpone a hearing in similar circumstances, because the tribunal considered the delays involved would be prejudicial to a particular party. Despite this decision, chairmen in Scotland have a practice of always postponing proceedings until after the Sheriff's Court case has been heard.

Spent convictions

27.2   You should also be aware that under the provisions of the Rehabilitation of Offenders Act 1974 a witness cannot be asked about a conviction which is 'spent' and if asked he cannot be required to reveal the spent conviction. You will have to refer to the Act to see to what convictions this applies. Broadly a spent conviction is where there has been a non-custodial sentence or a custodial sentence of less than 30 months.

Previously determined identical cases: 'issue estoppel'

27.3   What happens when there has been an identical case in another court which has already been determined? Where in all material respects the case is identical then the parties should not be allowed to re-open the issue. This is known as 'issue estoppel' (*Green v Hampshire County Council [1979] ICR 861*), and could arise where, for example, both cases involved the same breach of a term in a contract of employment. It is extremely unlikely however that any two cases will be identical; and anyway the tribunal hearing will usually come first (for an example see *Turner v London Transport Executive [1977] IRLR 441*).

Chapter 28

Arriving at the Tribunal

Steps to be taken

28.1   The following steps should be taken when arriving at the tribunal:

1. Book in by informing the tribunal you have arrived.

2. If available, find a conference room where you and your witnesses can have privacy. Otherwise go into the waiting room set aside for 'applicants' or 'respondents', whichever is appropriate.

3. Inform the usher of your whereabouts so that any late witnesses can be directed to your room.

4. Find the tribunal clerk (or, more accurately, the clerk will find you). He will require to know your name, whether you are a representative, and the name and position of any witnesses.

5. The clerk will also note the names of the other party's representative and witnesses. Even at this late stage you may wish to seek a settlement (*see* Chapter 29). If you have not heard of any of their witnesses before, ask your own witnesses who they are and what evidence it is thought they will give.

6. You should also check the timing of your case with the clerk. You may have been asked to come at 10 a.m. but find other cases down for hearing before you. These may only be short technical hearings, such as a pre-hearing assessment.

7. This is your opportunity to find out as much as possible about the tribunal members before whom you will appear. You should ask the clerk the names of the chairman and the two lay members and write these down (if you have not already obtained this information from the 'listing sheet' on the notice board listing cases to be heard that day with the names of tribunal members). If you have not appeared before them previously, you should inquire as to the degree of formality the chairman prefers. The occupations and positions of the lay members should also be ascertained as the subject matter of the case may fall particularly within the province of a lay member, and you may be able to make use of that knowledge in your presentation. This information would be important to you where one of the lay members is absent and you are asked to consent to the hearing taking place without that member. Finally, you may wish to

object to a member if you know he or she has some connection with the case.

8. If you will be referring to authorities or citing cases (*see* 37.5) the clerk will require a list of them with appropriate law report citations. You should ask for sight of the other side's list, and if any are unfamiliar request the clerk to supply you with copies in order to have an opportunity to peruse these before the hearing commences.

9. Witnesses are usually required to swear an oath or affirm. If a witness requires a special holy book, let the clerk know at this stage in order to avoid the possibility of delay later.

10. The clerk will want to know the DHSS or DE office from which an applicant received payment of benefits for the purposes of recoupment (*see* 39.25).

11. Collect expense forms from the clerk relating to travel, loss of wages etc. for each witness and the parties to the action, as you may forget these when the case is over.

12. If there are any other procedural matters you want clarified ask the clerk before the hearing begins.

13. Explain to the witnesses the composition and format of the tribunal and the procedure they are likely to encounter. Emphasise the informality compared with other courts, and generally try to put them at their ease. Also explain that their manner in and out of the witness box is important and can influence the tribunal.

14. You should make sure each witness is supplied with pen and paper and that any points which arise during the hearing on which they may wish to comment, should be written down and passed to you at the time. Explain that if they try to communicate by word of mouth you may miss some evidence as it is difficult to concentrate on more than one person speaking at a time. Also emphasise that a note must be passed to you at the time a point arises, and not at the lunch adjournment, for example, when it may be too late to raise it.

15. If there has not been a recent opportunity to go through a witness's evidence with him, do so now, particularly where the start of the hearing is delayed.

16. If witnesses have not turned up use the public telephone you will find in the building. Let the clerk know. If the witness is important, explain why you may have to ask for an adjournment.

Perhaps it can now be appreciated why it is so important to arrive at the tribunal in plenty of time.

The press

28.2   Nearly all cases are open to the public. Therefore there is a strong likelihood that members of the press will be present. You should advise the parties and their witnesses not to speak to the press before and

Figure 30: Illustration of tribunal hearing

during the hearing. It may also be advisable for none of you to speak to the press after the hearing, depending on the outcome and findings of the case. It has been known for press photographers to be waiting outside the tribunal building at the end of a hearing!

The case is called

28.3 When the tribunal is ready, the clerk will call you into the tribunal room, which will look something like the illustration depicted in figure 30 opposite. If you are a representative, then seat the applicant or principal witness next to you, and all other witnesses behind you. In Scotland witnesses are not allowed into the hearing until they are required to give their evidence. If there is a conflict in the evidence this procedure would seem more conducive to the truth. In England and Wales it is possible to apply for witnesses to remain outside but this is rarely granted unless you can maintain that the other side's witnesses are likely to commit perjury.

Then set out your papers in an easily accessible way, with your bundles of documents (*see* 13.9, 13.10) ready to hand to the tribunal in triplicate.

When both parties and all their witnesses are ready the clerk will inform the tribunal members and they will enter the tribunal room very soon after the clerk returns. (Today, it is not uncommon for the tribunal members to be waiting for you.) On their entrance you and your witnesses should stand and remain standing until invited to sit. After this the proceedings will be conducted seated except:

— when witnesses are being administered the oath or affirmation, and then only that witness and the clerk will stand;

— when the tribunal adjourns, or for some other reason the tribunal members leave the room, then you will stand as they leave and when they return.

Chapter 29

'Tribunal-Door' Settlements

Last minute settlements

29.1　There is nothing to prevent the parties settling the case at the last minute at the door of the tribunal or even during the hearing. In these situations it is common for tribunals to be asked by the parties to dismiss the originating application on withdrawal by the applicant and the tribunal then producing a decision similar to figure 26 on page 129. There is always the risk then that the respondent could renege on the settlement, and it has been known for an applicant to insist that the respondent repair to the nearest bank, return with a briefcase full of banknotes, and pay the monetary settlement before going before the tribunal and withdrawing.

In the more common case the agreement to settle is wholly executory (i.e. performed later) and it leaves the applicant without a remedy in a tribunal if the respondent does not perform his undertakings. The proceedings are at an end, and the agreement to settle, since it is invalidated by the terms of Section 140 of EPCA cannot be sued upon before the High Court or County Court.

Therefore it is not surprising to find tribunals are beginning to adopt new forms of decisions in these sorts of situations where ACAS is unlikely to be involved. They tend to follow the form of wording of the precedents considered next.

Precedent forms

29.2　Set out below are two precedents for settlement decisions used by tribunals:

Decision (1)

Terms of settlement having been agreed between the parties, by consent, this originating application is withdrawn upon payment by the respondent to the applicant on or before . . . of the sum of £. . . in full and final settlement of the applicant's claim. Liberty to apply on or before . . ., and if no application is made by this date, this originating application is dismissed on withdrawal by the applicant.

Decision (2)

Terms of settlement having been agreed between the parties in accordance with the terms set out in the Schedule hereto, by consent, this originating application is withdrawn upon compliance by the respondent with the terms of settlement on or before . . . Liberty to apply on or before . . . and if no application is made by this date, this originating application is dismissed on withdrawal by the applicant.

These decisions still give the applicant the opportunity to return to the tribunal within certain time limits if the respondent's undertakings are not performed.

Chapter 30

The Informality of the Hearing

Simplifying tribunal proceedings

30.1 Perhaps the most consistent criticism of tribunal procedure from both sides of industry has been that tribunal hearings are too legalistic and therefore too long, contrary to the procedure originally envisaged by the Donovan Report. The Tribunal Regulations encourage tribunals to feel able to be less formal by making it clear that they are not bound to observe the more formal court procedures. Rule 8(1) reads:

> 'The tribunal shall conduct the hearing in such manner as it considers most suitable to the clarification of the issues before it and generally to the just handling of the proceedings; it shall so far as appears to it appropriate seek to avoid formality in its proceedings and it shall not be bound by any enactment or rule of law relating to the admissibility of evidence in proceedings before the courts of law.'

The rules of natural justice

30.2 This means that ITs, in contrast to other courts, should make it easier to have lay representation. However, hearings still have to be conducted fairly and follow what are known as the 'rules of natural justice', which among other things means that:

(a) tribunal members must be impartial and be seen to be unbiased;

(b) both parties should be given the right to be heard;

(c) no party shall be taken by surprise by an allegation against him of which he is unaware or be denied the opportunity of bringing evidence to refute it;

(d) justice must be seen to be done.

Tribunals and courts compared

30.3 In practice the degree of formality very much depends on the individual tribunal chairman. Perhaps the really true test of whether an IT is less formal than other courts is where the tribunal adopts an 'inquisitorial' role rather than depending on an 'adversary' system. Courts in England and Wales consider the prime responsibility for determining the course of hearings and the presentation of evidence and legal argument should be taken by the representatives. Such a system is adversary because it is practised on accusatorial lines. When tribunal members, particularly the chairman, take over this prime responsibility so as to ensure all relevant matters of evidence, fact and law have been brought out, and those that are in dispute have been argued at the hearing, then the procedure really becomes less legalistic. This type of inquisitorial system is already practised to a large extent by tribunals in Scotland and is becoming much more common in England and Wales.

Chapter 31

What Tribunal Members Know

Information known to tribunal members before the hearing begins

31.1   The tribunal members will usually have read the pleadings before entering the tribunal room. In other words, they will have read the IT 1, IT 3 and any documents attached to these. Also they may have read any interlocutory papers which have passed through ROIT, such as a reply to an order for further particulars. However, they may not have read through a bundle of documents submitted to ROIT before the hearing, even if this has been agreed between the parties. In any case, it is inadvisable to send bundles of documents to the tribunal (as opposed to an index of documents) before the hearing as it has been known for lay members to draw incorrect inferences before hearing the evidence. So you should not assume the tribunal members have any detailed knowledge of your case, only the basic information contained in the originating application and notice of appearance.

Chapter 32

The Hearing

Preliminary matters

32.1 The chairman will first establish who is the applicant and the respondent or their respective representatives. From now on, the chairman is referred to as Sir or Madam or Mr Chairman. There may be occasions where you wish to refer to particular lay members and they should be called by name, e.g. Mrs Jones. However, most of your applications and representations will be addressed to the chairman, unless you are replying to a specific question from a lay member.

Tribunal's discretion with unrepresented parties

32.2 If a party fails to appear or to be represented, the tribunal has discretion under Rule 8(3) to:

(*a*) dismiss the claim if the absent party is the applicant; or

(*b*) dispose of the claim in the absence of either party; or

(*c*) adjourn the hearing to a later date.

Where the tribunal decides to dismiss or dispose of the claim it must consider any pleadings before it and any written representations submitted in accordance with Rule 7(3) (*see* 17.3). Where one party does not appear there is no duty on the tribunal, whether or not it exercises its discretion under Rule 8(3), to turn itself into an investigatory body and ask questions of the party appearing before it. (*Mason v Hamer EAT 161/81*).

Obviously, a respondent who attends will prefer to discourage a tribunal from adjourning the hearing. Also, under Rule 11(2) the tribunal only has power to award costs against the absent party 'on the application of a party to the proceedings'. If the tribunal adjourns on its own initiative, it has no power to award costs. Therefore, the first matter with which you may have to deal, if you are the respondent, is to ask the tribunal to use its discretion to dismiss the case.

Other applications

32.3 There may be other applications you wish to make before the case really starts. For example, where your opponent has not complied with an order of the tribunal under Rule 4(1), you should bring this to the tribunal's attention, and perhaps apply for part of the IT 1 or IT 3 to be struck out under Rule 4(4) (*see* 13.6). Alternatively, you may wish to apply for the IT 1 or IT 3 to be amended where certain grounds have been omitted. If you are successful, the other side may then wish to apply for an adjournment or reserve the right to be heard on the amended matter only, at a later date.

You may wish to object to the introduction of a statement by a witness who is unable to attend because you have only been handed a copy at the hearing (*see* 17.3). Perhaps the most likely event to arise is the non-appearance of one of your own witnesses or a subpoenaed witness. You may have to prove service of a subpoenaed witness (*see* 16.4–16.6). If he is crucial to your case you must ask for an adjournment so as to have an opportunity to contact him. If unsuccessful, you may have to apply for a postponement and costs are more than likely to be awarded against you under Rule 11(2).

These instances however are rare and it is most likely the merits of the case will be dealt with straight away, unless there is a preliminary point of jurisdiction.

Preliminary points of jurisdiction

32.4   If there is a preliminary point you should already have prior notice of this, because either you raised it yourself or have been notified by ROIT that this is a preliminary hearing (*see* 19.3) or preliminary matters will be dealt with first. If there is any dispute as to whether the applicant is qualified to bring the claim it will be considered at this stage. For example, if a woman teacher of 62 is claiming unfair dismissal she will have to show that the normal retiring age at her school is over 60.

The preliminary stage may be a full-scale hearing in its own right, and may necessitate all the procedures of a full hearing which are discussed in the following chapters. This will be particularly true in a constructive dismissal case where the applicant has to show there has been a dismissal. Only employees who have been dismissed can bring a claim for unfair dismissal. Therefore the question of dismissal is technically a preliminary point of jurisdiction. However, such cases should be treated in the same way as those involving a full hearing since nearly all the evidence will be needed to determine the issue. Really the only thing in common with other preliminary matters is that the applicant has to start first, in other words he who asserts that he is qualified must prove it. This is invariably the applicant.

Who starts the full hearing?

32.5   In contrast to a preliminary hearing, the normal rule in unfair dismissal cases is that the employer goes first. Since the Employment Act 1980, the burden of proving that a dismissal is reasonable is no longer on the employer. However, the employer still has to prove that there is a permitted reason for dismissal [*EPCA s 57(2)*], such as misconduct or ill health, and therefore usually starts.

Where the employee admits the reason for dismissal (e.g. incapability) but disputes the reasonableness, the employer would still normally go first as he has knowledge of why he dismissed the employee in a particular way.

In redundancy payment cases the applicant has to prove dismissal. If dismissal is admitted then it is presumed to be by reason of redundancy and the employer again goes first.

With anti-discrimination and employment protection rights the employee usually goes first.

The tribunals, however, have a degree of flexibility in the way they handle who starts. In *Hawker Siddeley Power Engineering v Rump* [*1979*] *IRLR 425*, for example, the 'dismissal' was contested, which would normally mean the employee starting first. The EAT upheld the chairman's decision insisting on the employer starting which was within his discretion under Rule 12(1): this rule allows tribunals to regulate their own procedure.

Hand in bundle of documents

32.6   The party who starts should then hand to the clerk the agreed bundle of documents, or if not agreed, his own bundle, in triplicate so that there is one for each member of the tribunal. These may then become exhibits.

Stages of the hearing

32.7   Some tribunals require the hearing to take part in two stages. First, evidence is given as to the merits only, i.e. whether the claim succeeds or fails. Secondly, if it does succeed, then evidence is required in relation to remedies. In Scotland the hearing is not divided in this way and both stages are dealt with at the same time. This is now becoming the practice with many ITs in England and Wales. However, where the remedies involved are reinstatement or re-engagement this may be difficult and a second stage more likely. Therefore ask the chairman whether evidence as to remedies should also be given at this stage or left to later. In either case the evidence required is discussed in Chapter 39.

Chapter 33

Order of Hearing

33.1　In general proceedings in an unfair dismissal case will follow an order like this:

(*a*)　The employer (or his representative) makes an *opening statement*.

(*b*)　The employer calls his witnesses and asks them questions. This is called *examination* or *examination-in-chief*.

(*c*)　The employee's side then *cross-examines*, i.e. gets the opportunity to ask questions of those witnesses.

(*d*)　The *tribunal* members, if they feel it necessary, ask the witnesses *questions* about the evidence they have just given.

(*e*)　If the employer feels that it is necessary, then he can *re-examine* a witness.

(*f*)　The employee (or his representative) then puts his case and may make an opening speech, although this is becoming less frequent.

(*g*)　The employee then calls his witnesses and a similar procedure to steps (*b*), (*c*), (*d*) and (*e*) above are followed.

(*h*)　The employee then gives a *final address* in effect summarising his case.

(*i*)　The employer likewise gives a final address.

(*j*)　There may be some *discussion* as to remedies, although this is often discussed after the decision.

(*k*)　The tribunal *adjourns* to consider the decision.

(*l*)　The tribunal returns and announces its *decision*.

Under Rule 12(1) a tribunal has power to regulate its own procedure and therefore you should not be surprised if occasionally this order is varied, or that at some stage in the proceedings the chairman invites the parties to consider settling the case.

The next few chapters look at the procedure on the basis of the usual order of proceedings set out above.

Chapter 34

The Opening Speech

Tribunals' discretion to allow opening statements

34.1   A party no longer has the right to make an opening speech or statement. Rule 8(2) has cut out this right. However, as tribunals have power to regulate their own procedures under Rule 12(1) they may allow a party to make an opening statement.

Why should they do this? As already pointed out in Chapter 31 you should not assume any detailed knowledge of the case by tribunal members. Therefore they are unlikely to be aware of the full nature of the case at the start of the hearing. As a result it is probable they will ask the party who starts (*see* 32.5) to make a brief, succinct statement putting them in the picture.

In Scotland there has always been a tendency to discourage the use of opening statements, particularly where they refer to what the witnesses are going to say. The logic behind this is that if the witnesses are there, let them say it.

Opening statement checklist

34.2   If you are faced with the task of making such a statement because you are invited to do so by the tribunal or have asked them to allow you to, then the following checklist should prove useful.

(*a*)   Where there is some interesting point of law or an especially interesting aspect of fact, it is as well to draw this to the tribunal's attention from the outset, so that they may anticipate (possibly with relief) that this is not just a run-of-the-mill case.

(*b*)   In any event, inform the tribunal what you consider are the main legal issues to be determined and show what you have to prove. Do not refer to sections or schedules of Acts unless the case is unusual and be concise.

(*c*)   Then outline the facts which you know you can prove or are not in dispute. This should include the main events behind the matters in dispute. Also outline the background to the case, for instance if you are the respondent give a general description of the applicant's job, the size and type of resources of the organisation, the management structure, the products manufactured etc.

(*d*) Then identify your principal witnesses and the relevance of their evidence to your task of proving what has to be proven. Include a very brief description of the nature of the evidence they will give and indicate where any conflicts may lie.

(*e*) You should explain briefly the nature of the documents in your bundle, and particularly refer the tribunal to the relevant parts in each.

(*f*) Having given the tribunal the gist of the case you are presenting you may endeavour to anticipate the nature of the case to be presented by your opponent, suggesting, perhaps, possible answers to his arguments (by doing this you are recognising any weaknesses in your case and offering explanations for them).

(*g*) Finally, you may like to suggest the questions which you consider the tribunal members will have to ask themselves when the evidence has been given.

You do not have to deal with all these matters, only those which you feel are necessary to put the tribunal in the picture. Even if requested by the chairman to make a statement there is no penalty as such for declining to do so. However, unless the tribunal knows what the case is about, your early evidence may be out of context and have less impact than if the tribunal was in the picture. The tribunal may refuse to allow you to make an opening speech. Where you have good reasons for wanting to make one, explain this to the chairman. If the tribunal still refuses to give you the opportunity there is really nothing further that can be done since ITs can regulate their own procedure.

Example of a hypothetical opening speech in an unfair dismissal claim

34.3   If you wish to write the statement out beforehand in anticipation of being allowed to make one, it is usually quite acceptable to read it to the tribunal. The example below provides a guideline of the sort of statement which might be given in a hypothetical unfair dismissal case.

> I represent CTU Ltd in resisting Mr Quinn's claim against us that he was unfairly dismissed. Let me first say that this is an unusual case in that it involves the European Commission who are providing financial assistance to CTU in relation to research into micro-chip technology.
>
> This case concerns the failure of the applicant to obey what I would suggest were the reasonable orders of his employer, in particular, he refused to represent them in Brussels at a seminar to be held by the Commission. Therefore, it will be necessary for the respondent to show that such failure was a permitted reason for dismissal, and then for you to decide whether in all the circumstances having regard to equity and the substantial merits of the case we acted reasonably in treating it as a sufficient reason for dismissing Mr Quinn.
>
> CTU is a small research and development company in the computer field. We have 25 employees, half of whom are highly skilled engineers, and the

company is a subsidiary of Videotape plc. The applicant was recruited as a research engineer in May 1980, subject to the company's normal terms and conditions of employment for 'S' members of staff. These conditions are contained in document 3 of the bundle starting on page 34. I would particularly like to draw your attention to condition 6 on page 35 in relation to travel.

In June 1982 the EEC agreed to financially support the company to carry out further research into micro-chip technology. Mr Quinn agreed to be the research engineer responsible for the project. One of the conditions of receiving funds was that the company should submit progress reports every six months. It was estimated the project would take two years.

The research started well. The applicant produced an excellent first six-monthly report. He was then requested in April 1983 to present it at a conference in Brussels to be held by the Commission on 11 and 12 August 1983, but he refused. The managing director, Mr Card will give evidence to the effect that he tried on several occasions to explain the importance of attending the conference, and that EEC support might be withdrawn if a paper was not presented. However, Mr Quinn still refused to go. The disciplinary procedure was then put into motion, see pages 12–13 of the bundle, and despite several warnings and a disciplinary hearing he still refused to attend. Eventually he was dismissed by letter on the 5 August which is at page 51 of the bundle. He exercised his right to appeal but his dismissal was confirmed.

Mr Quinn may well argue that he was not contractually obliged to travel or work abroad. I will seek to show that it was part of the applicant's contractual obligation to undertake overseas travel. He may also argue that someone else could have presented the paper in Brussels. In this respect I will bring evidence to show that it was management's decision that he was the most suitable person to present the paper.

Sir, in my submission, the questions the tribunal members will have to apply their minds to when the evidence has been heard are:

(*a*) was there an express or implied term in the applicant's contract of employment relating to overseas travel and work?

(*b*) whether or not there was such a term, was it reasonable for the respondent to insist on the applicant travelling to Brussels to present his report?

(*c*) was his refusal a sufficient reason to dismiss?

The party who does not have to prove his case, and who starts second, may also be asked to make an opening statement. However, this is extremely unlikely as the tribunal will be familiar with the evidence and issues involved by the time such a statement might be appropriate. For similar reasons this party (second) is unlikely to want to make a statement.

Chapter 35

The Advocate's Checklist

Procedures to be dealt with

35.1   The representative or party in person who may have made an opening statement, now conducts the rest of the hearing as an 'advocate'. The following is a checklist of procedures and points which will have to be mastered and dealt with by the advocate:

(*a*) taking notes

(*b*   giving and calling evidence

(*c*) avoiding leading questions

(*d*) witnesses not coming up to proof

(*e*) using manuscript notes

(*f*) introducing documents

(*g*) the worth of hearsay evidence

(*h*) the art of cross-examination

(*i*) tribunal questioning

(*j*) re-examination

(*k*) objecting/interrupting

(*l*) seeking adjournments

(*m*) no case to answer.

Taking notes

35.2   In addition to a large notebook you will be well advised to have a pen and at least two coloured pencils. You should take a full and accurate note of the evidence given by the other side's witnesses, the replies your witnesses give when questioned by your opponent and the tribunal, and the evidence given during re-examination. You should also try to take a full note of any additional evidence given by your witnesses which is not in the prepared statement (*see* Chapter 15), the replies of the other side's witnesses to your questions and the tribunal's questions and the replies to any re-examination of your witnesses.

Some of this note-taking is particularly difficult because you cannot easily speak and take notes at the same time. So it may be useful to take a colleague with you or ask one of your witnesses to take full notes at paticular times or throughout the proceedings. Otherwise, do not be afraid to ask the witness to repeat the answer so that you can write it down. Similarly, do not be afraid to interrupt the other side to ask for an answer to be repeated so that you can record it correctly.

The coloured pencils should be used to mark passages of the evidence upon which you propose to question the other party's witnesses (known as cross-examination) and to underline those parts which might be useful for reference when you come to your final address. Use a different colour for each purpose so that later on you can easily pick out the points.

It is also advisable to leave a margin on the left of your notes in which you can add a short note indicating the line of cross-examination you hope to pursue.

You are not the only one who will be taking notes. The chairman (in England and Wales) has to take a full note of all the relevant evidence because the EAT requires him to submit notes of the proceedings on appeal. The result is that the proceedings are generally slow because you must make sure the chairman has time to write down the evidence; so WATCH HIS PEN. In Scotland the EAT does not require such notes, so the flow of evidence is not interrupted in the same way and the proceedings tend to be quicker.

Giving and calling evidence (examination-in-chief)

35.3   After making the opening statement, the same party is then obliged to call his evidence. In other words, to give evidence himself if appearing in person, or to call witnesses to give evidence if a representative, or both. You should now call your first witness who will be directed into the witness box by the clerk. Nearly all tribunals exercise their discretion under Rule 8(4) to require evidence to be given on oath or affirmation. The clerk will administer this and it is essential that you do not talk while the oath is being administered.

If you are a party appearing in person, it is difficult to give evidence unaided. Most chairmen will allow you in such situations to read a prepared written statement and it is advisable to make copies available for the tribunal members (*see* Chapter 17). This statement should take a similar form to that suggested in 15.3–15.6. A written statement of evidence read by a party is not the same thing as a written representation where seven days' notice must be given as described in 17.3. If you are a representative calling evidence, your witnesses will rarely be allowed to read from a prepared statement and will usually be required to give evidence from memory, because tribunals prefer unaided recollections. However, some tribunals allow witnesses to read out their evidence for the sake of convenience and speed.

The prepared statement will act as your aid only to prompt the witness to give the evidence required. If the witness has been prepared properly this part of the hearing should be straightforward.

The first thing to bear in mind is that the tribunal is not bound by any strict rules of evidence. As mentioned on a number of occasions already, the tribunal has power to regulate its own procedure.

Secondly, there are no hard and fast rules about the order in which witnesses are called, and this will be your decision. You should call your witnesses in an order enabling your case to be presented to its best advantage. A tribunal should not dictate the order in which a party calls witnesses. (*Barnes & Taylor v BPC (Business Forms) Ltd (1975) 10 ITR 110*).

Thirdly, always keep the witness under your control. Experience shows that the witness who is left to tell his own story may not. Take him up to the essential points and only then leave him to give his own account. If necessary interrupt, taking care not to put him out of his stride, in order to bring him back under your control and maintain a precise and chronological account.

Fourthly, phrase your questions simply and briefly. Take care only to put one question at a time and in a logical sequence.

Fifthly, avoid peculiar mannerisms like repeating the witness' answer. This also applies when cross-examining. However, take your time and pause to let answers sink in.

Sixthly, depending on how your evidence is going, decide whether it is necessary to call all your witnesses to give evidence.

Avoiding leading questions

35.4   What is a leading question? It is one which suggests a particular answer, usually yes or no. For example: 'Did the applicant swear as the manager approached?' or 'When the manager approached, did the applicant swear?' Both these are leading questions, and it can be very difficult for the inexperienced, perhaps nervous, advocate to avoid asking questions in this way. Luckily, unlike other courts, ITs have discretion to allow such questions and will encourage them in respect of:

— introductory matters such as the name, address and description of your witness;

— matters which are clearly not in dispute; and

— where you are trying to get a specific denial of a particular allegation.

In the average case there are only a few areas of dispute. This gives the advocate plenty of opportunity to lead in order to save time.

Because of the informality of tribunals leading questions are often allowed even where evidence is in dispute (except perhaps where the advocate is a lawyer!). However, they will weaken the strength of the testimony. ITs rely to a great extent on witnesses and their credibility is vital. Therefore, it is much better to let them tell the events in their own words.

If a chairman or your opponent objects to the leading nature of your question, just stop to think how it can be rephrased. Taking the above examples:

Q   Did you see the applicant?
A   Yes.

Q   Was anyone else around?
A   The manager was approaching us.

Q   What happened then?
A   The applicant swore at the manager.

Witnesses not coming up to proof

35.5   What happens when a witness fails to give the evidence you supposed? Unfortunately this often happens but you may be able to correct the position. The written statement you are using may read: 'As I entered the stock room, I saw the applicant asleep under the stairs'. When you ask, 'When you entered the stock room, was there anything unusual happening?' and you get the answer 'No', it may take you by surprise. You may not be able to correct this by asking a leading question as the chairman may prevent you from doing so, especially if this is essential disputed evidence. However, there are two methods of dealing with this situation:

(*a*)   Proceed something along these lines:

Q   You have told us you entered the stockroom
A   Yes.

Q   Did you see the applicant there?
A   Yes.

Q   What was he doing?
A   He was asleep.

Q   Where was he asleep?
A   Under the stairs.

(*b*)   Ask a leading question:

e.g. 'Did you see the applicant asleep?'
It may be allowed. If not, the witness will have heard the question and hopefully take the cue and give the answer required.

The first method is preferable as the tribunal may not give much weight to evidence given by the second method. Despite the aggravation caused by a witness not coming up to proof always put your questions quietly and civilly.

Using manuscript notes

35.6 It can be difficult for witnesses to recall events in the unfamiliar environment of a tribunal, especially if they are nervous. Therefore, if there are any written notes which can be referred to by a witness to refresh his memory these should be used, provided they were made contemporaneously with or soon after the event. This is a little like a police officer referring to his notebook. Some managers keep a diary of daily events and this could be used to help recall dates of interviews and of oral warnings. Documents in the bundle before the tribunal can be used in the same way and this will be discussed below. However, the written notes referred to here will not usually be disclosed or included in an agreed bundle.

ITs do not have to accept such notes or allow a witness to refer to them. However, they will usually exercise their discretion to do so if you can show the witness kept a record, he made it himself, and the notes were made up at the time of or shortly after the events (this could be a matter of minutes, or in some cases, days).

Introducing documents

35.7 During your examination of witnesses you will want to introduce any documentary evidence. This is done simply by referring the witness, in the course of a question, to a page in the bundle (a copy of which you should have provided for those giving evidence). Alternatively, if no bundle has been prepared hand the individual document to the witness with copies to the tribunal members and to your opponent. Depending on the nature of the document you may allow the tribunal to read it, you may read it to the tribunal, or the witness may read it. The witness can then be asked to explain the document or any matters relating to it. The individual document will become an exhibit (unless the bundle has already become so) and will be marked for ease of reference. Respondents' documents are usually marked 'R' followed by a number representing the order of the documents produced; applicants' documents are correspondingly marked with an 'A' followed by a number.

Although this is the usual way to introduce documents, it may not be necessary. For example, an agreed bundle is likely to include documents not in dispute and which contain agreed evidence. No witness need introduce these and it will usually be sufficient to refer to them only in the opening statement or final address or both.

The worth of hearsay evidence

35.8 According to the strict rules of evidence 'hearsay evidence' (evidence as to what someone else heard or saw) is not admissible. The EAT has made it clear that industrial tribunals are not bound to follow such strict rules of evidence. (*Coral Squash Clubs Ltd v Matthews [1979] IRLR 390*). This has been clarified by Rule 8(1) of the 1980 Regulations which states that ITs 'shall not be bound by any enactment or rule of law relating to the admissibility of evidence in proceedings before the courts of law'.

What does this mean? It means that tribunals can admit evidence which is second or third hand, e.g. Y told me that X said to him. It does not mean tribunals have to accept such evidence for they can regulate their own procedure. What now appears to be the present law was summarised by the EAT in the *Matthews* case:

> 'It seems to us clear that an industrial tribunal is not bound by the strict rules of evidence but should exercise its good sense in weighing the matters which come before it unless it feels that the evidence which it is proposed to tender is such that its admission could in some way adversely affect the reaching of a proper decision in this case.'

Tape recordings may be admitted as hearsay evidence, subject to the tribunal's discretion. (*Jones v Trust House Forte Hotels Ltd EAT 58/77*). The tribunal will, however, take into account the fact that those recorded might have made statements they would *not* have made with more consideration.

First hand evidence, however contradictory is usually given more weight by a tribunal than hearsay evidence. So if possible you should rely on and try to obtain first hand evidence.

The art of cross-examination

35.9   Once your opponent has completed the examination of one of his witnesses you will be entitled to question that witness. In other courts this is usually known as 'cross-examination', which is defined by the Oxford English Dictionary as 'subjecting (a witness) to an examination with the purpose of shaking his testimony or eliciting facts not brought out in his direct examination'. From this definition cross-examinations can be seen to be a tool of the adversary system.

Reference to it is omitted from the 1980 Regulations. Rule 8(1) only refers to the right to 'question' witnesses called by the other side, with the caveat that even this right is subject to the tribunal conducting the hearing in the way 'it considers most suitable to the clarification of the issues before it'. This is a further attempt to reduce formality and encourage a more inquisitorial hearing.

What does this mean in practice? Basically lay persons should be able to cope more easily with this difficult stage of the hearing. For example, one of the strict rules of evidence connected with cross-examination (which presumably will no longer apply and even if it did is no longer binding on a tribunal) is that you must *put your side's version of the facts to the other side's witnesses*. This involves putting forward every disputed fact so that these witnesses have an opportunity of dealing with them. This is not only a mammoth task but is very difficult to do in practice. The possible penalties for failure are implied acceptance of the other side's evidence and a possible bar on your witnesses giving evidence about those disputed facts. Although the penalties are no longer strictly applied, you should still try and put your version of the facts to the other side's witnesses in order to avoid the possibility of these witnesses having to be recalled at a later stage in the hearing.

So the apparent change in the Regulations is rather significant.

Objectives of questioning a witness

35.10 Your objectives at this stage of the hearing will be similar to that required from an *actual* cross-examination, namely:

(*a*) *Highlighting the conflict of facts.*
Where it is apparent from the evidence given by the other side's witnesses that this will be in conflict with the evidence to be given by your witnesses highlight this so the tribunal knows what to expect. For example evidence is given by a manager that his supervisor did not get on with his subordinates. But you will be calling contrary evidence. So put it to him: 'Despite what you say about Mr Jenkins' poor relationship with his workmates I put it to you that you are mistaken as several of his colleagues will give evidence to the contrary.'

(*b*) *Exposing inconsistencies in the evidence.*
You must not expect a direct admission of a lie or a dramatic collapse of the witness. This generally only happens on television. However, a lie may be detected or inferred from facts which do not immediately seem important. For example, it is alleged an oral warning was given at a certain meeting, which you dispute. You note from the disciplinary procedure that an investigation must be held before any warnings are given. Through your questioning it transpires the investigation took place after that meeting. The tribunal may now infer there was no warning prior to the investigation.

(*c*) *Showing that procedures have not been followed.*
Any discrepancy in the following of internal company procedures in unfair dismissal claims may be fatal to an employer's case. This can be easily shown, where witnesses are not lying, by taking the witness through the procedural documents and comparing them with what actually happened.

(*d*) *Bringing the worth of hearsay evidence to the tribunal's attention.*
The worth of hearsay evidence is explained in 35.8 above. It may not be apparent to the tribunal that evidence is hearsay. Bring this out by asking the witness whether the recollection of facts is from the witness's own knowledge. If not, you can put it to the witness that you will be calling first hand contradictory evidence. By doing this the tribunal will be on guard as to the weight to be given to the evidence.

(*e*)   *Showing the tribunal where evidence or opinions have been based on invalid assumptions.*
If the witness has jumped to an incorrect conclusion this should be shown up. This can happen where the witness has relied on what someone else told him, who later denies having said anything of the sort.

(*f*)   *Refuting allegations.*
Where there is a conflict of fact it is likely that witnesses will make damaging allegations. If your evidence refutes this, it is best to put it to the witness that his allegation is not accepted.

(*g*)   *Putting evidence into proper context.*
Following the example in 35.4 and 35.5 above, the evidence is that the former supervisor did not get on with his workers. It is your case that the reason why he did not get on was because he was instructed to implement unpopular practices. Prior to that there were excellent relations between him and his staff. By putting that evidence into its proper context it will be easier for you to refute the allegation that the supervisor has a personality defect.

(*h*)   *Correcting misleading or confusing testimony.*
It may be misleading to suggest that a work-to-rule was the applicant's fault, when the industrial action was principally motivated by a campaign by the union involved against new legislation being introduced to restrict secondary picketing. Also such misleading evidence may suggest a reason for a particular course of action which was not the real reason. This should be brought out by appropriate questioning.

Checklist for questioning witnesses

35.11   In order to maximise the effectiveness of your cross-examination there are certain guidelines:

(i)   You should be *in control* of this part of the proceedings. After all, you can choose the parts of the evidence to question and the form and substance of the questions themselves. This does not mean you should bully or browbeat the witness. Just *be firm with the witness* and give the witness a fair chance to answer your questions. If it becomes clear the witness is being evasive, then you are entitled to a straight answer by repeating the question.

(ii)   Where possible you should *prepare points which must be taken up.* By the time of the hearing you should have a clear indication of your opponent's case and have some idea which questions will have to be asked to achieve the objectives referred to above. Also remember you should still try and put your version of the facts to your opponent's witnesses. Much of this preparation can be done before the hearing relying on the evidence you have to hand. Also by underlining the relevant parts in your notes of the other side's evidence that will have to be taken up at this stage, you will have 'prepared' a further list of points to be raised.

(iii)   *Never prepare actual questions* for this stage of the hearing. It is most dangerous to arrive at the tribunal with the questions you intend to ask already written out. What questions and how you ask them is best decided during the conduct of the case. Prepared questions may prove irrelevant or unnecessary once you have heard the evidence, and the realisation of this may put you out of your stride. There is perhaps only one exception to this rule and that relates to the opening question. This is the moment when the untruthful witness will be ill at ease. The right question could put him off balance. For example, at an interim hearing where a respondent is denying dismissing an employee for proposed trade union membership but has no union membership in his factory, it may be appropriate to ask whether he believes in trade unionism. If he answers 'Yes' it will be difficult to explain why there are no TU members other than the applicant. If he answers 'No' it is strong evidence that he would disapprove of the applicant's membership. The untruthful witness may not recover from this realisation.

(iv)   *Is there a need to ask any questions at all?* This is something you must decide. If the opponent's witness has said nothing that harms your case, questioning at this stage may achieve no more than eliciting an answer which will!

(v)   *Is the question necessary?* If the witness has already given the answer you want or one which could be interpreted to give the meaning desired, do not push your luck by asking the same or further questions or you may get a different answer. In other words, think before putting a question and remember discretion is the better part of valour.

(vi)   Evidence in dispute is not the only area which should be subject to questioning. *Areas of omission or gaps* in the evidence may be raised provided they are relevant; for example, where one party fails to refer to a written statement of terms and conditions or the lack of such a statement.

You may ask questions about any other relevant matter. The tribunal will be the ultimate determinant as to whether it is relevant.

(vii)   A basic rule of cross-examination which also applies to questioning is: *never ask a question to which you do not know the answer*, or have a shrewd idea of the answer. The better your preparation, the more likelihood of being able to comply with this rule. However, it is often impossible to keep to this rule and sometimes risks will have to be taken in order to get out the evidence required.

(viii) In contrast to examination-in-chief, *you may lead* to your heart's content when questioning. Despite this, keep your questions short and do not make a statement. Some advocates address the tribunal on the evidence at this stage, but this should be left to a more appropriate time.

(ix) The reason for keeping questions *short and sharp* is so that the witness understands the question but is not given much opportunity of thinking out the answer. If a question is long it will often indicate where it is leading and give ample time to produce a protected answer.

(x) Once you ask the question you must *let the witness have a fair chance to answer.* You cannot interrupt because you don't like the answer you are getting, unless it is irrelevant. This is another reason for brief and to the point questions.

(xi) It is very easy to ask several questions at a time. This tends to confuse the witness and you do not get a straight answer to any of your questions. So ask not only short, sharp questions, but *ask one at a time.*

(xii) *Do not* try to *discredit a witness* because of minor contradictions and discrepancies, or get over exultant when you gain a point or admission. Just let the point sink in and then move on. You can stress its importance in your final address.

(xiii) A good test of the effectiveness of your questioning is the *reaction of the chairman.* If he is recording the witness' replies, you have some indication he considers the evidence relevant – although not necessarily to the advantage of your case! If he and the other members appear bored and are getting impatient, it may be a sign that this line of questioning is getting nowhere.

Despite it no longer being strictly accurate to describe this part of the procedure as 'cross-examination', for ease of reference most of the following chapters in this book will continue to use the old label.

Tribunal questioning

35.12 When your questioning is complete, it is the tribunal's turn to ask questions. The chairman will usually invite each of the lay members to ask the witness questions if they wish, then he will do the same. Listen carefully to these. They will deal with issues not answered to their satisfaction in previous questioning. They may indicate areas you will have to put more emphasis on later. Their questions should not indicate any bias, but merely be used to help clarify the issues. If there is an apparent bias, this could be a ground for a review or appeal (*see* Chapter 42).

You may find that the chairman in particular asks questions throughout the proceedings; in the middle of examination-in-chief or your questioning. As stated previously, the chairman has a wide discretion on how he conducts the hearing and he may involve himself in the conduct of the case for a variety of reasons. It may be simply that he likes to run his tribunals that way or in order to speed up the hearing. It is more likely that the case is not being conducted very well and he is trying to establish the issues so that he and the other members can come to a just and correct decision. Because ITs are designed for lay persons, he will often take an active role where, for example, the representatives are not lawyers. He will particularly take this role where there is a party appearing without representation. The amount of involvement also depends on the particular chairman. In Scotland the chairman tends to intervene more specifically at an early time in order to clarify the issues and tends to take a more inquisitorial role than in England and Wales. Since the 1980 Regulations this seems to be happening to a greater extent in England and Wales. However, you cannot rely on the chairman doing your advocate's job because he and the other members may take a formal approach to the extent of leaving you to conduct your case without help. The tribunal does not have a duty to ensure that all relevant evidence is before it. This is the responsibility of the parties whether or not they are represented. (*Craig v British Railways Board (1973) 8 ITR 636*).

Again, watch the chairman's pen to see if he records any of the witnesses' replies. If he does, it is because he considers the evidence relevant. Much can also be gleaned about the tribunal's attitude towards your case and how it is proceeding by the questions they ask. Watch the members carefully. If they do not appear to be impressed by the evidence given so far, you may have to reconsider your approach.

Re-examination

35.13   If the tribunal have asked questions it is usual for the chairman to invite the cross-examiner to further question on any new matters arising from their questions. If this opportunity is not offered and you require it, ask the chairman to allow you to ask a few more questions; if he is reluctant, be prepared to give him your reasons for requiring to do so.

Finally, the examiner or party whose witness is giving evidence will be given the opportunity to re-examine. During questioning by the other representative or by the tribunal, suitable notes should have been taken. Some answers may have been ambiguous, others out of context and even others admitting certain adverse facts without qualification. These matters should be underlined in your notes and then at this stage an attempt can be made to clear them up.

In other words, the object of re-examination is to explain inconsistencies, put misleading remarks into proper context, or minimise damaging statements. Also use this opportunity to re-emphasise any points weakened during questioning and allow the witness to expand in full any points the other side prevented him from developing if it is to your advantage. The ability to do this will depend on careful observation of replies to questions. There are certain rules identified with re-examination which no longer bind the tribunal but of which you should be aware:

— leading questions are not usually allowed (similar to examination-in-chief, but more strictly adhered to);

— it may not be used as an opportunity to introduce new evidence;

— it should only relate to really important and essential matters which emerge from replies to questioning and which are adverse to your case.

It can be appreciated that often re-examination will be unnecessary, or one or two questions only need be asked. Chairmen will get extremely impatient with advocates who use this part of the hearing incorrectly, although it should be emphasised that they have discretion to override the rules previously mentioned. It often happens that one realises during the course of cross-examination that crucial evidence has been left out. There is no reason why you should not now apply for it to be given in the interests of justice, and hopefully the chairman will exercise his discretion to allow this new evidence.

Occasionally tribunal questioning only occurs after re-examination. If this happens always ask for a further opportunity to re-examine if needed.

Releasing witnesses

35.14   Once re-examination has been completed, you may wish to apply for the witness to be released before calling your next one. The case may involve the majority of the members of a management team or full-time officials of a trade union who will wish to return to their work as soon as possible.

One word of caution: the evidence may develop in such a way that the released witness ought to be recalled and this may cause delays or prove very difficult, and may necessitate asking for an adjournment.

How and when to object and/or interrupt

Objections

35.15   There may be times when it is necessary to object to the way your opponent is conducting his case, or the chairman is conducting the proceedings. For example, your opponent may continually lead his witnesses on disputed evidence, introduce new evidence on re-examination, cross-examine your witnesses on irrelevant matters and so on. If such action appears to prejudice your case, then object. This can be done by interrupting your opponent politely, and making a case to the tribunal as to why such a line of questioning should be disallowed. If the chairman agrees with you, he will stop the line of questioning. He may do this on his own initiative anyway. Again, it must be emphasised that ITs are designed for lay representation, and the chairman will not be bound by rules of procedure where he feels they will obstruct justice. Your objection therefore may be overruled, although valid. If the only reason for your objection is that it is wasting the tribunal's time (but not adversely affecting your case), then let the chairman take the initiative.

Interruptions

35.16   What happens if you are interrupted? If you disagree with your opponent's objection, give reasons, say why you are pursuing the particular line of questioning and, where necessary, argue the matter out. The chairman will eventually make a decision as to whether or not you can proceed.

Often it is the chairman, not your opponent, who interrupts. As already mentioned, you may find him taking over the conduct of the case, or preventing you asking questions you consider relevant. Courteously, but firmly, argue why you must be allowed to present your case in that particular way. If you believe your line of questioning is essential, stick to your guns and explain why this is so. In these situations you will usually get your way if there is any substance in your reasoning.

Coping with a difficult chairman

35.17   There may be however the rare occasion when this sort of atmosphere does not prevail. This may happen where the tribunal appear to be unreasonably refusing to accept your objections or to be particularly difficult in allowing you to present your case. The chairman should not interfere with your cross-examination, as long as it is relevant to the case and is not repetitive or unfairly harassing.

Where you are having severe problems with the chair and feel the tribunal is dealing with you so unreasonably as to affect the success of your case, then make a formal application for the matter to be noted on the record. Or in an extreme case ask the tribunal to stand aside on the grounds you no longer have confidence in the fairness of the hearing. Where the chairman will not make such a note or agree to stand down, make it clear you are recording the matter and may take it up further after the hearing (i.e. by challenging his decision, *see* Chapter 42). Above all, do not just walk out – this may mean you lose your case.

Where a fair hearing is not being allowed it will usually involve a breach of the rules of natural justice (*see* Chapter 30). In the constructive dismissal case of *Mortimer v Reading Windings Ltd [1977] ICR 511*, the applicant who appeared in person was greeted by the chairman with words to the effect: 'Why are we here today, because you obviously resigned'. Thereafter the chairman interrupted his cross-examination and rather over-zealously encouraged him to finish his case. The applicant appealed successfully to the EAT on the basis that he did not have a fair hearing and the case was sent back to a differently constituted tribunal to be reheard.

Seeking adjournments

35.18   There may be many situations where an adjournment is required (some have already been mentioned), for example:

— When new evidence (such as a fresh allegation) is introduced for the first time (e.g. *Grieves v Coldshield Windows Ltd EAT 218/82, IRLIB 234*).

— Where a released witness needs to be recalled.

— Where the respondent is not in a position to deal with the remedies of reinstatement or re-engagement (*see* 39.3–39.7).

— Where you wish to seek a settlement.

— Where you need time to prepare your final address (*see* Chapter 37).

— Where one of your witnesses has not turned up for the case.

— When you need to relieve yourself!

At an appropriate time, ask the chairman for an adjournment; provided there is a good reason and it is in the interests of a fair hearing your request will usually be granted. The chairman will give you a set time of say five or ten minutes and retire with his colleagues. The clerk will see if you are ready at the appointed time so that the tribunal can be recalled. If you are not ready, tell the clerk you will need another five minutes and invariably the chairman will grant this extra time.

A short adjournment may prove to be inadequate. You may find it necessary to ask for the actual hearing to be adjourned to another day. The tribunal has discretion to grant such an adjournment but must be mindful this could lead to long delays because of the necessity of constituting the tribunal with the same members. (Remember that the lay members and some chairmen are part-timers.) However, the adjournment is likely to be granted if a refusal would either defeat the rights of the parties or would be an injustice to one of them. (*M(J) v M(K)* [*1968*] *3 AER 878*). Under Rule 11(2) the tribunal has power to make an award of costs against the party requesting the adjournment.

Remember that where a witness is being cross-examined when the tribunal adjourns, even if only for lunch, that witness is not permitted to speak to fellow witnesses or the party or his representative about the case.

No case to answer

35.19   It may become apparent that the party who starts first has given no evidence which substantiates his case, i.e. has provided no case which you have to answer. In this situation do you still need to call your witnesses? In other courts there is a procedure whereby the party upon whom the burden of proof does not lie can make a statement or submission to the court at the end of his opponent's case to the effect that there is 'no case to answer'. This procedure has been adopted by ITs to a very limited extent. It is now doubtful whether a tribunal will risk not hearing the evidence of both parties where there is the slightest possibility of an arguable case. In fact, in sex and race discrimination cases the EAT has laid down specifically that the procedure should not be used (*George A Palmer Ltd v Beeby* [*1978*] *ICR 196*), and it appears that this view has now been extended to other IT claims (*Golden Cross Hire Co Ltd v Lovell* [*1979*] *IRLR 105*).

However, you may be faced with the rare case where you feel justified in making a submission, or are invited to do so by the chairman before you call your evidence. This could happen where in cross-examination your opponent's witness contradicts his own evidence. For instance, where originally the witness maintained that the applicant resigned, now he agrees he was dismissed. In this situation you would give your final address after the other side had finished calling their witnesses. The tribunal will then retire to consider your submission. If it does not succeed, you would then have to call your witnesses in the normal way. In other words by making such a submission you would not usually lose the right to call your witnesses. (*Walker v Josiah Wedgwood & Sons Ltd* [*1978*] *IRLR 105; Stokes v Hampstead Wine Co Ltd* [*1979*] *IRLR 298*).

What is more likely to happen today is that the tribunal having formed a preliminary impression of the facts that there is no case or a weak case, will invite the two parties to investigate the possibility of settling, although maintaining that they have not come to any decision. The chairman will normally expand this view off the record in camera, i.e. with only the representatives present. He will adjourn the case to give you this opportunity. It is advisable to consider it seriously.

Chapter 36

The Standard of Proof

Standard of proof in tribunals

36.1   The standard of proof required in an IT is similar to that of other civil courts, in other words, proof on a 'balance of probabilities'. (*Hindle v Percival Boats Ltd (1969) 4 ITR 86*). In criminal cases, a very high standard of proof is required ('beyond reasonable doubt') where the court must be 'sure' that a person is guilty. This is not the case in civil courts, and especially ITs. They enjoy considerable discretion in determining a question of fact. They are expected to apply the accepted standards of industry operating at the relevant time and place, in other words are expected to act as 'industrial juries'. (*Grundy (Teddington) Ltd v Willis [1976] IRLR 118*). Therefore an applicant may be found innocent of an alleged criminal offence, which also amounts to misconduct, but still be fairly dismissed because, among other things, the degree of proof is different. (*Ferodo Ltd v Barnes [1976] IRLR 302*).

Chapter 37

Closing Speeches

Introduction

37.1   When both sides have completed giving their evidence, there is one final stage left: the closing speech (or final address). Many tribunals would be happy without this stage. They would argue that in most cases the law is not in dispute, and as the tribunal is an experienced industrial jury there is no need to reiterate the facts already heard. In other words the tribunal members are specialists who know what has to be decided and by now know what the case is about. Also it is the duty of the chairman to consider on his own accord all relevant points of law and to discuss them with the two lay members when considering the decision (*see* Chapter 38). This is so whether or not these points have been raised in your closing statements or during the hearing.

Therefore it is tempting to pass over this final opportunity to address the tribunal. No doubt there are occasions when the specialists can be left to decide without further aid from you, for example in a case which would have been suitable for a submission of no case to answer. However, you are out to achieve your objectives and it is advisable to build your final address around these, and not to leave matters to chance.

Purpose of closing speech

37.2   It is customary for the last party to complete giving his evidence to sum up first. This gives the final opportunity to address the tribunal to the person on whom the burden of proof lies, or who started first. It may be appropriate to apply for a short adjournment to collect your thoughts. It is very difficult to sum up a case without a chance to reflect between one stage of the proceedings and the next.

So what is the purpose of the closing speech?

(*a*)   To remind the tribunal of the legal issues and of what the tribunal has to decide.

(*b*)   To review the salient evidence supporting your case.

(*c*)   To present the arguments and legal submission as to why the case should be decided in your favour.

(*d*)   To dispose of the other side's arguments and legal submissions as to why the case should be decided in their favour.

(*e*) To consider alternatives.

The law

37.3   You may have mentioned the basic law relating to the case in the opening statement. Whether or not this was done, it is a good idea to refer briefly to the Section(s) or Schedule(s) of the relevant Act involved. Also state clearly what you see as the main legal issues of the case and what the tribunal is being called upon to decide.

The salient facts

37.4   Bearing in mind the legal issues the tribunal has to decide upon, briefly review the facts relevant to these issues. In other words do NOT review ALL the factual evidence or you will find a bored and restless tribunal.

You should bring to the tribunal's attention all facts that are helpful to your case and mention clearly the points which your opponent has not challenged. You should also point out weaknesses or inconsistencies in his case. Where there is a conflict of evidence, you should bring out why your evidence is to be preferred, the contradictions that have been exposed in questioning of the other side's witnesses and why the tribunal should accept the version of facts given by your witnesses. In an unfair dismissal case an applicant may well go on to suggest how a more reasonable employer would have handled the matter which resulted in the dismissal and may even point out an alternative to dismissal. If you are the applicant, also bring out disparities between the employer's procedure (if any) and a code of practice, or if a respondent, why failure to follow the procedure would have made no difference to the decision to dismiss.

Present the arguments and legal submissions

37.5   Having reviewed the relevant facts supporting your case, it is then necessary to argue how these relate to the legal issues and in turn why the tribunal should find in your favour.

One of the best methods of achieving this is to use 'precedents'. A precedent is a previous judicial decision or case of a higher court. The hierarchy of courts is shown in the following diagram.

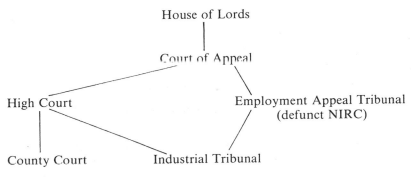

House of Lords

Court of Appeal

High Court

Employment Appeal Tribunal
(defunct NIRC)

County Court   Industrial Tribunal

37.6   *Closing Speeches*

An IT is bound by a previous decision of the House of Lords, Court of Appeal, EAT, High Court, but not the County Court or another IT. However, a well-argued IT decision may be very persuasive. If you can find a precedent which supports or is 'on all fours' with your case this can be cited as authority for your arguments. However, a word of caution, do not try and fit the facts of your case into a precedent when they will not fit. Also if you intend using a precedent know the whole case (*see* Chapter 12).

The reason for needing to know the whole case (and not just an isolated paragraph or headnote) is that you may be relying on something which later is contradicted in the same decision. Often judges in their decision reiterate the arguments of both representatives, finally accepting one set of arguments, or neither. There is no point in using a discredited argument!

In Scotland, there is not so much emphasis on precedent, Scottish ITs rely more on principle and therefore discourage the use of precedents.

There is now a similar trend in England and Wales. *Anandarajah v Lord Chancellor's Department [1984] IRLR 131* follows an increasing line of cases from the Court of Appeal which have upheld the right of ITs to be their own guide on issues of reasonableness.

> 'These cases implicitly declared that the days were passing when industrial tribunals were to be treated as dependent for the discharge of their fact finding role upon judicial guidelines extracted from reported decisions. Sometimes the judgement in a particular case expressed in concise and helpful language some concept which was regularly found in the field of employment law and it became of great illustrative value. But reference to such a case could never be a substitute for taking the words of the statute as the guiding principle.'

Therefore, in most cases there will be no need to refer to precedents.

Dispose of the other side's arguments or legal submissions

37.6   If the onus of proof is on you, the other side will have argued their case and made any legal submissions first. Then it is your opportunity to dispose of any adverse arguments or submissions by quoting perhaps a previous case from a higher court which overrides the precedent referred to by your opponent. A Court of Appeal case will override a decision of the EAT, for instance.

Even if you have to sum up first, your opponent's arguments may be known from his opening statement and therefore can be dealt with in advance.

Pleading in the alternative

37.7   You may have several lines of attack. If the first does not succeed, try the next. Unfortunately you cannot wait to find this out, because you will usually only have ONE opportunity for a closing speech. So, having made an argument on one line, it may be necessary to argue the next without conceding the first is unsuccessful. This may appear very illogical to the lay-person, but it is common practice for lawyers and is a form of pleading in the alternative. For example, where you have been required to give evidence as to remedies (*see* Chapter 39) and you represent the respondent, then although the case has not been decided in the applicant's favour, it may still be appropriate to address the tribunal on the extent of the applicant's contribution to his own dismissal if the tribunal should find against you.

Final speech by party with burden of proof

37.8   The party having to prove the case then has the final opportunit address the tribunal. Obviously, if the law has already been stated there is no need to repeat it. You should have been noting any points in your opponent's summing-up which will require answering. It is not unknown for the chairman to interrupt these final speeches to ask for clarification of an argument or submission, or to dispute your recollection of the evidence. However, the chairman will usually wait until you have finished addressing the tribunal before requiring further explanation.

Final speech by party who first summed up

37.9   The party who summed up first then has a final right (which is very rarely exercised) to address the tribunal on any legal point which has just been referred to by his opponent. For instance, in a typical unfair dismissal case the applicant will sum up first. He may make legal submissions. The respondent then has an opportunity to attack these submissions and make his own. The applicant will not have had a similar opportunity to respond to these submissions as he gave his summing-up first; therefore the tribunal will (if appropriate) give him a final chance to deal with these, but only where they relate to a point of law.

Part III

The Decision and After

Chapter 38

The Decision

Introduction

38.1 Once both parties have finished addressing the tribunal the main part of the case is complete. The tribunal members will usually retire at this stage to consider their decision. They can take with them their notes on the evidence, any documents which became exhibits and any relevant precedents or previous decisions. Some tribunals will require the parties to leave the tribunal room as there may be no other facilities available.

The tribunal may take from minutes to hours to come to their decision. The tribunal chairman will take his lay members through the evidence and documents and explain how the law relates to the case. Although the tribunal may come to its decision quite quickly, it may not reconvene immediately because the chairman will want to collect together the relevant facts and law so that the reasons for the decision can also be given.

Reserved decisions

38.2 As this process can take some time it may become necessary to 'reserve' the decision. Reserving the decision is where the tribunal declares that the decision will not be made after the close of the hearing but will be sent to the parties in writing some weeks later. This practice may be used where there is a sensitive or complex area of law or fact involved and the tribunal is in some doubt at the end of the hearing. Nevertheless, although tribunals have discretion to reserve decisions, this is officially discouraged as it is unsatisfactory to keep the parties waiting; so in some instances, the chairman announces the finding, e.g. the claim fails or succeeds, but states that the reasons will be sent to the parties later.

There is always the risk if this happens that the tribunal could reconsider their decision before it is registered. Although tribunals can do this it is only in exceptional circumstances that a case should be re-opened and only where the parties are invited to address further argument on precise questions which the tribunal makes clear it wishes to look at afresh. (*Lamont v Fry's Metals Ltd [1983] IRLR 434*).

Majority decisions

38.3 In most cases the decision is announced orally at the close of the tribunal

38.3   *The Decision*

THE   INDUSTRIAL   TRIBUNALS

BETWEEN

Applicant		Respondent
Mr J Rider	AND	Mason (UK) Ltd

DECISION OF THE INDUSTRIAL TRIBUNAL

HELD AT	London North	ON 19 April 1984
		2 May 1984

CHAIRMAN: Mr R A Sprout   MEMBERS: Mrs K Stern
                                             Mr L B Graham

RESERVED DECISION

The unanimous decision of the Tribunal is that the applicant succeeds and is awarded £4082 of which the prescribed element is £124.

REASONS

1   On 19 April 1984 the tribunal sat for the purpose of hearing the evidence and submissions of Mr Hitchcock who appeared for the applicant and Ms Hawkins the personnel manager of the respondent. The decision was reserved and the tribunal met again on 2 May to consider their decision and the reasons for it.

2   The applicant was employed by the respondents from 3 September 1970 until 13 January 1984. For the last seven years of his employment he occupied the position of warehouse supervisor. The respondents contend that they dismissed him because he unreasonably refused to obey reasonable and/or lawful orders, and that this amounted to misconduct sufficient to justify his dismissal.

3   The applicant contends that he did not refuse to carry out any orders except those which would have meant the Company breaking the law or which were outside the terms of his contract of employment and that he was therefore unfairly dismissed.

Figure 31: Decision after hearing

190

4   The basic issue is whether the orders or instructions were unlawful or outside the terms of employment and whether it was unreasonable for the respondent to expect him to undertake such orders.

5   Having considered the evidence called on behalf of both parties, we find that the respondents have not shown on the balance of probabilities that the applicant unreasonably refused to obey lawful orders which justified his dismissal on the grounds of misconduct.

6   We have considered the circumstances the parties put before us as relevant and inquired into such further matters as appeared to us to be relevant, and have taken into account the size and administrative resources of the respondents' undertaking. We find that the respondents acted unreasonably in treating the applicant's refusal to obey what in effect were mainly unlawful orders as a sufficient reason for dismissing the applicant. That question we have determined in accordance with equity and the substantial merits of the case.

7   The application succeeds and the applicant who no longer seeks reinstatement or re-engagement is awarded £ 4082 compensation made up as follows:

Basic Award (13 x £145)	£1885
Compensatory Award	
loss to date of hearing	124
future loss	1062
loss of pension rights	935
loss of statutory rights	50
expenses	26
	£4082

8   The total sums awarded by way of compensatory award is the sum which we consider just and equitable for this applicant to receive, having regard to the loss sustained by the complainant in consequence of the dismissal insofar as that loss is attributable to action taken by the employer.

Figure 31 (continued)

9   The prescribed element for the purposes of the recoupment regulations is £124. The balance of the award is payable forthwith.

_____
Chairman

Decision sent to the parties
on 24 May 1984
and entered in the register

2 May 1984 London North
Date and Place of decision

For Secretary of the Tribunals

Figure 31 (continued)

hearing together with the reasons for it. Under Rule 9(1) a majority decision is allowed, and where there are only two tribunal members the chairman has a casting vote. Despite this provision nearly all tribunal decisions are unanimous.

It can happen that all three members reach different decisions. In these unusual circumstances the tribunal may order a fresh hearing. (*R v IT, ex parte Cotswold Collotype Co Ltd [1979] ICR 190*). Where there is a majority decision the dissenter will be invited to give his reasons for dissenting, which will be announced by the chairman after giving the reasons for the majority decision. This is usually done without disclosing who took the minority view, unless this is the chairman himself.

Announcing the decision

38.4   The normal practice is for the chairman to record the decision and reasons on tape while announcing them. Afterwards the tape is transcribed into a typed statement and checked and signed by the chairman.

Reasons for decision

38.5   There is a duty under Rule 9(2) for tribunals to give reasons for their decisions. The CA described it thus:

'This involves making findings of fact and answering questions of law. It is helpful to the parties to give some explanations for the findings of fact, but it is not obligatory. So far as questions of law are concerned, the reasons should show expressly or by implication what were the questions to which the tribunal addressed its mind and why it reached the conclusion it did, but the way in which it does so is entirely a matter for the tribunal.' (*Martin v MBS Fastenings Ltd [1983] IRLR 198*).

In another case the CA said:

'There is no obligation on a tribunal to provide an analysis of the facts and arguments on both sides with reasons for rejecting those they did reject and for accepting those relied upon in support of their conclusion. Since there is no right of appeal on a question of fact, there is no use having a detailed recitation of the evidence. That reasons are often given in the decision of an IT which are very similar to those in a judgment of the court may be commendable as a public relations exercise but it does not follow that it is necessary as a matter of law'. (*Kearney & Trecker Marwin Ltd v Varndell [1983] IRLR 335*).

Figure 31 (pages 190–192) provides an abridged example of a decision along the lines of the minimum requirements set out above by the CA. Most tribunals, however, tend to give more detailed reasons in practice.

The decision

38.6   The typed, checked and signed decision is sent by the clerk to the Secretary of COIT who enters it in the register of cases. Under Rule 9(4) the reasons will be omitted from the register where the hearing was held in private and the tribunal so directs. Each ROIT also has a register and that office is responsible for sending copies of the decision to the parties by ordinary post, and where relevant under Rule 17(9) to the EOC and CRE.

Therefore it is unnecessary for you to write out the reasons in long-hand whilst they are being dictated by the chairman. However, it is advisable to record the main points in the event that you wish to take the case further.

At the end of figure 31 on page 192 is the date the decision was sent to the parties. This is an important date to note as it represents the base date from which time limits are calculated for reviewing or appealing decisions.

After the decision

38.7   If the application is successful the tribunal will then go on to consider the remedy as discussed in the next chapter. Approximately 30·7 per cent of all applications which reached a hearing in 1982 in GB were successful. (This statistic was provided by COIT in its Fact Sheet of February 1984.) If not, the case will be complete as far as the IT is concerned, except for possible questions of costs and expenses (*see* Chapter 40), a review or an appeal (*see* Chapter 42).

Chapter 39

The Remedy

Introduction

39.1   If the claim succeeds the tribunal can order a variety of remedies. The extent of these can be identified from column 8 of the Tribunal Table, Appendix A. They principally fall into four main categories:

(*a*) *Declarations* as to the legal entitlement of the parties, i.e. a statement as to their rights.

(*b*) *Orders* as to a course of action which must be taken.

(*c*) *Monetary awards.*

(*d*) *Recommendations* that the respondent should take a particular course of action.

The particular category of remedy available will depend on the nature of the claim. Some claims enable the tribunal to consider more than one category of remedy, others are restricted to one category. For example, whereas a successful equal pay claim may result in a declaration and a monetary award, a finding of persistent racial discrimination will only enable the tribunal to make a declaration to that effect.

Where the tribunal has power to make a declaration or recommendation only then these remedies normally form part of the decision referred to in the previous chapter and they are announced with it.

Where the tribunal's power extends to making orders and monetary awards then it may hear further evidence and submissions from the parties. This is the *second stage* of the hearing which only arises where the application is successful.

Whether such a second stage is held depends upon the practice of different tribunals. Some may hear the evidence relating to remedies before giving the decision. This is often due to the practice of leaving it to the parties to agree the amount of the award, although providing guidelines as to how it should be calculated. This is sensible where the decision is reserved or there is insufficient time at the hearing to hold this second stage and saves a further appearance at the tribunal. The parties will still be given the right, however, to return to the IT for it to determine the award if they cannot agree.

A detailed discussion of these remedies is out of context in a book on procedure. However, the following is a brief examination of each category of remedy and the evidence which may be required in relation to them. This is in order to help you understand the relevant procedural aspects and in particular to give an appreciation of how compensation in an unfair dismissal claim will be assessed.

Declarations

39.2   As can be seen from column 8 of the Tribunal Table (*see* Appendix A), these can take a variety of forms, for example:

— as to the terms and conditions of employment (claim 1(*a*));
— as to discrimination in recruitment or promotion (claims 7(*a*) and 8 (*a*));
— as to an entitlement to a redundancy payment (claim 14(*c*));
— as to what is reasonable time off to discharge union duties or safety representative functions (claims 2(*b*) and 12(*a*)).

Declarations may be accompanied by a monetary award, such as a protective award where there has been a declaration of non-compliance with EPA s 99 (*see* claim 14(*f*)). As the nature of the claim is usually in the form of a request for a declaration, sufficient evidence will already have been heard to enable the tribunal to make its declaration. The only circumstance where the parties may have to give additional evidence is where there is an accompanying monetary award. For example, if the tribunal is considering a protective award it will require evidence as to the weekly wage of the employee(s) involved in order to determine the entitlement. [*EPA s 102*].

Orders

39.3   Again, these can take a variety of forms, for example, an interim order stating that the contract of employment should continue [*EPA s 78*], or an order to permit an employee, absent due to maternity leave, to return to work. [*EPCA s 56*]. However, the two most important orders are those of *reinstatement* and *re-engagement*, which a tribunal *must* always consider if it finds a person unfairly dismissed. [*EPCA s 68*]. The tribunal must first examine whether the ex-employee is entitled to an order for reinstatement and, if it decides not to make such an order, it must next consider whether to make an order for re-engagement.

Order for reinstatement

39.4   An 'order for reinstatement' [*EPCA s 62(a)*] is an order to the effect that the employer restores the ex-employee to his former position, treating him in all respects as if he had never been dismissed. In addition to specifying the date for compliance, the tribunal must specify any benefits which the employee might 'reasonably be expected to have had' if he had not been dismissed and which must be restored. These could include arrears of pay and any rights and privileges such as seniority and pension rights. The tribunal must also require the ex-employee to be treated as if he had benefited from any improvements in terms and conditions of employment from which he would have benefited had he not been dismissed, such as a wage increase.

Order for re-engagement

39.5　An 'order for re-engagement' [*EPCA s 69(4)*] is a more flexible remedy. It can include an order that the ex-employee be engaged by the same employer, his successor, or an associate employer. It can also include an order to engage the ex-employee in work comparable to that from which he was dismissed or some other suitable employment. Further, the tribunal must specify the main terms on which re-engagement is to take place, i.e.:

(*a*)　the identity of the employer;

(*b*)　the nature of the employment;

(*c*)　any amount to be paid for 'reasonably expected benefits' lost owing to the dismissal;

(*d*)　any rights and privileges which might be restored;

(*e*)　the date for compliance.

The position differs from an order for reinstatement, in that a tribunal has some discretion in determining the terms of an order for re-engagement. The above orders can involve a monetary award and these remedies are, therefore, not exclusive of each other. However, any monetary award will take into account any money received between the dismissal and reinstatement or re-engagement in the form of:

— wages *in lieu* of notice;

— *ex gratia* payments paid by the employer;

— remuneration from another employer;

— other benefits the tribunal thinks appropriate.

[*EPCA s 71(9)*].

Whether reinstatement or re-engagement order appropriate

39.6　In order to determine the appropriateness of reinstatement and re-engagement as remedies [*EPCA s 69(5)(6)*], the tribunal will require the parties to give evidence and address it on the following matters:

(*a*)　*The wishes of the ex-employee*: although an applicant may have asked for compensation only in his IT 1, there is nothing to stop him changing his mind now and asking for one of these orders.

(*b*)　*The practicability of compliance by the employer*: matters which may be raised in evidence in relation to non-practicability could include the employee's incompetence or illness, or where a replacement has been employed on a permanent basis, or whether there are suitable alternative jobs (but *see Timex Corp v Thompson [1981] IRLR 522*).

(c) *Whether the ex-employee caused or contributed to some extent to the dismissal*: the tribunal will take into account the degree of 'fault' of the applicant. This is a most important factor as many cases will contain some element of fault by the employee. For example an applicant may have been dismissed unfairly where there was misconduct but no proper procedure was followed. The employee's misconduct will have contributed towards his dismissal, albeit unfair. In such circumstances the tribunal must consider whether it would be 'just' to order reinstatement or re-engagement.

The parties, in particular the respondent, will be expected to be in a position to deal with these matters without the necessity for an adjournment. In other words, as these remedies *must* be considered by the tribunal, the parties are on notice that they may have to deal with them if the claim succeeds. That is why this was referred to in the pre-hearing checklist in 25.3.

It may be necessary to call witnesses, exhibit documents and go through the same procedures of examination and questioning as described in Part II. If you are a respondent and had notice of the applicant's desire to obtain reinstatement or re-engagement at least seven days before the hearing, costs of any adjournment made necessary because you were not ready with evidence as to the availability of the job will be awarded *against you* (Rule 11(3)).

Very few such orders actually made

39.7   Although much emphasis is placed on the tribunal's powers to make these orders, only 1·1 per cent of successful applications in 1982 in GB resulted in orders of reinstatement or re-engagement. (This statistic was taken from COIT's Fact Sheet of February 1984.) However, this does not mean you can avoid penalisation in relation to costs if you are unprepared!

Monetary awards

39.8   The remedy used for the vast majority of cases is some form of monetary award. This is primarily because over 78 per cent of all applications to ITs relate to unfair dismissal and most applicants in these cases are only interested in a monetary award. These awards take a wide variety of forms as can be appreciated from column 8 of the Tribunal Table (*see* Appendix A). For example:

— An employer who fails to give written reasons for dismissal although requested to do so will have an award of two weeks' (gross) pay made against him unless the failure was reasonable (claim 13(*a*)).

— Where a payment has been wrongly withheld in respect of a lay-off, an award of up to £10 per day may be made up to a maximum of five days in any three month period (claim 9(*a*)).

— Where an applicant has been dismissed and discriminated against on

Figure 32: Unfair dismissal – assessment of compensation form

---

Basic awards [*s 73*] (based on gross pay £
£145 pw max from 1.2.84) (no minimum
age limit).

   Less contributory fault, unreasonable £
   refusal of reinstatement or
   conduct prior to dismissal
   [*s 73(7)(7A)(7B)*] %

   Less redundancy award/payment £
   [*s 37(9)*]

   Less possible ex-gratia payment in £
   commutation (see *Chelsea
   Football Club v Heath [1981]
   IRLR 73*).

              Net basic award A = £ _____

Compensatory award [*s 74*] (max
£7,500 from 1.2.84).
Loss of wages to date of hearing/promulgation or prior date to which an
award for loss of wages is made (after
allowing for failure to mitigate).

Net average wages £   pw:

From   to-   (weeks) £
   Less earnings/money in lieu of £
   notice/ex-gratia payment
   Less contributory fault by applicant £
   [*s 74(6)*]   %
                Balance £
   Less any balance of (i) and (iii) not £
   deducted from *C* below.
       Prescribed element B = £ _____

1 Estimated future loss of wages (after
  allowing for failure to mitigate)
  Net average wages £   pw for
    weeks   = £
2 Loss of other benefits (before and
  after hearing)   = £

3 Loss of statutory industrial rights
  (including redundancy rights in
  excess of statutory entitlement)
  [*s 74(3)*]   = £
4 Loss of pension rights   = £
5 Expenses incurred.   = £
         Total (1 to 5) = £ _____

   Less (i) Any other payment by £
         respondent (e.g. any balance
         of ex-gratia payment which
         can be set off)
   Less (ii) Contributory fault by
         applicant [*s 74(6)*] %
   Less (iii) Excess of redundancy
         payment over basic award
         [*s 74(7)*].
            Net total C = £ _____

Additional awards
(1) Unreasonable refusal to provide £
    reasons for dismissal [*s 53(4)*]
(2) Unnotified deductions from salary £
    [*s 11(8)(b)*]
(3) Applicant not reinstated/ re- £
    engaged under Order. Award:
    13–26 weeks' pay [*s 71(2)(b)*].
           Total *D* = £ _____

(a) Monetary award		
Grand Total £		
(b) Prescribed element £	Total *A* =	£
(c) Period of prescribed	*B* =	£
element	*C* =	£
to	*D* =	£
(d) Excess of (a)		
over (b) £		

          Grand total = £ _____

*Note: In both sections covering loss of wages and loss of future wages the deductions in respect of earnings/money in lieu
of notice/ex-gratia payment should be made before the deduction for contributory fault. This appears to be the effect of*
Parker & Farr Ltd v Shelvey [1979] IRLR 435 *until a more authoritative decision replaces it.*

the grounds of sex or race, compensation may be awarded for any expenses, loss of earnings, injured feelings, etc., up to a maximum of £19,390 (claims 7(*a*) and 8(*a*)).

Each claim has its own special provisions. In order to illustrate the procedural aspects of this remedy, *unfair dismissal* claims have been chosen because they represent the vast majority of monetary awards.

If an IT finds a dismissal unfair and does not make an order for reinstatement or re-engagement, it *must* make an award of compensation under three separate heads. [*EPCA s 68(2)*].

1. A basic award [*EPCA s 73*];

2. A compensatory award [*EPCA s 74*];

3. A special award [*EPCA s 75A*].

It will be easier to follow the discussion of these awards by looking at figure 32 on page 199.

The basic award

39.9   The basic award (under *EPCA s 73, as amended*) provides an element of compensation for the value of accrued service lost by the unfair dismissal. The rules for calculation are similar to that of a redundancy payment. There are three variables: the employee's length of service, the employee's age, and the amount of the week's pay. These are considered below.

Length of service

39.10   The calculation of the basic award starts by establishing the effective date of the termination as explained in 3.9, and counting backwards the number of complete years worked.

> *Example*: Mrs Edwards began work with her employers on 25 May 1964 and was dismissed on 5 April 1984 without notice. She is entitled to 12 weeks' notice (one week for each complete year of employment up to a maximum of 12 weeks). She is therefore treated as being employed until 27 June 1984. Her length of service for the calculation of a basic award is 20 years.

It does not matter that she actually completed the last year of her service during the period of statutory notice.

Age

39.11   The next stage of the calculation depends upon the employee's age. The following should be noted:

(*a*) In calculating the length of service up to 22 years of age, all years of employment are included even below the age of 18;

(*b*) In calculating years of employment which straddle the employee's

22nd or 41st birthday (or both) it will be correct to count as full years those in which those birthdays occurred. It is not entirely clear, however, whether those years can be multiplied by the higher or the lower number of weeks in order to arrive at the total which underlies the basic award calculation.

For each year of completed service up to a maximum of 20 years [*EPCA s 73(4)*], the employee is entitled to receive varying multiples of a week's pay according to his or her age during employment. The scale is:

For men	*For women*
Up to 22 years ½ week's pay	Up to 22 years ½ week's pay
23 – 41 years 1 week's pay	23 – 41 years 1 week's pay
42 – 64 years 1½ week's pay	42 – 59 years 1½ week's pay

Example: Mrs Edwards was born on 1 April 1929 so her 41st birthday was 1 April 1970. Counting backwards from 27 June 1984 there are five complete years of employment before Mrs Edwards was 41 (she began work on 25 May 1964) and 14 complete years after she was 41. The calculation is as follows:

Number of complete years after 41st birthday:

$$14 \times 1\frac{1}{2} = 21 \text{ weeks}$$

Number of complete years after 22nd birthday:

	5 weeks
Total	26 weeks

A week's pay

39.12   The final stage in the calculation of the basic award is to ascertain what is a week's pay. In the majority of cases it is simply the gross basic wage or salary, based on normal working hours (*see* 3.12). Normal working hours will include overtime hours only where these are compulsory on both sides. (*Lotus Cars Ltd v Sutcliffe* [*1982*] *IRLR 381*). Pay can also include bonuses, commissions and attendance allowances, but not fringe benefits, such as a car. Where hours or pay (such as piece-work) vary the average weekly pay over the 12 weeks immediately prior to dismissal is taken. Backdated pay awards are not taken into account.

The most important point to remember is that basic awards are calculated as a multiple of *gross* wage per week, subject to a present maximum of £145 per week.

Reductions in basic award

39.13   The basic award will be reduced in five circumstances:

   (i)   Women in their 59th year and men in their 64th year will have their awards reduced by the following fraction: 12 minus the number of whole months between the 59th/64th birthday and the effective date of termination, divided by 12. Although there is no lower age limit in respect of the basic award there is an upper age limit (i.e. 60 for women and 65 for men).

Example: If Mrs Edwards (see 39.10 above) was born on 1 April 1925 (59 on 1 April 1984) and was receiving £50 gross per week at the date of her dismissal 27 June 1984, her basic award would be: £50 $\times$ 26 = £1,300 $\times$ $\frac{9}{12}$ = £975.

(ii)   By the amount of any redundancy payment already received by the employee. [*EPCA s 73(9)*].

(iii) Where the tribunal finds the employee contributed to his dismissal, by such amount as the tribunal considers just and equitable.

(iv)   Where the tribunal finds the employee unreasonably refused an offer of reinstatement by the employer, by such amount or further amount as the tribunal considers just and equitable. [*EPCA s 73(7A)*].

(v)   Where the tribunal finds that the employee's conduct before the dismissal (other than referred to in (*iii*) above), although only discovered subsequently, then by such amount or further amount as the tribunal considers just and equitable. [*EPCA s 73(7B)*]. This reduction will not apply if the reason for dismissal is redundancy, unless it is also unfair. [*EPCA s 73(7C)*].

Maximum basic award

39.14   The maximum basic award (at present) is 30 weeks $\times$ £145 = £4,350. In most cases there is no minimum award. The major exception is where the employee has been dismissed for trade union membership or activities or non-membership of a union where there is a minimum award of £2,000. [*EPCA s 75A*].

Evidence relating to the basic award

39.15   In order to establish entitlement to a basic award evidence on age, length of service and weekly wage will have to be given. Most of this information will be contained in the IT 1 subject to any correction in the IT 3. Even if these facts are unchallenged, further evidence may have to be given. The tribunal should be addressed on whether the employee's conduct contributed to the dismissal or he unreasonably refused an offer of reinstatement. If the employer suggests one of these, the onus is then on the employee to show that he did not contribute to his dismissal or refuse an offer. By contrast it will be for the employer to show that, say, the former employee had been dishonest although this was not discovered until after the dismissal.

The compensatory award

39.16   The purpose of the compensatory award is to restore the employee's financial position to what it would have been had the dismissal not taken place. [*EPCA s 71(1)(2)*]. It is, therefore, likely to be the most important part of the monetary package. There is no punitive element in it: the award is not intended to punish the employer. As the EAT pointed out in *Lifeguard Assurance Ltd v Zidronzny [1977] IRLR 56*, compensation should not be increased either out of sympathy for the employee or as a means of expressing disapproval of the employer's industrial relations policy. This award is meant to compensate the ex-employee for the *loss* suffered as a consequence of the unfair dismissal.

The tribunal will award an amount which it 'considers just and equitable in all the circumstances having regard to the loss sustained' up to a present maximum of £7,500. (This amount is reviewed annually). There is a present minimum award in union membership dismissal cases of £2,000, *see* 39.14 above. The tribunal will assess this loss under five main heads:

1. loss of earnings prior to the hearing (see 39.17 below);

2. loss of future earnings (see 39.18 below);

3. loss of potential statutory rights (see 39.19 below);

4. loss arising from the manner of dismissal (see 39.20 below);

5. loss of contractual benefits other than pay (see 39.21 below).

(*Norton Tool Co Ltd v Tewson [1972] IRLR 86*).

The onus is on the employee to raise the particular 'head of loss' and produce evidence to support it. This may often be difficult where the employer is in possession of the evidence, for instance as to pension rights. Once the employee has provided reasonable evidence of a head of loss it should be compensated unless the employer produces evidence strong enough to rebut the employee's claim. The heads are assessed by the tribunal as set out below.

Loss of earnings prior to the hearing

39.17 The former employee will have lost wages from the date of dismissal to the date of the hearing. In order to appreciate how tribunals assess this loss it is necessary to see how a week's pay is calculated.

The definition here is less rigorous than compared with 'a week's pay' under a basic award (*see* 39.12 above). It includes all payments which an employee may reasonably expect to earn in the course of employment, but is assessed on the *net* figure after deduction of tax and national insurance contributions. Unlike the basic award, other benefits such as non-compulsory overtime pay (*Brownson v Hire Service Shops [1978] IRLR 73*), tips (*Palmanor Ltd v Cedron [1978] IRLR 303*), and holiday pay (*Tradewinds Airways Ltd v Fletcher [1981] IRLR 272*), may be included.

The loss can also take into account backdated pay awards as well as anticipated pay rises. (*Leyland Vehicles Ltd v Reston [1981] IRLR 19*). However, tax rebates which are usually small are ignored (*see MBS Ltd v*

Calo [1983] IRLR 1898). Where payments fluctuate from week to week there is no statutory formula for assessing the weekly loss. As a general rule, however, the average net weekly pay over the last three months prior to dismissal is taken.

The total sum of the loss assessed under this head will be reduced by any money received by the employee as a direct result of the dismissal, such as wages in lieu of notice, ex gratia payments (*see Chelsea Football Club & Athletic Co Ltd v Heath [1981] IRLR 73; IRLIB 261.2*), and large tax rebates (*Lucas v Lawrence Scott Electromotors Ltd [1983] IRLR 61*).

Loss of future earnings

39.18   The applicant may still be unemployed at the date of the hearing. Alternatively he may have found a new job but at a smaller salary. The tribunal will assess the weekly amount and duration of this continuing loss. If the applicant is still out of work the weekly amount of the loss will be the amount of a week's net pay in the previous job. If he has a new job on lesser terms it will be the difference.

The more difficult decision for the tribunal to assess is the continuing loss of earnings which might be weeks, months or years. The applicant will want to bring evidence to point out any disadvantages that he is likely to suffer in the job market such as age (*Isle of Wight Tourist Board v Coombes [1976] IRLR 413*), state of health and special skill (*Fougère v Phoenix Motor Co Ltd [1976] IRLR 259*). He will also want to give evidence about the state of local industry with regard to job opportunities. There is no reason why a representative of a local jobcentre or Department of Employment should not be required to give evidence if necessary by means of a witness order. The respondent will no doubt wish to bring evidence to refute these disadvantages. The tribunal will take this evidence into account and can also rely on its own knowledge and experience. If it does rely on its own knowledge and experience, because, for instance, one of its members has specialised knowledge, then not only should the tribunal indicate this, but also bring the facts known to that member to the attention of the parties so that they have an opportunity of dealing with them or asking for an adjournment. (*Hammington v Berker Sportcraft Ltd [1980] ICR 248*).

Loss of potential statutory benefits

39.19   An unfair dismissal will result in a loss of statutory rights in the short-term. For example it will take normally one year in any new employment before the applicant will have acquired the right to bring a claim for unfair dismissal again. Similarly, a women will lose her right to maternity leave for at least two years.

Usually only a nominal award is made under this head (£20 – £50) because the basic award takes into account the loss of redundancy rights. However, there is a strong argument that the loss of some of the rights under the EPCA is substantial.

Loss owing to manner of dismissal

39.20 The manner in which the employee was dismissed may make his task of finding a new job more difficult. For example, if a person is dismissed in humiliating circumstances which become well publicised, this may add to the loss suffered by making it harder to find new employment (*Vaughan v Weighpack Ltd [1974] IRLR 105*), or a dismissal just before the completion of an apprenticeship, (*Colin Johnson v Baxter EAT 492/82*). It is possible that additional compensation could be awarded for emotional upset under this head where the employee would not be fit for similar work for some time. (*John Millar & Sons v Quinn [1974] IRLR 107*).

Loss of contractual benefits other than pay

39.21 Most prominent among these are fringe benefits such as the use of a car, travel allowance, medical insurance, share ownership, free food, subsidised accommodation and cheap rate loans. (The AA will provide a schedule of estimated standing and running costs for cars — *Shove v Down Surgicals Plc [1984] IRLR 17* — or the Inland Revenue scales charges might be used, or as canvassed in the *Shove* case, the difference between the purchase price of a new car and the resale price of the car at the end of the period of assessment.) Perhaps the most important element today relates to the loss of pension rights covered by a private pension scheme. This can today make up the largest part of the compensatory award.

As with other contractual benefits, the employee has the responsibility of proving any loss. This loss must be considered, as with earnings, in two parts: the loss prior to the hearing, and the loss for the future.

Pension rights

39.22 The two most common methods of assessing pension loss are:

(*a*) the contributions method, based on the value of lost contributions to the fund; and

(*b*) the benefits method, based on the value of benefits the employee would have received but for the dismissal.

A paper issued in 1980 by the Government Actuary's Department is now widely used by tribunals to calculate pension loss but its legal status is uncertain (*Manpower Ltd v Hearne [1983] IRLR 281*). Where the paper is used by a tribunal, the parties are entitled to ask for a copy (*Todd & Duncan Ltd v Toye EAT 185/80, IRLIB 253, 3*), and perhaps they should obtain a copy in any case.

The following guidelines come from decided cases:

— the closer an employee is to retirement age the more likely the assessment is to be based on the cost of purchasing an annuity which will yield an equivalent pension (*John Millar & Sons v Quinn [1974] IRLR 109*);

— the award for both past and future loss must be discounted to allow for the possibility of withdrawal from the old scheme as a result of resignation or fair dismissal (*Linuar Ltd v Hammersley EAT 226/83 IRLIB 253.8*);

— in assessing future loss, tribunals must take into account the chance that employees may subsequently find a new job with an equivalent pension scheme and the possibility that inferior provisions in a new job may be improved (*Sturdy Finance Ltd v Bardsley [1979] IRLR 65*);

— the award may be discounted to allow for the accelerated receipt of the benefits which otherwise would not have been payable until retirement (*Smith, Kline & French v Coates [1977] IRLR 220*);

— generally refusal to accept a deferred pension will not be in breach of the statutory duty to mitigate loss (*Willment Bros Ltd v Oliver [1979] IRLR 393*).

Although the tribunal will raise the loss of pension rights as a head of loss along with other heads of compensation the employee will need to establish the loss by presenting evidence before the tribunal. The problem is that most information relating to a pension scheme is in the hands of the employer, so it is up to the employee to use the tribunal machinery to get production of the relevant documentation. (*Copson v Eversure Accessories Ltd [1974] IRLR 247*).

Expenses resulting from dismissal

39.23   There is also one further minor head of loss and this relates to *expenses* incurred as a result of the dismissal (but not in bringing the claim). It is not unusual for awards of £20 – £50 to be given for expenses incurred in seeking new jobs or larger amounts for setting up the former employee's own business. (*Gardiner-Hill v Rolland Berger Technics Ltd [1982] IRLR 498*). The employee must bring evidence of interviews, travelling expenses, etc.

Reductions in compensatory award

39.24   Compensation awarded under all these heads may be reduced:

— on the ground that the employee did not suffer great injustice by reason of the dismissal [*EPCA s 74(1)*];

— by any contributory element [*EPCA s 74(b)*];

— by the applicant's failure to mitigate his loss [*EPCA s 74(4)*].

Tribunals have a very wide discretion to achieve what they consider to be a *just and equitable* result. This means that a tribunal may award little or no compensation if it so chooses as a proper exercise of its discretion. Tribunals may do this where the dismissal is procedurally unfair, but the proper procedure would have made no difference, or where it is discovered after the dismissal that there was a valid reason for dismissal such as dishonesty. (*Devis & Sons Ltd v Atkins [1977] IRLR 315*). So in effect the tribunal is recognising in its award that the employee is not suffering any major injustice by his dismissal.

The tribunal may also reduce the award by such proportion as it considers just and equitable where the applicant *contributed* towards his dismissal in other words to the extent that he was to blame for his dismissal. The tribunal is entitled to take into account any of the employee's conduct and actions when assessing the extent of his blame-worthiness, not just the specific conduct relied upon by the employer for the dismissal. (*Nelson v BBC [1979] IRLR 346*). Where the tribunal finds such contribution it will reflect this by means of a percentage reduction (*see Hollier v Plysu Ltd [1983] IRLR 260*).

Industrial tribunals have adopted different procedures for determining issues of contributory fault. Some maintain a 'wait and see' policy leaving the employer to raise the issue if he wishes; some give directions at the outset as to the course of the hearing. This direction may be to hold a split hearing as described in 39.1 above, with issues of fairness dealt with at one session and remedy at another. In this situation the chairman should give evidential direction as to whether the evidence on fairness and contributory fault is to be taken together or whether the evidence is to be treated as divided into separate categories with evidence relating to compensation being taken at a second hearing. (*Iggesund Converters Ltd v Lewis EAT 298/83*).

The applicant is under a duty to do all he reasonably can to lessen the loss caused by his dismissal. He may fail to *mitigate* his loss by refusing to adopt an internal company appeal procedure before dismissal (*Hoover Ltd v Forde [1980] ICR 239*), or by refusing a reasonable offer of re-employment (*Martin v Yeomen Aggregates Ltd [1983] IRLR 49*). An ex-employee can mitigate his loss by becoming self-employed in his own business even though in the short-term this increases the liability of the employer to pay compensation. (*Gardiner-Hill v Roland Berger Technics Ltd [1982] IRLR 498*). An employee does not necessarily fail to mitigate loss by refusing the first job offered after dismissal if this is unsuitable.

The burden is on the employer to prove that the applicant has failed to mitigate. (*Bessenden Properties Ltd v Corness [1974] IRLR 338*). An employer may have difficulty in identifying what steps an employee has taken to mitigate loss. During the preparation of the case he should have asked 'what steps and measures it is alleged the applicant took to mitigate his loss (if any), identifying all relevant documents relied on?'

The employer should also come to the industrial tribunal armed with details of vacancies appropriate to the dismissed employee in the area, and, where appropriate, job advertisements from specialist publications.

The employee, by the same token, is well advised to keep a full list of posts applied for, with the reasons for any refusals and be prepared to exhibit all relevant letters at the hearing.

Not infrequently the combined loss suffered under the above heads is greater than the current maximum which can be awarded. In this situation the maximum only will be awarded. [*EPCA s 75(3)*].

Recoupment of benefits paid to employee

39.25   The tribunal will use a form such as figure 32 on page 199 to set out its calculation of the monetary award. It will be noted that the form refers to four totals. Alongside total B are the words 'prescribed element'. The Employment Protection (Recoupment of Unemployment and Supplementary Benefit) Regulations 1977 (SI 1977; No 674 *EPCA s 132*) allows the DHSS or DE to recoup any unemployment and supplementary benefit paid to a successful applicant between the date of dismissal and the hearing.

It works like this. The tribunal must assess the compensatory award under the first head (loss of earnings prior to hearing, less reductions), and give it a special designation known as the prescribed element. This will be stated as such in the decision. The applicant is required within certain time limits to give to the tribunal clerk the address of the DHSS or DE from which he received payment of benefits. The tribunal then sends a copy of the decision to that address. The employer also has to provide certain information directly to the DE explained in the 'annex' to the tribunal decision.

The employer must retain the prescribed element for a period of 21 days from the date of the decision or until the expiry of nine days from the date he receives a copy of the decision, whichever is the later. The rest of the compensatory award should be paid to the successful applicant.

Within the time period, the DHSS or DE must serve a recoupment notice setting out the amount of benefit they are claiming (a copy of which is also sent to the applicant). The employer should then deduct this from the prescribed element and send it to the DHSS, and the balance can then be paid to the applicant. If the employer does not receive a recoupment notice, he should pay over the whole of the prescribed element to the applicant after the time limit has expired.

The ex-employee may not accept the figures contained in the notice, and has a right to appeal to a Social Security Appeal Tribunal (SSAT) within 21 days of the date the notice was sent to him if he thinks that the amount of benefit recouped is more than he in fact received. If the parties settle the case before a hearing, these recoupment regulations do not apply.

The idea behind these regulations is that the State avoids subsidising an unfair employer and the tax-payer does not bear the burden of the employer's unfairness to his employee. There is no recoupment provision relating to future loss, as employees who are in receipt of compensation are not regarded as having a day of unemployment for the period of that future loss and are therefore ineligible for unemployment benefit during that period.

Additional award

39.26 The monetary awards so far described are based on the need to compensate the successful applicant for actual loss sustained. There is no punitive element. However, there are circumstances where a form of exemplary damages can be awarded. These are when there has been complete non-compliance with an order for reinstatement or re-engagement [*EPCA s 71*], where the tribunal found the principal reason for dismissal was either sex or race discrimination.

In such cases an 'additional award' may be made on a scale from a minimum of 26 weeks' to a maximum of 52 weeks' pay. The maximum amount of week's pay is at present fixed at £145. The base date for the purposes of calculating a week's pay is the date on which notice is given if the dismissal was with notice. In all other cases it is the effective date of termination.

An additional award will only be made at a subsequent hearing. It will arise where the successful applicant informs ROIT that there has been non-compliance with an order for reinstatement or re-engagement (*see* Chapter 41).

The special award

39.27 The special award (under EPCA s 75A) is only available if it can be shown that trade union membership or activities or non-membership is the reason (or the principal) reason for the dismissal of the employee. [*EPCA s 58, as amended by EA 1982, s 3*]. When such an award is made it may be additional to the basic and compensatory awards, and is triggered automatically by an application for reinstatement by the applicant. The amount of compensation varies according to whether the tribunal makes an order for reinstatement and if so whether the order is complied with. It does not depend on an employee's age or length of service like a basic award, although it does have similar scaling down provisions and therefore in effect an upper age limit. However, there is no lower age limit.

There is no limit to the maximum amount which qualifies in calculating a week's pay. Where there is no order of reinstatement the special award may be up to 104 weeks' pay subject to a minimum award of £10,000 and a maximum of £20,000. Where there is an order for reinstatement which is not complied with the award may be up to 156 weeks' pay subject to a minimum of £15,000 but with no maximum.

As with a basic award, the tribunal has power to reduce the award where the conduct of the employee contributed to the dismissal (cf 39.13 above).

Total awards

Non-union membership dismissals

39.28 Adding up the maximum award in each category results in:

basic award	4,350
compensatory award	7,500
additional award	7,540
	£19,390

Union membership dismissals

39.29 For union membership dismissals there are four possible variations on compensation:

(*a*) *Where reinstatement is not sought*

	Minimum	*Maximum*
basic award	2,000	4,350
compensatory award	2,000	7,500
	£4,000	£11,850

(*b*) *Where reinstatement is sought but no order is made*

basic award	2,000	4,350
compensatory award		7,500
special award	10,000	20,000
	£12,000	£31,850

(*c*) *Where reinstatement is ordered by the tribunal and the order is complied with*

compensatory award	£7,500

(*d*) *Where reinstatement is ordered by the tribunal and the order is not complied with*

basic award	2,000	4,350
compensatory award		7,500
special award	15,000	no max.
	£17,000	no limit

Awards in practice

39.30 Although some of the above totals seem very high, in practice monetary awards in Great Britain are very much less than the maximum, particularly as special awards are so far rare. The Table on the next page provided by COIT in its Fact Sheet published in February 1984 shows, in bands, the awards made in 1980, 1981 and 1982 in unfair dismissal cases.

Table of awards

Amount	1980 No.	1980 %	1981 No.	1981 %	1982 No.	1982 %
Not known	—	0·0	18	0·9	36	1·8
Less than £50	7	0·4	12	0·6	9	0·4
£50–£99	83	4·2	44	2·3	35	1·7
£100–£149	135	6·8	76	3·9	58	2·8
£150–£199	141	7·1	67	3·4	50	2·4
£200–£299	212	10·6	125	6·4	110	5·4
£300–£399	172	8·6	123	6·3	117	5·7
£400–£499	140	7·0	110	5·7	99	4·9
£500–£749	272	13·6	240	12·3	211	10·3
£750–£999	192	9·6	195	10·0	193	9·5
£1,000–£1,499	258	12·9	303	15·6	305	14·9
£1,500–£1,999	138	6·9	183	9·4	220	10·8
£2,000–£2,999	132	6·6	209	10·8	287	14·0
£3,000–£3,999	45	2·3	98	5·0	147	7·2
£4,000–£4,999	20	1·0	52	2·7	51	2·5
£5,000–£5,999	19	1·0	39	2·0	39	1·9
£6,000–£6,999	18	0·9	27	1·4	34	1·7
£7,000–£7,999	6	0·3	15	0·8	27	1·3
£8,000–£8,999	2	0·1	5	0·3	11	0·5
£9,000 and over	2	0·1	4	0·2	6	0·3
All	1,994	100·0	1,945	100·0	2,045	100·0
Median award		£598		£963		£1,201
Cases where basic award only made	334	16·8	180	9·3	145	7·1
Cases where compensatory award was the maximum £6,250 (from 1 Feb 1980) £7,000 (from 1 Feb 1982)	8	0·4	17	0·9	38	1·9

These figures show that whereas in 1980 the percentage of awards at £1,000 and over was 32%, by 1982 it had risen to 55·1%.

Decisions on awards

39.31 When tribunals give their decision on the amount of any award, they are obliged to explain in sufficient detail how they arrived at their assessment of the award. (*Norton Tool Co Ltd v Tewson*). There is also an obligation on tribunals to make some reference to the question of contribution in their written decisions, even if the award is not reduced. (*Portsea Island Mutual Co-operative Society Ltd v Rees [1980] ICR 260*). However, tribunals do not have power to award interest at present

(*UCATT v Brain [1981] IRLR 224*), although the Secretary of State has power to make a statutory instrument providing that tribunal awards should carry interest [*EPCA 9 Sch 6A; EA 1982, 3 Sch 7*]. Now a 1983 consultation paper 'Interest on County Court Judgments and Orders' issued by the Lord Chancellor's Department suggests that successful applicants should be able to apply for simple interest on tribunal awards exceeding £500. The Secretary of State, therefore, may soon exercise this power.

Recommendations

39.32   This remedy principally applies to race and sex discrimination cases. It will take the form of a recommendation that the respondent should take action to obviate or reduce the adverse effect on the applicant of the discrimination complained of. For example, a recommendation that a particular job should be open to all age groups and not just to applicants between ages 24 and 32 which happen to be the main child-bearing years for women. (For another example *see Prescold Ltd v Irvine [1980] IRLR 267*.)

Chapter 40

Costs

Tribunals' power to award costs

40.1   In practice, very few awards of costs are made by tribunals. This is in line
with the underlying objective for extending the jurisdiction of industrial
tribunals as expounded by the Donovan Commission, namely 'to make
available to employers and employees, for all disputes arising from their
contracts of employment, a procedure which is easily accessible,
informal, speedy and *inexpensive*'. So it is argued that if costs were
automatically awarded to the innocent party, as in other civil courts, this
would not only increase the cost of proceedings but also discourage the
resolution of disputes through ITs. Not surprisingly, in view of
Donovan, the Tribunal Regulations reflect this argument, hence the
lack of awards of costs.

Rule 11 directs that 'a tribunal shall not normally make an award in
respect of the costs or expenses incurred by a party to the proceedings'.
The tribunal, however, does have discretion to award costs 'where in its
opinion a party (and if he is a respondent whether or not he has entered
an appearance) has in bringing or conducting the proceedings acted
frivolously, vexatiously or otherwise unreasonably.'

What costs are recoverable?

40.2   Rule 11 refers to awards in respect of 'costs or expenses'. 'Costs' has
always been understood to cover the successful party's *legal* costs. In
Wiggin Alloys Ltd v Jenkins [1981] IRLR 275, the EAT held that in the
case of employers such costs could be recovered whether they used
outside or in-house lawyers. And in a House of Lords decision on
taxation of costs, *Malloch v Aberdeen Corporation (No 2) [1973]
1 AER 304*, it was held that a party appearing in person could
nonetheless, if awarded costs, recover legal costs which were reasonably
necessary to spend in equipping himself to appear in person and present
his own case. It is unclear, however, whether that principle applies to
awards of costs to parties appearing in person before industrial
tribunals.

Prior to 1976, a litigant in person could, in addition to *Malloch* costs,
recover only his bare out-of-pocket expenses and no more in the County
Court. The Litigants in Person (Costs and Expenses) Act 1975 extended
the powers of the County Court so that such a litigant could recover

sums in respect of any work done and not just actual expenses and losses incurred in connection with the proceedings. The successful litigant was thereby put in a position vis-à-vis costs roughly comparable to that of his fellow litigant who was represented by a solicitor. The 1980 Regulations gave similar powers to industrial tribunals by adding the words 'or expenses', so that an award of costs would not necessarily be restricted to legal costs. Tribunals can now make an award for time and labour expended in preparing a case and out-of-pocket expenses. It is likely that the time covered by such an award will be limited to that reasonably spent in doing work which a legal representative would have done and for which costs could have been recovered. It is most unlikely, however, that 'expenses' extends to all management time spent on a case, and still less to the value of lost production suffered as a result of defending a tribunal application. The precise meaning of 'expenses' must, however, await a ruling from the EAT.

The Scottish Tribunal Regulations refer only to 'expenses'. However, this terminology covers broadly the same costs and expenses as do the Regulations for England and Wales.

Costs distinguished from allowances

40.3   Allowances are paid out of public funds to parties and witnesses, in respect of attendance *at the hearing* and are paid irrespective of the success or failure of a party. They are paid, on the authority of the clerk to the tribunal, on the scale fixed by the Secretary of State for Employment. Such allowances cover travelling expenses, subsistence, and loss of earnings. The current scale of allowances or expenses can always be obtained from the clerk to your tribunal.

Where costs are awarded against a party, however, the tribunal may, under Rule 11(1)(*b*), order a party to repay all or part of the allowances to the Secretary of State. It is obviously right that the successful party should not be paid both costs and allowances in respect of the same out-of-pocket expenses. Accordingly, when an award of costs is made, this is usually stated to be in respect of costs only and not in respect of those matters which were covered by allowances.

However, by the very nature of having scales of allowances these may not necessarily cover a party's actual expenses. Rule 11 allows tribunals to award expenses in respect of matters usually covered by allowances where current scales are insufficient to cover actual costs.

Claiming allowances or expenses

40.4   If you have not already obtained claim forms from the clerk (*see* 28.1(11), ask him for these at the end of the hearing. Where possible complete them for each eligible witness and party and hand them back to the clerk. It is also advisable to add the case number (e.g. 269/84) on the top of each form. This procedure tends to prevent delays in reimbursement. If this is not possible you can send the completed forms later to ROIT by post. Although these forms do not cover expenses of representatives such as solicitors, they do cover interpreters' fees.

When can costs be recovered?

40.5 There are several circumstances where a tribunal has power to make an award of costs, although to date tribunals have used this power sparingly. These are considered separately below.

Party acted 'frivolously or vexatiously'

40.6 A tribunal has power to award costs where, in its opinion 'a party has in bringing or conducting the proceedings acted frivolously [or] vexatiously'. In *E T Marler Ltd v Robinson [1974] ICR 72*, the NIRC considered these terms in the following way:

> 'If the employee knows that there is no substance in his claim and that it is bound to fail, or if the claim is on the face of it so manifestly misconceived that it can have no prospect of success, it may be deemed frivolous and an abuse of the procedure of the tribunal to pursue it. If an employee brings a hopeless claim not with any expectation of recovering compensation but out of spite to harass his employers or for some other improper motive, he acts vexatiously, and likewise abuses the procedure. In such cases the tribunal may and doubtless usually will award costs against the employee . . . It is for the tribunal to decide if the applicant has been frivolous or vexatious and thus abused the procedure. It is a serious finding to make against an applicant, for it will generally involve bad faith on his part and one would expect the discretion to be sparingly exercised.'

That decision was extended by the EAT in *Cartiers Superfoods Ltd v Laws [1978] IRLR 315*, so that the meaning of frivolous applies not only to a party who knows that there is no substance in his claim or defence and that it is bound to fail, but also to parties who *ought to have known* that there was no substance or it was bound to fail. In this case Mrs Laws was dismissed because she rewarded members of staff for overtime by giving them food from the shop rather than cash. She was dismissed without notice or an opportunity to offer an explanation, the employers taking the view that she had been guilty of some criminal offence. The company threatened her with a suit for damages if she took legal advice, but she started a claim. At the tribunal hearing she was represented by a solicitor and barrister and the employers failed to give evidence. She was found to be unfairly dismissed and was awarded compensation. She was also awarded costs because the tribunal found that the employers had acted frivolously. The employers appealed against the award of costs, but the EAT upheld the tribunal's decision on three main grounds. In the first place, the employers had failed to give Mrs Laws a chance to explain her behaviour. In the second, their approach had been such as to make it inevitable that solicitors and counsel would be instructed, and finally, they very early on in the case should have realised that they had no chance of success and withdrawn, or settled at a stage which would have dramatically reduced costs.

Legal advice

40.7   Legal advice is a relevant factor in determining whether a party has acted frivolously. For example, in *Lothian Health Board v Johnstone* [*1981*] *IRLR 321*, the Scottish EAT commented on the conduct of solicitors who represent parties before tribunals and did not exclude the possibility that in certain circumstances such conduct might be frivolous. In particular the Appeal Tribunal was referring to solicitors who 'insist in their pleas beyond the stage where a tribunal deems appropriate,' where their client knew or ought to have known that such pleas of, say, misconduct were bound to fail.

In *Ur v The Medical Research Council EAT 477/80*, the applicant was advised by solicitors and counsel that he had a very good prospect of success. They ceased to act for him after eleven days of the hearing because Dr Ur could not afford to continue paying them. The hearing went on for another thirty-seven days. The tribunal felt that Dr Ur should have accepted an offer to settle the case prior to the hearing and found he had not told the truth concerning one crucial aspect of evidence. As a result they found that he knew what he was doing and that he should have known that his conduct was frivolous. In their reasons for awarding costs they did not mention the role of his legal advisers.

On appeal, the EAT said that in considering whether an employee knew or ought to have known that the claim was bound to fail, it was right to bear in mind whether or not he had taken any legal advice. While this in itself would not be conclusive, it must be considered a relevant factor.

The EAT went on to suggest that the tribunal in deciding whether Dr Ur's claim was frivolous should have asked themselves the following question:

> 'To what extent did he act under legal advice, and to what extent was that legal advice prejudiced by the misinformation that he gave either to the tribunal or to his legal advisers?'

As they did not address themselves to that question, there was an error of principle which prevented the EAT upholding the tribunal's decision to award costs.

Striking out 'scandalous, frivolous or vexatious' applications

40.8   The word 'frivolous' is also found in Rule 12(2)(*e*) where tribunals are given power to strike out originating applications on the grounds that they are 'scandalous, frivolous or vexatious' (only 'vexatious' in Scotland). In *Mulvaney v London Transport Executive* [*1981*] *ICR 351*, the applicant complained he was unfairly dismissed after being absent from work due to ill-health. He withdrew this claim a short while later, and then presented a second application based on the same grounds.

The respondents (employers) asked the tribunal to strike out his second application under this sub-rule on the grounds that Mr Mulvaney's attendance record at work was so poor that he had no reasonable prospects in succeeding in this case. On appeal, the EAT asked:

'On the face of it, is this claim so manifestly misconceived that it can have no prospect of success?'

The EAT said that sickness cases require careful consideration of the facts to show whether an employer has acted reasonably in all the circumstances. It would thus appear unlikely that a tribunal would find proceedings in 'ill-health' cases frivolous, even where the claim is the subject of two identical applications.

Twofold test

40.9 From the above decisions it seems that tribunals apply two different tests. The first is an objective test where the tribunal decides whether the claim or defence is meritless, i.e. manifestly misconceived. The second is a subjective test where the party knows the case is meritless, i.e. the party has acted in bad faith. In the first test the tribunal examines the merits of the case, whereas in the second the tribunal examines the attitude of the parties. Tribunals have been reluctant to find that a party has acted in bad faith and therefore they have tended to take the objective approach in deciding whether to award costs under the 'frivolous' or 'vexatious' heads.

'Conduct which is otherwise unreasonable'

40.10 Rule 11 was extended in 1980 to include 'otherwise unreasonable' conduct in bringing or conducting proceedings. There is no doubt that one of the principal reasons for widening the rule was to facilitate the awarding of costs following an opinion given at a pre-hearing assessment. Rule 6(2) envisages opinions being given where an applicant knew or should have known his claim was 'unlikely to succeed' or that a particular contention put forward by a party had 'no reasonable prospect of success'. The extension of Rule 11 allows tribunals to consider awards of costs without having to decide whether there is an element of bad faith or that a case is manifestly misconceived, something which they are reluctant to do.

So tribunals now perhaps find it easier to award costs where an application is withdrawn at the last moment. Even before the extension of Rule 11 the EAT in *Rocha v Commonwealth Holiday Inns of Canada Ltd, EAT 13/80* had sounded a warning note:

'Applicants to Industrial Tribunals and appellants before this Employment Appeal Tribunal must take notice that if they withdraw their applications at a late stage they will be at risk of an application being made for costs, and if they desire to contend that application it is their duty to appear before the Industrial Tribunal or this Employment Tribunal in order to do so. If they do not turn up, then they must take the consequences if an application is made. It simply will not do for applicants or appellants to complain after the event and to say that they ought to have been given notice that the application might be made. We desire to give them notice here and now that, if late withdrawals take place, such applications may be made and, excepting cases where the Tribunal feels it would not be just to go ahead, are likely to be dealt with by the Tribunal.'

(See also the comments of the EAT in *Walsall Metropolitan Borough Council v Sidhu, EAT 600/79*). In view of the *Rocha* case it would appear a similar view could now be taken by tribunals under the extended Rule 11.

There have been very few cases where tribunals have awarded costs under the 'otherwise unreasonable' head. One of these is *Stein v Associated Dairies Ltd [1982] IRLR 447* where the morning after Mr Stein was given a final warning he was 67 minutes late in arriving at work. The tribunal found the dismissal fair and the majority of the Scottish tribunal awarded expenses on the grounds that the applicant had 'acted unreasonably'.

The extended power to award costs under the 'otherwise unreasonable' head may be compared with the power of the EAT to award costs where it appears that any proceedings were unnecessary, improper or vexatious, or that there has been unreasonable delay or other unreasonable conduct. [*Employment Appeal Tribunal Rules (SI 1980 No 2035), Rule 27(1)*]. In *Croydon v Greenham (Plant Hire) Ltd [1978] IRLR 415*, although noting that this power was the only safeguard against irresponsible litigation, the EAT said that costs should only be awarded under this rule in exceptional circumstances.

Postponements and adjournments

40.11   Under Rule 11(2) tribunals can award costs for or against a party who applies for a postponement of the hearing or an adjournment of the hearing. This will not necessarily relate to whether that party is ultimately successful.

In *Rajguru v Top Order Ltd [1978] ICR 565*, two reasons were given by the respondent for dismissing Mr Rajguru. At the hearing, a further two reasons were put forward. Mr Rajguru's lawyer applied for an adjournment, which was granted on the condition that the applicant paid the cost of the day's hearing; the reason given by the tribunal for this decision was that Mr Rajguru's lawyer had had the details of the case weeks earlier, and if it had appeared to him to be necessary for further details to be obtained, he should have asked for further and better particulars of the allegations. The other matters would have then come to light. Not surprisingly, the EAT allowed the appeal, saying that the failure to ask for further and better particulars begged the question whether an adjournment should have been allowed in the first case, rather more than the question of costs. The IT should have considered that, in the circumstances, if an adjournment was to be granted at all, it was hardly the type which should be penalised by the award of costs.

This was possibly the sort of adjournment which the sub-rule envisaged would result in an award of costs against the respondent rather than the applicant. So where a large bundle of documents was handed to the applicant's counsel only 45 minutes before the hearing was due to begin as happened in *Ladbroke Racing Ltd v Hickey* [*1979*] *IRLR 273*, it was not surprising to find the tribunal granting an adjournment and ordering the employers to pay costs in respect of that adjournment. The EAT upheld the tribunal's order, saying:

'While we have some sympathy for Mr Burroughs [the employers' counsel] in the way that he prepared his documents and delivered them only 45 minutes before, he really must not be surprised if that is regarded by an industrial tribunal as taking the other side by surprise. If he has a large bundle of documents, on which Ladbrokes wish to rely, it is really essential, in order that the other side can have the opportunity of taking instructions and appreciating what is involved in these documents, that they should be passed over, if they are going to be passed over at all, sufficiently long beforehand to make it possible. To deliver them only 45 minutes before the case is due to be called on, while it has obvious administrative convenience, really is not giving the other side a chance. We feel bound to say that if Mr Burroughs has managed to get away with this before, the sooner he stops the less expensive it is likely to be for Ladbrokes. We do not find that there was an error of law or, indeed, otherwise, in the order making the adjournment and in the order charging Ladbrokes with the cost of the adjournment, subject of course, to the second important point.'

That point was whether the costs rule relating to adjournments and postponements was restricted to situations which were in the tribunal's opinion frivolous and vexatious, and now otherwise unreasonable. The EAT turned to the decision in the *Rajguru* case where it had been said:

'Rule 10(2) [now Rule 11(2)] specifically widens that type of limitation and enables a tribunal which is granting some form of adjournment, or amendments to proceedings, matters of that kind, in an appropriate case to make orders against the party who has caused a delay or has compelled an adjournment. It is therefore quite plain . . . that because of the enlargement of the rule with regard to costs there is an open discretion to an industrial tribunal in this area.'

However, a tribunal cannot impose as a condition for continuing a claim that the costs awarded against the applicant in relation to an adjournment have to be paid first. (*Northeast v Grundy Auto Products Ltd, EAT 811/83; IRLIB 257.15*).

Circumstances when IT must award costs

40.12 Whereas a tribunal has discretion whether to award costs under Rule 11(2), a tribunal *must* award costs for any postponement or adjournment of the hearing caused by the two circumstances referred to in Rule 11(3). The first circumstance is where the applicant has expressed a wish to be reinstated or re-engaged which has been communicated to the respondent at least seven days before the hearing, say, in the originating application, and the employer at the hearing is unable to produce reasonable evidence as to the availability of jobs. The second circumstance is where the employer has similarly failed to produce evidence as to the availability of jobs arising out of a failure to permit the applicant to return to work after an absence due to pregnancy or confinement.

Cost awards in PHA cases

40.13   Chapter 14 described the provisions of Rule 6 which introduced PHAs. Briefly, these are oral hearings designed to discourage meritless claims by, where appropriate, issuing a written warning to either party that their contention appears to have no reasonable prospect of success or, to the applicant, that his claim is unlikely to succeed, and that in the tribunal's opinion the party in question by pursuing the contention or claim may have an order for costs made against him at the full hearing. The costs figures available from COIT for the first three years of the operation of PHAs are set out below.

Costs awarded against applicant

	Applicant warned at PHA	No warning against applicant at PHA
1.10.80 – 25.9.81 (Average amount of costs awarded)	37 (£108)	11 (£66)
28.9.81 – 24.9.82 (Average amount of costs awarded)	51 (£115.50)	5 (£125)
27.9.82 – 30.9.83 (Average amount of costs awarded)	74 (£83)	13 (£120)

These figures do not include two cases in 1982/83 and one case in both 1981/82 and 1980/81 where costs were awarded under a County Court scale (*see* 40.15 below). Although the number of cost awards against warned applicants is increasing, the average scale of costs is not. There have been only three cost awards against respondents in the three years PHAs have operated, and they were all cases where no warning was given.

Level of costs awards — other than PHAs

40.14   Unfortunately there are no available statistics other than those for PHAs which give an exact indication of the levels of awards by tribunals.

Many of the reported decisions are several years old and therefore cannot provide a realistic indication of current costs award levels. However, it would seem that awards are of relatively small amounts although there are exceptions like the *Ur v Medical Research Council* case where the tribunal awarded costs of £5,000 against Dr Ur where the hearing lasted 48 days in 1981. In any event, this order was revoked on appeal.

Under Rule 11(1) the tribunal has the power to award a specified sum or that costs or expenses are 'taxed'. Under sub-rules (2) and (3) the tribunal only has power to award a specified sum.

So what are taxed costs? These are costs assessed by the County Court if the parties themselves cannot agree an appropriate sum. County Courts operate four scales of costs which reflect the amount of costs which can be awarded. In other words the higher the scale of the award the larger the amount which will be assessed by the County Court, or, put in another way, the more punitive the award.

How does the tribunal decide the amount or scale of a costs award?

40.15   A tribunal will usually take into account the following factors. First, the actual costs incurred by the successful party; secondly, the loser's means to pay, and finally the extent to which the loser is to blame. In *Ellis v Clarke Chapman and Thompson Charlton Ltd EAT 677/77*, the EAT rejected the argument 'that as the respondents did nothing wrong, once an order for costs is made it ought to be commensurate with the costs incurred by the innocent party. Regulation 11(1) clearly gives to an industrial tribunal a wide area over which to exercise discretion. It seems to us that the Regulation contemplates a balancing operation setting the entitlement to costs against the element of blame on the part of the other litigant.'

And in *Wiggin Alloys Ltd v Jenkins* the tribunal refused to make an order for costs against an applicant who was in prison. The EAT, upholding the tribunal's decision, said:

> 'In our view, the inability of the applicant to meet any order for costs is a matter which is properly to be taken into consideration and, therfore, we cannot see that they have erred in any way in law in exercising their discretion. We should emphasise that it is no consequence of our decision that the mere fact that for the time being an applicant is penniless is in every case a sufficient ground for refusing an order for costs. Each case depends on its own circumstances and lies within the discretion of the Tribunals.'

In *Carr v Allen-Bradley Electronics Ltd [1980] IRLR 263*, the tribunal awarded costs on the highest County Court scale giving as a principal reason for this that the applicant was union-assisted. The tribunal seems to have given as a basis for this reason a High Court practice in personal injury claims. On appeal the EAT did not think it was helpful to try to adapt principles applied in the High Court to the quite different circumstances that arise in litigation before industrial tribunals'. The Appeal Tribunal went on to give the following guidance:

'The normal rule is that there is no order for costs. In the comparatively infrequent case in which the claimant has acted frivolously or vexatiously, we think that the tribunal should consider the means of the claimant himself rather than of his trade union, in deciding, first of all, whether or not to make an order in respect of the costs, and secondly, the form of the order to be made.'

The County Court scales themselves are based on the amount of damages or compensation awarded and the latest scales are as follows:

Lower scale	£26 to £100
Scale 1	£101 to £500
Scale 2	£501 to £3,000
Scale 3	exceeding £3,000

So in the ordinary County Court case where a sum of, say, £2,000 is awarded this would automatically be taxed on scale 2 which is the second highest scale. As far as industrial tribunals are concerned it does not work this way because generally a successful respondent is not awarded any compensation. In *Field v Brush Electrical Machines, EAT 321/79*, the applicant's Counsel took the point that 'if compensation had been awarded under the Race Relations Act the amount of compensation would have been relatively modest'.

The tribunal in the *Field* case had awarded costs on scale 4 (which was then the highest scale) and the respondent's solicitors had prepared a bill of costs, which, if upheld, was a substantial sum of money. The EAT commented that: 'In many of these cases it is more convenient to award a fixed sum. It saves the need for the parties to incur further costs in taxation'. However, they continued: 'We do not think that it is necessary for the tribunal to be satisfied that the amount of compensation, or damages likely to be awarded, would exceed £1,000 [£3,000 today] before they can order scale 4 . . . It seems to us that they are entitled to take into account the nature of the claim and the extent of the investigation which was required in deciding the appropriate scale.'

Therefore the higher the scale awarded the more punitive the award. Only an award under scale 3 will allow a party to recover anything like his actual costs.

Applying for costs

40.16   There is no formal procedure for making an application for costs. The parties should consider the possibility of such an application even prior to the hearing. As very few awards are made, there is little point applying unless the case comes within the narrow provisions of Rule 11. However, where the successful party wishes to apply for costs all that is necessary is that he or his representative ask the chairman of the tribunal for an award of costs immediately after the decision is announced. The chairman will allow both parties to make oral representations, and then the tribunal will make a decision on this particular application which will usually be announced there and then. Their decision on costs will be recorded together with their decision on the substantive issues of the case which is sent to the parties some three to six weeks after the hearing. The tribunal will usually give reasons for making or refusing a costs award.

Sometimes decisions are reserved and parties do not find out the decision until it arrives by post. It is usually inappropriate for a party to apply for costs until he knows whether or not he is successful. Therefore an application in these circumstances would have to be by letter to the Regional Office requesting an order for costs. The tribunal will then usually invite the parties to deal with the application either at a further hearing, or alternatively by written representations in order to save costs. Even where a party who has the opportunity to apply for costs at the hearing fails to do so he is not prevented from applying at a later stage. In *Zakia v The Home Office* the EAT gave some guidance on when applications should be made:

> 'Now it is right to say that an application for costs should be made promptly and, of course, the tribunal will normally deal with it as expeditiously as in the circumstances is possible. It might well be a ground for refusing an order for costs that it is made at a very late and unreasonably late stage, but we find it quite impossible to say that an application for costs must be made during the course of the hearing itself. It is really only for a party to consider whether an application is justified when the decision of the tribunal has been given and the grounds of the decision are staged. Moreover, we do not think that it would be right to say that there must be an application within 14 days of the entry on the register by analogy to the position where a review is sought. The tribunal is not limited by the rules as to the time when it may deal with the application.'

From whom are costs recoverable?

40.17   Under Rule 11 it is only a 'party' against whom costs can be awarded. So in the *Carr v Allen-Bradley Electronics Ltd* case (see 40.15 above), even if the tribunal had been allowed to take into account that the applicant was union-assisted there could have been no costs order against that union.

However, Rule 14(1) was extended in 1980 to allow trade unions to be joined as respondents in order to facilitate the changes to Section 76 of EPCA (referred to in 11.2). Also Rule 14(1) enables trade unions or union officials to be joined in proceedings relating to closed shop dismissals where the employer was induced to dismiss by industrial pressure. [*EA 1982, s 7*]. So there can be a number of parties against whom costs might be awarded.

Furthermore, in the case of *Lowbey v Lindo* [*1981*] *ICR 216*, the EAT under their own rules on costs were asked to join the solicitors acting for the employer as a party to the proceedings so that an award of costs could be made against them. The EAT was not prepared to grant such an application in that case, but did not rule out the possibility that solicitors could be joined as parties. This may surprise lay persons, but in view of Rule 14(1), giving a tribunal the power to join in 'any person against whom relief is sought' this may be possible. In the *Lowbey* case counsel for the employee argued that the solicitors acting for the employer must have given him such wrong advice that they ought to pay the costs. The EAT did not accept that there was any evidence to show this, but did not rule out the possibility that where they were on the record at the time costs were incurred an award could be made against them.

This reflects the power of County Courts to make an order against a solicitor to pay his client's costs which the client has been ordered to pay to other parties in the case. This could happen where costs are incurred improperly or without reasonable cause or are wasted by undue delay or any other misconduct or default by a solicitor. [*CCR Order 47, r 50(1)*].

Who can recover costs?

40.18   Only a party to the proceedings can recover costs or expenses, and only where that party has 'incurred' costs or expenses. *The Walsall Metropolitan Borough Council v Sidhu* case is an example of a situation where the applicant had not incurred costs or expenses. The EAT found:

> 'In the exercise of powers given to them under the Race Relations Act 1976, the Commission for Racial Equality undertook the case and gave assistance to Miss Sidhu. They did so, . . . on the terms that she would herself not incur any expenses. It is quite plain that the Commission for Racial Equality did incur expenses, and, indeed, did incur costs in connection with these proceedings. Miss Sidhu has incurred no costs. Can we make an order that the Council shall pay the costs incurred by the Commission for Racial Equality? It seems to us quite plain that they are not a party to the proceedings within the meaning of the Rule, and therefore, in the ordinary way, as Miss Sidhu has no liability to them, their costs and expenses are not her costs and expenses.'

Appealing against costs

40.19   As will be appreciated from the EAT cases quoted in this chapter it is possible for either party to appeal against a costs order or alternatively against a tribunal's refusal to make such an award. On appeal the EAT will be looking to see whether the tribunal has exercised its discretion on costs properly. The scope for intervention by the EAT in most cases is therefore quite narrow. However, where the EAT is satisfied that the tribunal's exercise of its discretion was improper, it can dismiss an order for costs or vary the extent of the order by, say, reducing an award of costs. This happened in *Ellis v Clarke Chapman and Thompson Charlton*, where the EAT reduced the award of costs from £250 to £100. Conversely, it would seem possible for the EAT to make an award of costs in circumstances in which an industrial tribunal had refused to exercise its discretion to do so.

Chapter 41

Enforcement

Introduction

41.1 How does the IT enforce its remedies? The answer is it does not do so. It has no jurisdiction to enforce its own remedies.

What happens if an 'order', for example, to reinstate, is not complied with? In this situation the IT can penalise the offending party by awarding some monetary compensation or penalty. Therefore at the end of the day most remedies can be reduced to a monetary award. This can then be enforced in the County Court. However, this is rarely necessary as in practice most awards are paid without the need for legal coercion.

Non-compliance with declarations

41.2 You may wonder how this conversion to an award can apply to a declaration. Let us take as an example a declaration by a tribunal as to the terms and conditions of employment. [*EPCA s 11*]. The IT has declared that these terms include a basic wage of £110 per week and an entitlement to four weeks' paid holiday. After the declaration the employer continues to pay the old wage of £95 per week and only allows three weeks' paid holiday. In these circumstances, the employee could sue the employer for the arrears of wages and non-payment of holiday pay in the County Court on the basis that the arrears and non-payment amount to a breach of contract. Alternatively, he could resign and claim constructive dismissal on the basis of a fundamental breach of two principal terms of the contract, and if successful could then receive a monetary award. In addition, he could sue as mentioned before in the County Court for any loss which occurred prior to the effective date of termination, such as arrears of wages or outstanding holiday pay.

Non-compliance with orders

41.3 What happens if a woman who has been on maternity leave is not allowed to return to work despite an order of the IT that she should be reinstated? Here she should write to the tribunal informing them of the position. A new hearing will then be arranged where the tribunal will consider an appropriate monetary award which, if necessary, can be enforced in the County Court.

The penalty for non-compliance with the remedies of reinstatement and re-engagement is exclusively financial as outlined in Chapter 39.

If an order for reinstatement or re-engagement is not complied with in any way it is up to the employee to write to ROIT informing them of this fact. A new hearing will then be held and the onus only shifts to the employer once there is a finding of non-compliance. It is then up to him to satisfy the tribunal that there was a defence in terms of practicability. [*EPCA s 71*].

The hearing will be conducted in a similar way to the first and second stages already described and will be a complete hearing in its own right.

Non-implementation of recommendations

41.4   Unfortunately there is no way of enforcing recommendations, except that, if a subsequent case materialises out of the non-implementation of a recommendation, the tribunal may reflect this in its subsequent award.

County Court enforcement of financial awards

41.5   At the end of the day therefore, nearly all remedies can be reduced to a financial award, which can then be enforced in the County Court. The procedure to be recommended is as follows:

1.   On the assumption that the employer received a copy of the tribunal decision containing the financial award at approximately the same time as the applicant, the employee should wait a reasonable time (about two weeks) for a cheque to arrive.

2.   If nothing has been sent, the employee should telephone and then write to the employer asking whether he proposes to pay or take any other action. The other action basically relates to an appeal. The employer will have 42 days from the date the decision was sent to the parties to appeal against the tribunal decision. The effect of an appeal will be to stay or hold in abeyance any order or award until the appeal has been heard.

3.   If there are no proposals or appeal within 42 days, the employee should write another letter threatening to take legal proceedings without further notice if the sum awarded is not paid within about seven days from the date of that letter. Such a letter will result in any costs of the proceedings being recoverable from the employer.

4.   If this letter does not have the desired effect the employee should issue proceedings.

It is not difficult for an applicant himself to sue in his local County Court. The staff of the County Court are usually extremely helpful and there are a variety of books available providing the necessary guidance. The action is *ex parte* (i.e. it is unnecessary to notify the employer) for the sum claimed plus any court fees. [*CCR Or 25, r 7A*]. It is made by way of originating application supported by an affidavit similar to figure 33 on page 228 which can be sworn at the court where it is filed.

41.5   *Enforcement*

AFFIDAVIT

IN THE MARYLEBONE COUNTY COURT

Plaint No ....0000/84....

Between :   JOHN RIDER   Plaintiff

and

MASON (UK) LTD   Respondents

I, John Rider, of 34 Westmount Road London NW11 9DX, make oath and say as follows:

1.   I was applicant in the case of Rider v Mason (UK) Ltd (No 269/84) in the Industrial Tribunal. By a decision entered in the register at the Central Office of Tribunals on 24 May 1984 I was awarded £4,082 by the said Tribunal. (A copy of the said decision is now produced and shown to me marked JR 1.)

2.   Despite a request for payment of the said award sent by my representative, the Warehousemen's Trade Union, to the Respondents herein dated 21 June 1984 to which no reply has been received, the said award remains unpaid. (A copy of the said letter of 21 June 1984 is now produced and shown to me marked JR 2.)

3.   I hereby ask this Honourable Court for judgment in the sum of the said award plus the fixed costs of this application.

John Rider

Sworn at London   )
this ...... day of   )
June 1984   )
)
Before me   )

J. Thomas   A Solicitor

[Author's note: a copy of both the decision and the letter should be exhibited to the affidavit.]

Figure 33: Affidavit supporting County Court summons

Judgment is usually a formality and can be enforced by levying execution against the employer's goods or making him bankrupt or any other method available to the County Court. [*EPCA 9 Sch 7*].

Insolvency of employer

41.6 What happens if the employer becomes bankrupt or goes into liquidation? Is there any point in suing in the County Court? The answer is 'no'. The former employee should first apply to the employer's representative (who is likely to be either a receiver, liquidator or trustee) for payment. If there is no representative, or the payment has only been received in part or not at all, the applicant can apply for payment from the Secretary of State for Employment in respect of the following tribunal awards (*see* Tribunal Table, Appendix A):

  (i) guaranteed payments;

 (ii) payments for suspension on medical grounds;

(iii) payments for time off work;

(iv) protective awards;

 (v) basic awards;

(vi) redundancy payments.

The Secretary of State has power to pay these amounts in full out of the Redundancy Fund.

Part IV

Challenging the Decision

Chapter 42

Challenging the Decision

Introduction

42.1   A decision on an IT can be challenged in one of three ways, considered separately in this chapter:

(*a*) by an application to alter or modify (see 42.2 below);

(*b*) by a review (see 42.3–42.7);

(*c*) by an appeal (see 42.8–42.18 below).

Application to alter or modify

42.2   Where a clerical mistake or a simple error is discovered in the document recording the decision, the chairman has power under Rule 9(6) to correct the matter. Either one of the parties can point out the mistake or error, or the tribunal can make the correction on its own initiative.

Under the 1980 Regulations it does not matter if the decision has been promulgated before being corrected. The chairman can make the correction at any time by certificate under his hand. The most common use of this procedure is where there is a mistake in a mathematical calculation in a monetary award. (*Thomas & Betts Manufacturing Co Ltd v Harding [1978] IRLR 213*).

The EAT in *Lamont v Fry's Metals Ltd [1983] IRLR 434* seems to have extended this power where ITs are convinced on later reflection that the original decision is or may be wrong or may require further consideration of authorities. Here tribunals may have jurisdiction before the decision is registered to make alterations. Before any change is made, however, the parties should be invited to address further argument to the tribunal and the tribunal should take steps to make clear to the parties the precise questions on which further submissions can be made and the findings which have to be looked at afresh.

An illustration of this power is provided by *Hanks v Ace High Productions Ltd [1979] IRLR 32*. In that case the tribunal announced at the conclusion of the hearing that Mrs Hanks was entitled to a redundancy payment of £532.12. In accordance with Rule 9(3) (previously Rule 8(3)) the next step was for the decision and reasons to be recorded in a document to be signed by the chairman. The tribunal clerk was then to transmit the document to the secretary for the purpose of entering it in the COIT register, and to send a copy to each party as described in Chapter 38. Before this was done, the chairman wrote to the parties through the clerk:

> Having given the matter further consideration the chairman of the tribunal is of the opinion that further argument on the law would be desirable from the representatives; accordingly the original tribunal will be reconvened to hear such further submissions as the representatives may wish to make.

The chairman had discovered when writing the decision that the legal argument at the hearing had not covered a material matter, hence the letter to the parties. The chairman's right to reconvene to correct the omission was challenged in the EAT. The Appeal Tribunal supported the chairman's right to correct the 'plain omission' in this way but went on to say that such a right should be used 'carefully, sparingly and not as a matter of course'.

Review

Grounds for a review

42.3   Tribunal decisions may be challenged relatively simply and quickly by means of a 'review'. The grounds on which an application to review can be accepted are set out under Rule 10(1):

1. 'The decision was wrongly made as a result of an error on the part of the tribunal staff.' It should be noted that the rule refers to staff and not to the chairman or members of the tribunal. Any error on their part can be made the subject of an appeal to the EAT (see below). In *Sherringham Development Co Ltd v Browne [1977] ICR 20*, it was held that the failure to send a copy of an amended originating application to a conciliation officer was *not* a sufficient error for a review.

2. 'A party did not receive notice of the proceedings leading to the decision.' This would include not receiving a copy of forms IT 1 or IT 3 as well as the notice of hearing. (*Migwain Limited v TGWU [1979] ICR 597*). In *Hancock v Middleton [1982] ICR 416*, the EAT held that where the respondent had not received notice of the original hearing and the decision was made in his absence, then a review of the case by a fully constituted tribunal was appropriate.

3. 'The decision was made in the absence of a party or person entitled to be heard.' This was one of the grounds for review in the *Hancock* case. In another case, *Holland v Cypane Ltd [1977] ICR 355*, a party who had been genuinely unaware of his right to ask for a postponement and who, as a result, failed to make an appearance, was able to apply for a review on this ground.

4. 'New evidence has become available' since the decision was made but only if 'its existence could not have been reasonably known of or foreseen' at the time of the hearing. The new 'evidence must be such

that, if given, it would probably have an important influence on the result of the case, though it need not be decisive': per Lord Denning in *Ladd v Marshall* [*1954*] *AER 745, p 748*. It must also be of a kind 'as is presumably to be believed, or in other words, it must be apparently credible, although it need not be incontrovertible'; and it must be shown that it would have been difficult to have had the evidence available for use at the hearing. According to the cases of *Craig v British Railways (Scottish Region) (1973) 8 ITR 636* and *Brown v Southall & Knight* [*1980*] *IRLR 130*, it is the duty of the parties, not of the tribunal, to ensure that all relevant evidence is before the tribunal notwithstanding that the tribunal, if properly aware, should point out to a party taken by surprise at the hearing in respect of new evidence being introduced that an adjournment would be advisable. It would seem that, if the party in question fails to ask for an adjournment, he cannot then use the review procedure to call a witness who should have been called at the hearing or an adjourned hearing.

A tribunal has power to grant a review of its monetary award in the light of such new evidence. For example, in *Bateman v British Leyland (UK) Ltd,* [*1974*] *IRLR 101*, an applicant gave evidence at the hearing that he had obtained new employment and the tribunal assessed compensation accordingly. Within two weeks of the hearing he was out of work and this could not reasonably have been foreseen at the time of the hearing. It was held that this was a proper case for the tribunal to review his compensatory award in the light of the new evidence. Similarly in *Ladup Ltd v Barnes* [*1982*] *ICR 107* where the employee had been dismissed for gross misconduct connected with a drug offence of which he was found guilty subsequent to the tribunal decision that he had been unfairly dismissed, the EAT considered that the employer's application for a review of the monetary award, which he made on hearing of the conviction, was a proper case where the tribunal chairman should have exercised his discretion to hold the review.

5.   'The interests of justice require such a review.' Where it is alleged there has been an error in law in a decision which was reached after there had been a procedural mishap, then this could be the subject of a review on this ground. In *Trimble v Supertravel* [*1982*] *IRLR 451*, the tribunal reached its decision on mitigation without the appellant's solicitor having an opportunity to present his case on the point. The tribunal rejected the application for a review on the grounds that they did not have jurisdiction because the grounds for the review involved a substantial error of law and the correct course was to appeal to the EAT. On appeal the EAT held (allowing the appeal and remitting the case to the industrial tribunal to consider again on review):

'We do not think that it is appropriate for an industrial tribunal to review its decision simply because it is said there was an error of law on its face. If the matter has been ventilated and properly argued, then errors of law of that kind fall to be corrected by this Appeal Tribunal. If, on the other hand, due to an oversight or to some procedural occurrence one or other party can with substance say that he has not had a fair opportunity to present his argument on a point of substance, then that is a procedural shortcoming in the proceedings before the tribunal which, in our view, can be correctly dealt with by a review under Rule 10 however important the point of law or fact may be. In essence, the review procedure enables errors occurring in the course of the proceedings to be corrected but would not normally be appropriate when the proceedings had given both parties a fair opportunity to present their case and the decision had been reached in the light of all relevant argument.

It is suggested that there are authorities binding us to hold that it is inappropriate for an Industrial Tribunal to deal with anything other than minor slips or small points of detail . . . There is nothing in those words [in the authorities] to suggest that only minor errors of law fall to be corrected in the circumstances. As we have indicated, in our view the distinction is not between minor errors and major errors; what is relevant is whether or not a decision, alleged to be erroneous in law, has been reached after there has been a procedural mishap.'

A review will not be ordered 'in the interests of justice' if it is sought to introduce new evidence which is available at the hearing. It is not, in other words, possible to rehear the case, and, in effect, have 'two bites at the cherry'. (*Flint v Eastern Electricity Board* [*1975*] *IRLR 277*).

Applying for a review

42.4   An application for a review may be made at the hearing or any time afterwards provided the application is made within 14 days of the date the decision is sent to the parties. This latter date is the date referred to in 38.6 but may be extended by the tribunal under Rule 12(2)(*a*). (*Namyslo v Secretary of State* [*1979*] *IRLR 450*).

An application can be made verbally or in writing. In either case the application must give the reason for concluding that 'the decision was wrong on its merits'. (*Vauxhall Motors Ltd v Henry (1978) 13 ITR 332*).

It is insufficient to reiterate one or more of the grounds under Rule 10(1). It is necessary under Rule 10(2) to give a detailed supporting explanation of the grounds in full and in the case of the fourth ground mentioned above relating to new evidence, this will require the preparation of a full written statement of the evidence sought to be introduced.

If the application is not made orally at the hearing, it should be incorporated in a letter and sent to ROIT. The application will be considered under Rule 10(3) by the chairman of the tribunal which decided the case (or by the Regional Chairman or President in London or Glasgow) who may refuse it, if in his opinion the application has no reasonable prospect of success. If the application is not refused, it will be heard by either the original tribunal, or where that is impracticable, by another tribunal (Rule 10(4)). A review hearing, however, must be by a full tribunal, not a chairman sitting alone.

Tribunals can only review their own decisions, not interlocutory orders. (*Peter Simper & Co Ltd v Cooke EAT 259/82, IRLIB 245.10*). The latter can only be the subject of an appeal to the EAT.

Review procedure

42.5   The procedure at a review is similar to the procedures already described. Witnesses may be called, although usually only submissions will be required. In a straightforward case the tribunal may invite written representations to avoid unnecessary attendance. At the hearing the tribunal is free to review the whole of its decision and not just the part which is the subject of the application for review. (*Estorffe v Smith (1973) 8 ITR 627*).

Review powers

42.6   A review tribunal has power under Rule 10(4) to vary or revoke a decision and order a rehearing. But where on a review the tribunal finds that the original decision was wrong and the right decision is obvious, it has power to substitute the correct decision without ordering a rehearing. (*Stonehill Furniture Ltd v Phillippo* [*1983*] *ICR 556*).

Dissatisfaction with a review

42.7   As far as most claims are concerned a party can appeal to the EAT against a tribunal's refusal to review their decision provided that refusal amounts to an error in law (*see*, e.g. *Trimble v Supertravel Ltd*).

Appeals

42.8   The grounds for a review can involve questions of both fact and law. By contrast, an 'appeal' to the EAT can only succeed where there has been an error of law on the part of the IT (except in relation to claim 3(d) in the Tribunal Table, Appendix A). If the IT has reached its decision after due consideration of all relevant arguments, then errors of law become the subject of appeals. (*Trimble v Supertravel Ltd*). In *Lewis v John Adamson & Co Ltd* [*1982*] *IRLR 233*, it was confirmed that, at least in unfair dismissal cases, the EAT's function is 'to correct an error of law where one is established and identified' and it 'should not search around with a fine toothcomb for some point of law'. The tribunal's 'reasoning should not be subject to meticulous criticism'. The question is 'whether, looking at the matter broadly and fairly, the industrial tribunal directed themselves properly or fairly on the facts and did not make an error of law'. And in *Hollister v NFU* [*1979*] *ICR 542, at p 553*, Lord Denning MR gave it as his view that it 'is not right that points of fact should be dressed up as points of law so as to encourage appeals'.

How does one know what is fact and what is law? The higher courts have given some guidance in a number of cases, including *Palmer v Vauxhall Motors Ltd [1977] ICR 24* and *Woods v W M Car Services (Peterborough) Ltd [1982] ICR 693*. Thus, the following are regarded as questions of law and are alternative grounds of appeal (*Dobie v Burns International Security Services (UK) Ltd, 14 May 1984 (CA), IRLIB 263.15*):

(*a*)   Where the tribunal misunderstood the law, or misapplied the law or misdirected itself in law; for example in relation to its interpretation of a statutory provision or to its exercise of a discretion as to whether to grant an adjournment. (*Masters of Beckenham Ltd v Green [1977] ICR 535*).

(*b*)   Where the decision was 'perverse' in the sense that no reasonable tribunal could have reached that decision.

(*c*)   Where the tribunal omitted to take into account particular relevant evidence, i.e. misunderstood the facts.

(*d*)   Where the tribunal considered wrong and/or irrelevant evidence, i.e. misapplied the facts.

The above grounds clearly indicate that an appeal cannot be used as a method of rehearing the case. An IT decision will not be interfered with merely because the Appeal Tribunal would have taken a different view of the evidence. Provided there is some evidence on which the IT could reach its findings of fact, the decision will not be disturbed. But the question of what is a proper inference from the facts is a question of law, which *can* be a ground of appeal. It should be noted that where both parties agree that the tribunal decision was in error and reach a proposed settlement, the parties themselves cannot reverse the decision. They must appeal to the EAT as with any other mistake of law. (*Comet Radiovision Services Ltd v Delahunty [1979] ICR 182*).

There are several further restrictions on the scope of appeals. The EAT will only vary an order for compensation if an error of law has resulted in a large discrepancy in the amount. It recognises that tribunals often have to decide in a rough and ready way. (*Fougère v Phoenix Motor Company Ltd [1976] IRLR 259*). The Appeal Tribunal will not accept new evidence unless it receives a reasonable explanation as to why it had not been offered to the IT, and such new evidence must be both credible and of decisive influence on the outcome. (*IAS (UK) Ltd v James [1979] ICR 371*).

Similarly, points of law which were not introduced at the tribunal hearing will only exceptionally be considered on appeal. (See, for instance, *Secretary of State for Employment v Newcastle CC [1980] ICR 447* and *House v Emerson Electrical Industrial Controls [1980] ICR 395*). Lastly, the EAT will not decide on issues which could not affect the actual decision in the case. (*Harrod v Ministry of Defence [1981] ICR 8*).

Although most appeals in relation to claims set out in the Tribunal

Table (*see* Appendix A) go to the EAT, a few appeals from tribunal decisions go elsewhere, mainly to the High Court.

Action to challenge IT decision

42.9   Procedures surrounding appeals should be studied. If you feel that the IT decision could be wrong on one of the above grounds then the following course of action is recommended.

Appeals procedure

Consult a solicitor

42.10   We are no longer dealing principally with facts but with points of law. Therefore it is advisable to consult the specialists in this field. Legal aid is available for applicants and information about this is contained in the notes accompanying the tribunal decision. Even as a lay representative or a party appearing in person you can appear before the EAT or High Court. It is not obligatory to seek a solicitor's help but it may be a wise step.

Time limits

42.11   An appeal to the EAT must be brought within 42 days of the date the decision was sent to the appellant. The time limit will only be extended under very exceptional circumstances. It will apply even if a review is pending or compensation has not yet been assessed. (*Blackpool Furniture Ltd v Sullivan [1978] ICR 558; Firestone Tyre Company v Challoner [1978] ICR 175*). It is therefore most important that you do not delay sending the notice of appeal, even if you have not yet been granted legal aid or the review has not been heard.

Papers to be handed over

42.12   If you do decide to consult a solicitor you will have to hand over to him the decision, all exhibits and your notes of testimony. These notes may be important. If they conflict with the chairman's 'notes of evidence' it is possible to apply for the latter to be amended if such an application can be based on a 'permissible' ground. (*Webb v Anglian Water Authority [1981] IRLR 494*). Permissible grounds would include the contention that a finding was unsupported by evidence or that the tribunal did not find in accordance with a relevant fact or that it misunderstood the evidence or that it reached a conclusion perversely.

Delaying compliance with a tribunal decision

42.13   If you are the respondent you may choose to delay compliance with a tribunal award. Lodging an appeal automatically suspends the award pending the outcome of the appeal. It is not clear whether an order is similarly suspended. Since it is likely to involve immediate action, for example reinstatement from the date of decision, it may only be possible to apply for an order to be suspended after a notice of appeal has been lodged.

42.14   *Challenging the Decision*

Statutory EAT powers

42.14   If the appeal is successful the EAT may substitute its own decision, reverse the original decision or remit the case back to the original tribunal or to a new tribunal to rehear the whole or part of the case.

Number of appeals

42.15   For the period 1 April 1982 to 31 March 1983, the EAT registered 841 appeals from the decisions of the ITs in England and Wales. Expressed as a percentage of tribunal cases heard in the same period (14,457) this indicates that about 5·8 per cent of cases determined following a hearing go to appeal:

(*a*)   14·4 per cent were allowed;

(*b*)   9·3 per cent were remitted to the tribunal for a rehearing;

(*c*)   46·5 per cent were dismissed;

(*d*)   29·8 per cent were withdrawn.

The majority of these appeals (60·3 per cent) had been lodged by employees. (These statistics were provided by COIT in its Fact Sheet published in February 1984.)

Appendices

Tribunal Table

1 No.	2 Nature of claim	3 Case brought by (applicant)	4 Case brought against (respondent)	5 Continuous service qualification
1	**Particulars of terms and conditions of employment**			
(a)	To determine the particulars of terms and conditions of employment	Employee or employer	Employer or employee	13 weeks
(b)	To determine the particulars of a change in terms and conditions of employment	As 1(a)	As 1(a)	As 1(a)
(c)	Right to receive itemised pay statement	As 1(a)	As 1(a)	None
2	**Rights relating to union membership or non-membership (outside a closed shop)**			
(a)	Action short of dismissal in relation to membership of an independent trade union or engaging in the activities of such a union	Employee	Employer	None
(b)	Action short of dismissal to compel employee to join any trade union or a particular trade union	As 2(a)	Employer (either party has an option to join a trade union or other person pressurising the employer)	As 2(a)

6 *Period in which claim must be commenced*	7 *Conciliation available*	8 *Tribunal powers*	9 *Source of rules*
During employment or within 3 months of employment ceasing	No	Declaration of particulars, which includes the power to confirm, amend or replace particulars already given	EPCA ss 1, 11
As 1(a)	As 1(a)	Declaration of particulars of change in terms and conditions	EPCA ss 4, 11
As 1(a)	Yes	Declaration and reimbursement of any unnotified deductions for the 13 weeks preceding the application	EPCA ss 8, 9 and 11
Within 3 months of the date of the action complained about (or the last action if one of a series)	Yes	Declaration and compensation considered just and equitable	EPCA ss 23–26; EA 1980, s 15
As 2(a)	As 2(a)	Declaration and compensation considered just and equitable (which may be apportioned between the employer and a joined party)	EPCA ss 23–26; EA 1980, s 15; EA 1982, ss 10, 11

Tribunal Table

No.	Nature of claim	Case brought by (applicant)	Case brought against (respondent)	Continuous service qualification
2	**Rights relating to union membership or non-membership (cont.d)**			
(c)	Dismissal for membership of an independent trade union or engaging in the activities of such a union	As 2(a)	As 2(a)	As 2(a)
(d)	Dismissal for non-membership of any trade union or of a particular trade union	As 2(a)	As 2(b)	As 2(a)
(e)	Interim relief after dismissal on the grounds of union membership or activities or non-membership	Employee (with certificate, if a member of an independent trade union)	Employer	As 2(a)
(f)	Failure to allow time off with pay for an official of a recognised independent trade union to carry out his or her duties or undergo training	As 2(a)	As 2(a)	As 2(a)
(g)	See also 16(a)			
(h)	Failure to allow time off for a member of a recognised independent trade union to take part in union activities	As 2(a)	As 2(a)	As 2(a)
3	**Closed shop rights**			
(a)	Action short of dismissal to compel an employee to join a specified independent trade union	Employee	Employer (either party has an option to join a trade union or other person pressurising the employer)	None

6 Period in which claim must be commenced	7 Conciliation available	8 Tribunal powers	9 Source of rules
Within 3 months of the effective date of termination	As 2(a)	Order for reinstatement or re-engagement and/or compensation of between £2,000 and £31,850 (in some cases unlimited)	EPCA ss 67–75; EA 1982, ss 3–6
As 2(c)	As 2(a)	As 2(c), but with discretion to apportion compensation between the employer and a joined party	EPCA ss 67–75; EA 1982, ss 3–7
Within 7 days of the effective date of termination	As 2(a)	Order for reinstatement or re-engagement or that contract continues	EPCA ss 77–79; EA 1982, s 8 and 3 Sch
Within 3 months of date of failure	As 2(a)	As 2(a)	EPCA ss 27, 30
As 2(f)	As 2(a)	As 2(a)	EPCA ss 28, 30
Within 3 months of the date of the action complained about (or the last action if one of a series)	Yes	Declaration and compensation considered just and equitable (which may be apportioned between an employer and a joined party)	EPCA ss 23–26; EA 1980, s 15; EA 1982, ss 10–11

Tribunal Table

1 No.	2 Nature of claim	3 Case brought by (applicant)	4 Case brought against (respondent)	5 Continuous service qualification
3	**Closed shop rights (cont.d)**			
(b)	Dismissal for non-membership of a specified independent trade union	As 3(a)	As 3(a)	As 3(a)
(c)	Interim relief after dismissal for non-membership of a specified independent trade union	As 3(a)	As 3(a)	As 3(a)
(d)	Refusal of, or expulsion from, membership	Employee or person seeking employment	Specified trade union	None
(e)	Compensation following declaration of admission or re-admission to membership which has been complied with	As 3(d)	As 3(d)	None
4	**Ballots**			
	Failure to allow secret ballot on employer's premises	Recognised independent trade union	Employer	Not applicable
5	**Equal pay**			
(a)	Failure to comply with an equality clause where employed on like work or work of equal value	Employee (or Secretary of State on his/her behalf)	Employer	None

6 Period in which claim must be commenced	7 Conciliation available	8 Tribunal powers	9 Source of rules
Within 3 months of the effective date of termination	Yes	Order for reinstatement or re-engagement and/or compensation of between £2,000 and £31,850 (in some cases no limit). Discretion to apportion compensation between the employer and a joined party	EPCA ss 67–75; EA 1980, ss 3–7
Within 7 days of the effective date of termination	Yes	Order for reinstatement or re-engagement or that contract continues	EPCA ss 77–79; EA 1982, s 8 and 3 Sch
Within 6 months of date of refusal or expulsion	Yes	Declaration that complaint well founded	EA 1980, s 4
Between 4 weeks and 6 months from 'Section 4 declaration' (see 3(d))	Yes	Compensation for loss suffered up to £11,850	EA 1980, s 5
Within 3 months of the date of the failure	No	Declaration that complaint well founded and compensation considered just and equitable	EA 1980, s 2
Within 6 months of effective date of termination	Yes	Declaration as to rights and compensation for arrears of wages or damages in respect of period (maximum 2 years) before proceedings commenced	EqPA ss 2, 2A

Tribunal Table

No.	Nature of claim	Case brought by (applicant)	Case brought against (respondent)	Continuous service qualification
5	**Equal Pay (cont.d)**			
(b)	Determination as to the effect of an equality clause	Employer	Employee	As 5(a)
6	**Pregnancy and maternity rights**			
(a)	Refusal to allow time off with pay for ante-natal care	Employee	Employer	None
(b)	See also 16(a)			
(c)	Dismissal on grounds of pregnancy	Employee	Employer	One year (or two years if no more than 20 persons employed) at effective date of termination
(d)	Non-payment of whole or part of maternity pay	Employee	Employer	Two years at the 11th week before the expected week of confinement
(e)	See 16(g)			
(f)	Failure to pay correct rebate for maternity payments made	Employer	Secretary of State	Not applicable
(g)	Appeal against recovery by Secretary of State of unpaid maternity pay	Employer	As 6(f)	Not applicable

6 Period in which claim must be commenced	7 Conciliation available	8 Tribunal powers	9 Source of rules
As 5(a)	No	Declaration as to rights	EqPA s 2
Within 3 months of day of appointment concerned	Yes	Order for reinstatement or re-engagement and/or compensation up to £15,620	EPCA ss 60, 67–75; EA 1980, s 8
Within 3 months of the effective date of termination	Yes	Order for reinstatement or re-engagement and/or compensation up to £15,620	EPCA ss 60, 67–75; EA 1980, s 8
Within 3 months of last day of payment period	Yes	Compensation of $\frac{9}{10}$ of a week's pay (less maternity allowance) per week up to 6 weeks	EPCA ss 34–36
Within 3 months of date Secretary of State's decision is communicated	No	Declaration as to amount of rebate owed	EPCA ss 39, 43
As 6(f)	No	Declaration as to amount recoverable	EPCA ss 41, 43

Tribunal Table

1 No.	Nature of claim	2 Case brought by (applicant)	3 Case brought against (respondent)	4 Continuous service qualification
6	**Pregnancy and maternity rights (cont.d)**			
(h)	Failure to permit a woman to return to work after confinement	Employee	Employer	As 6(d)
7	**Sex discrimination (including marital status)**			
(a)	Complaint by individual suffering discrimination	Employee	Employer	None
(b)	Appeal against non-discrimination notice	Employer	EOC	Not applicable
(c)	Complaint of discrimination as preliminary action in a County Court case	EOC	Employer	Not applicable
8	**Race discrimination**			
(a)	Complaint by individual suffering discrimination	Employee	Employer	None
(b)	Appeal against non-discrimination notice	Employer	CRE	Not applicable
(c)	Complaint of discrimination as preliminary action in a County Court case	CRE	Employer	Not applicable

6	7	8	9
Period in which claim must be commenced	*Conciliation available*	*Tribunal powers*	*Source of rules*
Within 3 months of notified day of return	Yes	As 6(c)	EPCA ss 45–48, 56 and 2 Sch; EA 1980, ss 11, 12
Within 3 months of act complained about	Yes	Declaration of rights and/or compensation up to £7,500 (£19,390 if dismissed) and/or a recommendation to take action	SDA ss 63–65, 76
Within 6 weeks of notice being served	No	Uphold, quash or vary the notice	SDA s 67; SI 1977 No 1094
Within 6 months of act complained about	No	Declaration that complaint well founded and of rights of employee and/or a recommendation to take action	SDA ss 71, 73, 76
Within 3 months of act complained about	Yes	Declaration of rights and/or compensation up to £7,500 (£19,390 if dismissed) and/or a recommendation to take action	RRA ss 54–56, 68
Within 6 weeks of notice being served	No	Uphold, quash or vary the notice	RRA s 59; SI 1977 No 1094
Within 6 months of act complained about	No	Declaration that complaint well founded and of rights of employee and/or a recommendation to take action	RRA ss 62, 64, 68

Tribunal Table

No.	Nature of claim	Case brought by (applicant)	Case brought against (respondent)	Continuous service qualification
9	**Guarantee payments**			
(a)	Right to receive if not provided with work	Employee	Employer	One month (or 3 months if contract for a fixed term or specific task) by day before payment claimed
(b)	See also 16(a)			
10	**Suspension on medical grounds**			
(a)	Failure to pay while suspended	Employee	Employer	One month (or 3 months if contract for a fixed term or specific task) by day before suspension began
(b)	See also 16(a)			
11	**Time off for public duties**			
	Failure to permit	Employee	Employer	None
12	**Occupational pensions**			
(a)	Equal access for men and women	Employee	Employer	None
(b)	Failure to consult recognised independent trade union if employer contracting out	Trade union	Employer	Not applicable
(c)	See also 16(f)			

6 Period in which claim must be commenced	7 Conciliation available	8 Tribunal powers	9 Source of rules
Within 3 months of last day of lay-off	Yes	Compensation of up to £10 per day for a maximum of 5 days in any period of 3 months	EPCA ss 12–17; EA 1980, s 14 and 1 Sch; EA 1982, 2 Sch
Within 3 months of day of non-payment	Yes	Compensation of up to 26 weeks' pay	EPCA ss 19–22; EA 1982, 2 Sch
Within 3 months of date of failure	Yes	Declaration and compensation considered just and equitable	EPCA ss 29, 30
Not applicable	No	Declaration of right to be admitted to scheme	SSPA s 53; SI 1976 No 142, Reg 12
None	No	Declaration	SI 1975 No 1927, Reg 4

1 No.	2 Nature of claim	3 Case brought by (applicant)	4 Case brought against (respondent)	5 Continuous service qualification
13	**Health and safety**			
(a)	Failure to permit a safety representative appointed by a recognised independent trade union to take time off with pay	Safety representative	Employer	None
(b)	Appeal against improvement or prohibition notice	Person served with notice	Health and Safety Inspector	Not applicable
14	**Dismissal**			
(a)	Written statement of reasons for dismissal	Employee	Employer	6 months at effective date of termination
(b)	Unfair (see also 2(c), 2(d), 2(e), 3(b), 3(c), 6(b), 7(a), 8(a))	As 14(a)	As 14(a)	One year (or two years if no more than 20 persons employed) at effective date of termination
15	**Redundancy**			
(a)	Failure to permit time off with pay to look for work or make arrangements for training	Employee	Employer	Two years by time notice due to expire
(b)	See also 16(a)			
(c)	Determination of entitlement to and amount of redundancy payment	As 15(a)	As 15(a)	Two years at the relevant date of termination
(d)	Failure of Secretary of State to pay rebate	Employer	Secretary of State	Not applicable

6 Period in which claim must be commenced	7 Conciliation available	8 Tribunal powers	9 Source of rules
Within 3 months of date of failure	No	Declaration that complaint well founded and compensation considered just and equitable	HSWA s 2(4); SI 1977 No 500
Within 21 days of notice being served	No	Affirm, modify or cancel notice	HSWA ss 21–24; SI 1974 No 1925
Within 3 months of effective date of termination	Yes	Declaration as to reasons and 2 weeks' pay	EPCA s 53; EA 1982, 2 Sch
As 14(a)	As 14(a)	Order for reinstatement or re-engagement and for compensation up to £15,620	EPCA ss 54–55, 57, 59, 61–75; EA 1980, ss 6, 8, 9 and 1 Sch; EA 1982, ss 4–6 and 3 Sch
Within 3 months of day on which it is alleged time off should have been allowed	Yes	Declaration that complaint well founded and an amount not exceeding $\frac{2}{5}$ of a week's pay	EPCA s 31
Within 6 months of relevant date of termination	No	Declaration of right to and amount of payment (maximum £4,350)	EPCA ss 81–101; EA 1980, 2 Sch; EA 1982, 2 Sch
	No	Determination of eligibility to rebate and amount owed	EPCA ss 104–108; EA 1982, 2 Sch; Redundancy Rebate Regulations 1965, 1976

1 *No.*	*2* *Nature of claim*	*3* *Case brought by* *(applicant)*	*4* *Case brought against* *(respondent)*	*5* *Continuous service qualification*
15	**Redundancy (cont.d)**			
(e)	Failure to consult representatives of a recognised independent trade union about proposed dismissals	Trade union	Employer	Not applicable
(f)	Failure to pay protective award	Employee	Employer	Not applicable
(g)	See also 16(a)			
(h)	Reduction of rebate on failure to notify redundancies	Employer	Secretary of State	Not applicable
16	**Employer's insolvency**			
(a)	Secretary of State has failed to pay arrears of pay owed (which includes a guarantee payment, remuneration for suspension on medical grounds, a payment for time off, a protective award, a statutory sick payment)	Employee	Secretary of State	Not applicable
(b)	Secretary of State has failed to pay notice money owed	As 16(a)	As 16(a)	As 16(a)
(c)	Secretary of State has failed to pay holiday money	As 16(a)	As 16(a)	As 16(a)

6 *Period in which claim must be commenced*	7 *Conciliation available*	8 *Tribunal powers*	9 *Source of rules*
Within 3 months of date dismissal takes effect	Yes	Declaration that complaint well founded and a protective award re wages for a specified period (maximum 90 days) beginning with date of first dismissal or date of award	EPCA ss 99, 101; SI 1979 No 958
Within 3 months of date of failure to pay	Yes	Order to pay remuneration owed (maximum 90 days' pay)	EPA ss 102, 103
Within 3 months of date Secretary of State's decision is communicated	No	Determination of level of rebate	EPA s 104
Within 3 months of date Secretary of State's decision is communicated	No	Declaration of amount that should be paid (maximum £145 a week for up to 8 weeks)	EPCA ss 122, 124; EA 1982, 3 Sch; SSHBA 2 Sch
As 16(a)	As 16(a)	Declaration of amount that should be paid	EPCA ss 122, 124
As 16(a)	As 16(a)	Declaration of amount that should be paid (maximum £145 per week for up to 6 weeks)	EPCA ss 122, 124; EA 1982, 3 Sch

Tribunal Table

1 No.	Nature of claim	2 Case brought by (applicant)	3 Case brought against (respondent)	4 Continuous service qualification	5
16	**Employer's insolvency (cont.d)**				
(d)	Secretary of State has failed to pay basic award of compensation	As 16(a)	As 16(a)	As 16(a)	
(e)	Secretary of State has failed to reimburse fee or premium to apprentice or articled clerk	As 16(a)	As 16(a)	As 16(a)	
(f)	Secretary of State has failed to pay unpaid contributions to occupational pension scheme	A person competent to act in respect of a scheme	As 16(a)	As 16(a)	
(g)	Secretary of State has failed to make maternity payments where employer insolvent	As 16(a)	As 16(a)	Two years at 11th week before expected week of confinement	
17	**Industrial training board**				
	Appeal against levy assessment	Company or organisation	Industrial Training Board	Not applicable	

6 Period in which claim must be commenced	7 Conciliation available	8 Tribunal powers	9 Source of rules
As 16(a)	As 16(a)	As 16(b)	As 16(b)
As 16(a)	As 16(a)	As 16(b)	As 16(b)
As 16(a)	As 16(a)	As 16(b)	EPCA ss 123, 124; EA 1982, 3 Sch
As 16(a)	As 16(a)	As 16(b)	EPCA ss 40, 43
As stated in levy order	No	Confirm, increase, reduce or rescind assessment	ITA s 12

1980 No. 884

INDUSTRIAL TRIBUNALS

The Industrial Tribunals (Rules of Procedure) Regulations 1980

Made - - - -	*26th June* 1980
Laid before Parliament	*8th July* 1980
Coming into operation	*1st October* 1980

ARRANGEMENT OF REGULATIONS AND RULES

REGULATIONS
1. Citation, commencement and revocation.
2. Interpretation.
3. Proceedings of tribunals.
4. Proof of decisions of tribunals.

SCHEDULE 1— RULES OF PROCEDURE
1. Originating application.
2. Action upon receipt of originating application.
3. Appearance by respondent.
4. Power to require further particulars and attendance of witnesses and to grant discovery.
5. Time and place of hearing and appointment of assessor.
6. Pre-hearing assessment.
7. The hearing.
8. Procedure at hearing.
9. Decision of tribunal.
10. Review of tribunal's decisions.
11. Costs.
12. Miscellaneous powers of tribunal.
13. Extension of time and directions.
14. Joinder and representative respondents.
15. Consolidation of proceedings.
16. Transfer of proceedings.
17. Notices, etc.

SCHEDULE 2
Regulations revoked.

The Secretary of State in exercise of the powers conferred on him by paragraph 1 of Schedule 9 to the Employment Protection (Consolidation) Act 1978(**a**) and after consultation with the Council on Tribunals hereby makes the following Regulations:-

---

(**a**) 1978 c.44.

1.—(1) These Regulations may be cited as the Industrial Tribunals (Rules of Procedure) Regulations 1980 (and the Rules of Procedure contained in Schedule 1 to these Regulations may be referred to as the Industrial Tribunals Rules of Procedure 1980), and they shall come into operation on 1st October 1980.

(2) The Industrial Tribunals (Labour Relations) Regulations 1974(a) and the other Regulations mentioned in Schedule 2 to these Regulations shall cease to have effect on 1st October 1980 except in relation to proceedings instituted before that date.

Interpretation

2. In these Regulations, unless the context otherwise requires, the following expressions have the meanings hereby assigned to them respectively, that is to say—

"the 1966 Act" means the Docks and Harbours Act 1966(b);

"the 1978 Act" means the Employment Protection (Consolidation) Act 1978;

"applicant" means a person who in pursuance of Rule 1 has presented an originating application to the Secretary of the Tribunals for a decision of a tribunal and includes:-

(a) the Secretary of State, the Board or a licensing authority,

(b) a claimant or complainant,

(c) in the case of proceedings under section 51 of the 1966 Act, a person on whose behalf an originating application has been sent by a trade union, and

(d) in relation to interlocutory applications under these Rules, a person who seeks any relief;

"the Board" means the National Dock Labour Board as reconstituted under the Dock Work Regulation Act 1976(c);

"the clerk to the tribunal" means the person appointed by the Secretary of the Tribunals or an Assistant Secretary to act in that capacity at one or more hearings;

"court" means a magistrates' court or the Crown Court;

"decision" in relation to a tribunal includes a declaration, an order (other than an interlocutory order), a recommendation or an award of the tribunal but does not include an opinion given pursuant to a pre-hearing assessment held under Rule 6;

"hearing" means a sitting of a tribunal duly constituted for the purpose of receiving evidence, hearing addresses and witnesses or doing anything lawfully requisite to enable the tribunal to reach a decision on any question;

"licensing authority" means a body having the function of issuing licences under the 1966 Act;

"the Office of the Tribunals" means the Central Office of the Industrial Tribunals (England and Wales);

"the panel of chairmen" means the panel of persons, being barristers or solicitors of not less than seven years' standing, appointed by the Lord

---

(a) S.I. 1974/1386, amended by S.I. 1976/661, S.I. 1977/911 and S.I. 1978/991.
(b) 1966 c.28.   (c)1976 c.79.

Chancellor in pursuance of Regulation 5 (2) of the Industrial Tribunals (England and Wales) Regulations 1965(a);

"party" in relation to proceedings under section 51 of the 1966 Act means the applicant and the Board or the licensing authority with which or (as the case may be) any person with whom it appears to the applicant that he is in dispute about a question to which that section applies and, in a case where such a question is referred to a tribunal by a court, any party to the proceedings before the court in which the question arose;

"person entitled to appear" in relation to proceedings under section 51 of the 1966 Act means a party and any person who, under subsection (5) of that section, is entitled to appear and be heard before a tribunal in such proceedings;

"the President" means the President of the Industrial Tribunals (England and Wales) or the person nominated by the Lord Chancellor to discharge for the time being the functions of the President;

"Regional Chairman" means the chairman appointed by the President to take charge of the due administration of justice by tribunals in an area specified by the President, or a person nominated either by the President or the Regional Chairman to discharge for the time being the functions of the Regional Chairman;

"Regional Office of the Industrial Tribunals" means a regional office which has been established under the Office of the Tribunals for an area specified by the President;

"Register" means the Register of Applications and Decisions kept in pursuance of these Regulations;

"respondent" means a party to the proceedings before a tribunal other than the applicant, and other than the Secretary of State in proceedings under Parts III and VI of the 1978 Act in which he is not cited as the person against whom relief is sought;

"Rule" means a Rule of Procedure contained in Schedule 1 to these Regulations;

"the Secretary of the Tribunals" and "an Assistant Secretary of the Tribunals" mean repectively the persons for the time being acting as the Secretary of the Office of the Tribunals and as the Assistant Secretary of a Regional Office of the Industrial Tribunals;

"tribunal" means an industrial tribunal (England and Wales) established in pursuance of the Industrial Tribunals (England and Wales) Regulations 1965 and in relation to any proceedings means the tribunal to which the proceedings have been referred by the President or a Regional Chairman.

Proceedings of tribunals

3. Except where separate Rules of Procedure, made under the provisions of any enactment, are applicable the Rules of Procedure contained in Schedule 1 to these Regulations shall have effect in relation to all proceedings before a tribunal where:—

(a) the respondent or one of the respondents resides or carries on business in England or Wales; or

(b) had the remedy been by way of action in the county court, the cause of action would have arisen wholly or in part in England or Wales; or

(a) S.I. 1965/1101 as amended by S.I. 1967/301.

(c) the proceedings are to determine a question which has been referred to the tribunal by a court in England or Wales; or

(d) in proceedings under the 1966 Act they are in relation to a port in England or Wales.

Proof of decisions of tribunals

4. The production in any proceedings in any court of a document purporting to be certified by the Secretary of the Tribunals to be a true copy of an entry of a decision in the Register shall, unless the contrary is proved, be sufficient evidence of the document and of the facts stated therein.

26th June 1980.

James Prior,
Secretary of State for Employment.

SCHEDULE 1

RULES OF PROCEDURE

Originating application

1.—(1) Proceedings for the determination of any matter by a tribunal shall be instituted by the applicant (or, where applicable, by a court) presenting to the Secretary of the Tribunals an originating application which shall be in writing and shall set out:—

(*a*) the name and address of the applicant; and

(*b*) the names and addresses of the person or persons against whom relief is sought or (where applicable) of the parties to the proceedings before the court; and

(*c*) the grounds, with particulars thereof, on which relief is sought, or in proceedings under section 51 of the 1966 Act the question for determination and (except where the question is referred by a court) the grounds on which relief is sought.

(2) Where the Secretary of the Tribunals is of the opinion that the originating application does not seek or on the facts stated therein cannot entitle the applicant to a relief which a tribunal has power to give, he may give notice to that effect to the applicant stating the reasons for his opinion and informing him that the application will not be registered unless he states in writing that he wishes to proceed with it.

(3) An application as respects which a notice has been given in pursuance of the preceding paragraph shall not be treated as having been received for the purposes of Rule 2 unless the applicant intimates in writing to the Secretary of the Tribunals that he wishes to proceed with it; and upon receipt of such an intimation the Secretary of the Tribunals shall proceed in accordance with that Rule.

Action upon receipt of originating application

2. Upon receiving an originating application the Secretary of the Tribunals shall enter particulars of it in the Register and shall forthwith send a copy of it to the respondent and inform the parties in writing of the case number of the originating application entered in the Register (which shall thereafter constitute the title of the proceedings) and of the address to which notices and other communications to the Secretary of the Tribunals shall be sent. Every copy of the originating application sent by the Secretary of the Tribunals under this paragraph shall be accompanied by a written notice which shall include information, as appropriate to the case, about the means and time for entering an appearance, the consequences of failure to do so, and the right to receive a copy of the decision. The Secretary of the Tribunals shall also notify the parties that in all cases under the provisions of any enactment providing for conciliation the services of a conciliation officer are available to them.

Appearance by respondent

3.—(1) A respondent shall within 14 days of receiving the copy originating application enter an appearance to the proceedings by presenting to the Secretary of the Tribunals a written notice of appearance setting out his full name and address and stating whether or not he intends to resist the application and, if so, setting out sufficient particulars to show on what grounds. Upon receipt of a notice of appearance the Secretary of the Tribunals shall forthwith send a copy of it to any other party.

5

(2) A respondent who has not entered an appearance shall not be entitled to take any part in the proceedings except—

    (*i*) to apply under Rule 13(1) for an extension of the time appointed by this Rule for entering an appearance;

    (*ii*) to make an application under Rule 4(1)(*i*);

    (*iii*) to make an application under Rule 10(2) in respect of Rule 10(1)(b);

    (*iv*) to be called as a witness by another person;

    (*v*) to be sent a copy of a decision or specification of reasons or corrected decision or specification in pursuance of Rule 9(3), 9(7) or 10(5).

(3) A notice of appearance which is presented to the Secretary of the Tribunals after the time appointed by this Rule for entering appearances shall be deemed to include an application under Rule 13(1) (by the respondent who has presented the notice of appearance) for an extension of the time so appointed. Without prejudice to Rule 13(4), if the tribunal grants the application (which it may do notwithstanding that the grounds of the application are not stated) the Secretary of the Tribunals shall forthwith send a copy of the notice of appearance to any other party. The tribunal shall not refuse an extension of time under this Rule unless it has sent notice to the person wishing to enter an appearance giving him an opportunity to show cause why the extension should be granted.

Power to require further particulars and attendance of witnesses and to grant discovery

4.—(1) A tribunal may—

    (*a*) subject to Rule 3(2), on the application of a party to the proceedings made either by notice to the Secretary of the Tribunals or at the hearing of the originating application, or

    (*b*) in relation to sub-paragraph (*i*) of this paragraph, if it thinks fit of its own motion—

        (*i*) require a party to furnish in writing to the person specified by the tribunal further particulars of the grounds on which he or it relies and of any facts and contentions relevant thereto;

        (*ii*) grant to the person making the application such discovery or inspection (including the taking of copies) of documents as might be granted by a county court; and

        (*iii*) require the attendance of any person (including a party to the proceedings) as a witness or require the production of any document relating to the matter to be determined, wherever such witness may be within Great Britain;

and may appoint the time at or within which or the place at which any act required in pursuance of this Rule is to be done.

(2) A party on whom a requirement has been made under paragraph (1)(*i*) or (1)(*ii*) of this Rule on an *ex parte* application, or (in relation to a requirement under paragraph 1(*i*)) on the tribunal's own motion, and a person on whom a requirement has been made under paragraph (1)(*iii*) may apply to the tribunal by notice to the Secretary of the Tribunals before the appointed time at or within which the requirement is to be complied with to vary or set aside the requirement. Notice of an application under this paragraph to vary or set aside a requirement shall be given to the parties (other than the party making the application) and, where appropriate, in proceedings which may involve payments out of the Redundancy Fund or Maternity Pay Fund, the Secretary of State if not a party.

(3) Every document containing a requirement under paragraph (1)(*ii*) or (1)(*iii*) of this Rule shall contain a reference to the fact that under paragraph 1(7) of Schedule 9 to the 1978 Act, any person who without reasonable excuse fails to comply with any such requirement shall be liable on summary conviction to a fine not exceeding £100.

(4) If the requirement under paragraph (1)(*i*) or (1)(*ii*) of this Rule is not complied with, a tribunal, before or at the hearing, may dismiss the originating application, or, as the case may be, strike out the whole or part of the notice of appearance, and, where appropriate, direct that a respondent shall be debarred from defending altogether: Provided that a tribunal shall not so dismiss or strike out or give such a direction unless it has sent notice to the party who has not complied with the requirement giving him an opportunity to show cause why such should not be done.

Time and place of hearing and appointment of assessor

5.—(1) The President or a Regional Chairman shall fix the date, time and place of the hearing of the originating application and the Secretary of the Tribunals shall (subject to Rule 3(2)) not less than 14 days (or such shorter time as may be agreed by him with the parties) before the date so fixed send to each party a notice of hearing which shall include information and guidance as to attendance at the hearing, witnesses and the bringing of documents (if any), representation by another person and written representations.

(2) In any proceedings under the 1966 Act in which the President or a Regional Chairman so directs, the Secretary of the Tribunals shall also take such of the following steps as may be so directed, namely—

(*a*) publish in one or more newspapers circulating in the locality in which the port in question is situated notice of the hearing;

(*b*) send notice of the hearing to such persons as may be directed;

(*c*) post notices of the hearing in a conspicuous place or conspicuous places in or near the port in question;

but the requirement as to the period of notice contained in paragraph (1) of this Rule shall not apply to any such notices.

(3) Where in the case of any proceedings it is provided for one or more assessors to be appointed, the President or a Regional Chairman may, if he thinks fit, appoint a person or persons having special knowledge or experience in relation to the subject matter of the originating application to sit with the tribunal as assessor or assessors.

Pre-hearing assessment

6.—(1) A tribunal may at any time before the hearing (either, subject to Rule 3(2), on the application of a party to the proceedings made by notice to the Secretary of the Tribunals or of its own motion) consider, by way of a pre-hearing assessment, the contents of the originating application and entry of appearance, any representations in writing which have been submitted and any oral argument advanced by or on behalf of a party.

(2) If upon a pre-hearing assessment, the tribunal considers that the originating application is unlikely to succeed or that the contentions or any particular contention of a party appear to have no reasonable prospect of success, it may indicate that in its opinion, if the originating application shall not be withdrawn or the contentions or contention of the party shall be persisted in up to or at the hearing, the party in question may have an order for costs made against him at the hearing under the provisions of Rule 11. A pre-hearing assessment shall not take place unless the tribunal has sent notice to the parties

to the proceedings giving them (and, where appropriate, in proceedings which may involve payments out of the Redundancy Fund or Maternity Pay Fund, the Secretary of State, if not a party) an opportunity to submit representations in writing and to advance oral argument at the pre-hearing assessment if they so wish.

(3) Any indication of opinion made in accordance with paragraph (2) of this Rule shall be recorded in a document signed by the chairman a copy of which shall be sent to the parties to the proceedings and a copy of which shall be available to the tribunal at the hearing.

(4) Where a tribunal has indicated its opinion in accordance with paragraph (2) of this Rule no member thereof shall be a member of the tribunal at the hearing.

The hearing

7.—(1) Any hearing of or in connection with an originating application shall take place in public unless in the opinion of the tribunal a private hearing is appropriate for the purpose of hearing evidence which relates to matters of such a nature that it would be against the interests of national security to allow the evidence to be given in public or hearing evidence from any person which in the opinion of the tribunal is likely to consist of—

(*a*) information which he could not disclose without contravening a prohibition imposed by or under any enactment; or

(*b*) any information which has been communicated to him in confidence, or which he has otherwise obtained in consequence of the confidence reposed in him by another person; or

(*c*) information the disclosure of which would cause substantial injury to any undertaking of his or any undertaking in which he works for reasons other than its effect on negotiations with respect to any of the matters mentioned in section 29(1) of the Trade Union and Labour Relations Act 1974(**a**).

(2) A member of the Council on Tribunals shall be entitled to attend any hearing taking place in private in his capacity as such member.

(3) Subject to Rule 3(2), if a party shall desire to submit representations in writing for consideration by a tribunal at the hearing of the originating application that party shall present such representations to the Secretary of the Tribunals not less than 7 days before the hearing and shall at the same time send a copy to the other party or parties.

(4) Where a party has failed to attend or be represented at the hearing (whether or not he has sent any representations in writing) the contents of his originating application or, as the case may be, of his entry of appearance may be treated by a tribunal as representations in writing.

(5) The Secretary of State if he so elects shall be entitled to apply under Rule 4(1), 13(1) and (2), 15 and 16(1) and to appear as if he were a party and be heard at any hearing of or in connection with an originating application in proceedings in which he is not a party which may involve payments out of the Redundancy Fund or Maternity Pay Fund.

(6) Subject to Rule 3(2), at any hearing of or in connection with an originating application a party and any person entitled to appear may appear before the tribunal and may be heard in person or be represented by counsel or by a solicitor or by a representative of a trade union or an employers' association or by any other person whom he desires to represent him.

(a) 1974 c.52.

Procedure at hearing

8.—(1) The tribunal shall conduct the hearing in such manner as it considers most suitable to the clarification of the issues before it and generally to the just handling of the proceedings; it shall so far as appears to it appropriate seek to avoid formality in its proceedings and it shall not be bound by any enactment or rule of law relating to the admissibility of evidence in proceedings before the courts of law.

(2) Subject to paragraph (1) of this Rule, at the hearing of the originating application a party (unless disentitled by virtue of Rule 3(2)), the Secretary of State, (if, not being a party, he elects to appear as provided in Rule 7(5)) and any other person entitled to appear shall be entitled to give evidence, to call witnesses, to question any witnesses and to address the tribunal.

(3) If a party shall fail to appear or to be represented at the time and place fixed for the hearing, the tribunal may, if that party is an applicant dismiss, or, in any case, dispose of the application in the absence of that party or may adjourn the hearing to a later date: Provided that before deciding to dismiss or disposing of any application in the absence of a party the tribunal shall consider any representations submitted by that party in pursuance of Rule 7(3).

(4) A tribunal may require any witness to give evidence on oath or affirmation and for that purpose there may be administered an oath or affirmation in due form.

Decision of tribunal

9.—(1) A decision of a tribunal may be taken by a majority thereof and, if the tribunal shall be constituted of two members only, the chairman shall have a second or casting vote.

(2) The decision of a tribunal shall be recorded in a document signed by the chairman which shall contain the reasons for the decision.

(3) The clerk to the tribunal shall transmit the document signed by the chairman to the Secretary of the Tribunals who shall as soon as may be enter it in the Register and shall send a copy of the entry to each of the parties and to the persons entitled to appear who did so appear and, where the originating application was sent to a tribunal by a court, to that court.

(4) The specification of the reasons for the decision shall be omitted from the Register in any case in which evidence has been heard in private and the tribunal so directs and in that event a specification of the reasons shall be sent to the parties and to any superior court in any proceedings relating to such decision together with the copy of the entry.

(5) The Register shall be kept at the Office of the Tribunals and shall be open to the inspection of any person without charge at all reasonable hours.

(6) Clerical mistakes in documents recording the tribunal's decisions, or errors arising in them from an accidental slip or omission, may at any time be corrected by the chairman by certificate under his hand.

(7) The clerk to the tribunal shall send a copy of any document so corrected and the certificate of the chairman to the Secretary of the Tribunals who shall as soon as may be make such correction as may be necessary in the Register and shall send a copy of the corrected entry or of the corrected specification of the reasons, as the case may be, to each of the parties and to the persons entitled to appear who did so appear and, where the originating application was sent to the tribunal by a court, to that court.

(8) If any decision is—

    (*a*) corrected under paragraph (6) of this Rule,

(*b*) reviewed, revoked or varied under Rule 10, or

(*c*) altered in any way by order of a superior court,

the Secretary of the Tribunals shall alter the entry in the Register to conform with any such certificate or order and shall send a copy of the new entry to each of the parties and to the persons entitled to appear who did so appear and where the originating application was sent to the tribunal by a court, to that court.

Review of tribunal's decisions

10.—(1) A tribunal shall have power to review and to revoke or vary by certificate under the chairman's hand any decision on the grounds that—

(*a*) the decision was wrongly made as a result of an error on the part of the tribunal staff; or

(*b*) a party did not receive notice of the proceedings leading to the decision; or

(*c*) the decision was made in the absence of a party or person entitled to be heard; or

(*d*) new evidence has become available since the making of the decision provided that its existence could not have been reasonably known of or foreseen; or

(*e*) the interests of justice require such a review.

(2) An application for the purposes of paragraph (1) of this Rule may be made at the hearing. If the application is not made at the hearing, such application shall be made the the Secretary of the Tribunals at any time from the date of the hearing until 14 days after the date on which the decision was sent to the parties and must be in writing stating the grounds in full.

(3) An application for the purposes of paragraph (1) of this Rule may be refused by the President or by the chairman of the tribunal which decided the case or by a Regional Chairman if in his opinion it has no reasonable prospect of success.

(4) If such an application is not refused under paragraph (3) of this Rule it shall be heard by the tribunal which decided the case or—

(*a*) where it is not practicable for it to be heard by that tribunal, or

(*b*) where the decision was made by a chairman acting alone under Rule 12(4),

by a tribunal appointed either by the President or a Regional Chairman, and if it is granted the tribunal shall either vary the decision or revoke the decision and order a re-hearing.

(5) The clerk to the tribunal shall send to the Secretary of the Tribunals the certificate of the chairman as to any revocation or variation of the tribunal's decision under this Rule. The Secretary of the Tribunals shall as soon as may be make such correction as may be necessary in the Register and shall send a copy of the entry to each of the parties and to the persons entitled to appear who did so appear and where the originating application was sent to a tribunal by a court, to that court.

Costs

11.—(1) Subject to paragraphs (2), (3) and (4) of this Rule, a tribunal shall not normally make an award in respect of the costs or expenses incurred by a party to the proceedings but where in its opinion a party (and if he is a respondent whether or not he has entered an appearance) has in bringing or conducting the proceedings acted frivolously, vexatiously or otherwise unreasonably the tribunal may make—

(*a*) an order that that party shall pay to another party (or to the Secretary of State, if, not being a party, he has acted as provided in Rule 7(5)) either a specified sum in respect of the costs or expenses incurred by that other party (or, as the case may be, by the Secretary of State) or the whole or part of those costs or expenses as taxed (if not otherwise agreed);

(*b*) an order that that party shall pay to the Secretary of State the whole, or any part, of any allowances (other than allowances paid to members of tribunals or assessors) paid by the Secretary of State under paragraph 10 of Schedule 9 to the 1978 Act to any person for the purposes of, or in connection with, his attendance at the tribunal.

(2) Where the tribunal has on the application of a party to the proceedings postponed the day or time fixed for or adjourned the hearing, the tribunal may make orders against or, as the case may require, in favour of that party as at paragraph (1)(*a*) and (*b*) of this Rule as respects any costs or expenses incurred or any allowances paid by that party as a result of the postponement or adjournment.

(3) Where, on a complaint of unfair dismissal in respect of which—

(*i*) the applicant has expressed a wish to be reinstated or re-engaged which has been communicated to the respondent at least 7 days before the hearing of the complaint, or

(*ii*) the proceedings arise out of the respondent's failure to permit the applicant to return to work after an absence due to pregnancy or confinement,

any postponement or adjournment of the hearing has been caused by the respondent's failure, without a special reason, to adduce reasonable evidence as to the availability of the job from which the applicant was dismissed, or, as the case may be, which she held before her absence, or of comparable or suitable employment, the tribunal shall make orders against that respondent as at paragraph (1)(*a*) and (*b*) of this Rule as respects any costs or expenses incurred or any allowances paid as a result of the postponement or adjournment.

(4) In any proceedings under the 1966 Act a tribunal may make—

(*a*) an order that a party, or any other person entitled to appear who did so appear, shall pay to another party or such person either a specified sum in respect of the costs or expenses incurred by that other party or person or the whole or part of those costs or expenses as taxed (if not otherwise agreed);

(*b*) an order that a party, or any other person entitled to appear who did so appear, shall pay to the Secretary of State a specified sum in respect of the whole, or any part, of any allowances (other than allowances paid to members of tribunals) paid by the Secretary of State under paragraph 10 of Schedule 9 to the 1978 Act to any person for the purpose of, or in connection with, his attendance at the tribunal.

(5) Any costs required by an order under this Rule to be taxed may be taxed in the county court according to such of the scales prescribed by the county court rules for proceedings in the county court as shall be directed by the order.

Miscellaneous powers of tribunal

12.—(1) Subject to the provisions of these Rules, a tribunal may regulate its own procedure.

(2) A tribunal may, if it thinks fit,—

(*a*) extend the time appointed by or under these Rules for doing any act notwithstanding that the time appointed may have expired;

(*b*) postpone the day or time fixed for, or adjourn, any hearing (particularly as respects cases under the provisions of any enactment providing for conciliation for the purpose of giving an opportunity for the complaint to be settled by way of conciliation and withdrawn);

(*c*) if the applicant shall at any time give notice of the withdrawal of his originating application, dismiss the proceedings;

(*d*) except in proceedings under the 1966 Act, if both or all the parties (and the Secretary of State, if, not being a party, he has acted as provided in Rule 7(5)) agree in writing upon the terms of a decision to be made by the tribunal, decide accordingly;

(*e*) at any stage of the proceedings order to be struck out or amended any originating application or notice of appearance or anything in such application or notice of appearance on the grounds that it is scandalous, frivolous or vexatious;

(*f*) on the application of the respondent, or of its own motion, order to be struck out any originating application for want of prosecution; Provided that before making any order under (*e*) or (*f*) above the tribunal shall send notice to the party against whom it is proposed that any such order should be made giving him an opportunity to show cause why such an order should not be made.

(3) Subject to Rule 4(2), a tribunal may, if it thinks fit, before granting an application under Rule 4 or Rule 13 require the party (or, as the case may be, the Secretary of State) making the application to give notice of it to the other party or parties. The notice shall give particulars of the application and indicate the address to which and the time within which any objection to the application shall be made being an address and time specified for the purposes of the application by the tribunal.

(4) Any act other than the holding of a pre-hearing assessment under Rule 6, the hearing of an originating application, or the making of an order under Rule 10(1), required or authorised by these Rules to be done by a tribunal may be done by, or on the direction of, the President or the chairman of the tribunal, or any chairman being a member of the panel of chairmen.

(5) Rule 11 shall apply to an order dismissing proceedings under paragraph (2)(c) of this Rule.

(6) Any functions of the Secretary of the Tribunals other than that mentioned in Rule 1(2) may be performed by an Assistant Secretary of the Tribunals.

Extension of time and directions

13.—(1) An application to a tribunal for an extension of the time appointed by these Rules for doing any act may be made by a party either before or after the expiration of any time so appointed.

(2) Subject to Rule 3(2), a party may at any time apply to a tribunal for directions on any matter arising in connection with the proceedings.

(3) An application under the foregoing provisions of this Rule shall be made by presenting to the Secretary of the Tribunals a notice of application, which shall state the title of the proceedings and shall set out the grounds of the application.

(4) The Secretary of the Tribunals shall give notice to both or all the parties (subject to Rule 3(2)) of any extension of time granted under Rule 12(2)(*a*) or any directions given in pursuance of this Rule.

Joinder and representative respondents

14.—(1) A tribunal may at any time either upon the application of any person or, where appropriate of its own motion, direct any person against whom any relief is sought to be joined as a party to the proceedings, and give such consequential directions as it considers necessary.

(2) A tribunal may likewise, either upon such application or of its own motion, order that any respondent named in the originating application or subsequently added, who shall appear to the tribunal not to have been, or to have ceased to be, directly interested in the subject of the originating application, be dismissed from the proceedings.

(3) Where there are numerous persons having the same interest in an originating application, one or more of them may be cited as the person or persons against whom relief is sought, or may be authorised by the tribunal, before or at the hearing, to defend on behalf of all the persons so interested.

Consolidation of proceedings

15. Where there are pending before the industrial tribunals two or more originating applications, then, if at any time upon the application of a party or of its own motion it appears to a tribunal that—

(*a*) some common question of law or fact arises in both or all the originating applications, or

(*b*) the relief claimed therein is in respect of or arises out of the same set of facts, or

(*c*) for some other reason it is desirable to make an order under this Rule,

the tribunal may order that some (as specified in the order) or all of the originating applications shall be considered together, and may give such consequential directions as may be necessary: Provided that the tribunal shall not make an order under this Rule without sending notice to all parties concerned giving them an opportunity to show cause why such an order should not be made.

Transfer of proceedings

16.—(1) Where there is pending before the industrial tribunals an originating application in respect of which it appears to the President or a Regional Chairman that the proceedings could be determined by an industrial tribunal (Scotland) established in pursuance of the Industrial Tribunals (Scotland) Regulations 1965(**a**) and that the originating application would more conveniently be determined by such a tribunal, the President or a Regional Chairman may, at any time upon the application of a party or of his own motion, with the consent of the President of the Industrial Tribunals (Scotland), direct that the said proceedings be transferred to the Office of the Industrial Tribunals (Scotland). Provided that no such direction shall be made unless notice has been sent to all parties concerned giving them an opportunity to show cause why such a direction should not be made.

(2) Where proceedings have been transferred to the Office of the Industrial Tribunals (England and Wales) under Rule 16(1) of the Industrial Tribunals (Rules of Procedure) (Scotland) Regulations 1980(**b**) they shall be treated as if in all respects they had been commenced by an originating application pursuant to Rule 1.

(a) S.I. 1965/1157.   (b) S.I. 1980/885.

Notices, etc.

17.—(1) Any notice given under these Rules shall be in writing.

(2) All notices and documents required by these Rules to be presented to the Secretary of the Tribunals may be presented at the Office of the Tribunals or such other office as may be notified by the Secretary of the Tribunals to the parties.

(3) All notices and documents required or authorised by these Rules to be sent or given to any person hereinafter mentioned may be sent by post (subject to paragraph (5) of this Rule) or delivered to or at—

(*a*) in the case of a notice or document directed to the Secretary of the State in proceedings to which he is not a party, the offices of the Department of Employment at Caxton House, Tothill Street, London SW1H 9NA or such other office as may be notified by the Secretary of State;

(*b*) in the case of a notice or document directed to the Board, the principal office of the Board;

(*c*) in the case of a notice or document directed to a court, the office of the clerk of the court;

(*d*) in the case of a notice or document directed to a party:—

(*i*) his address for service specified in the originating application or in a notice of appearance or in a notice under paragraph (4) of this Rule; or

(*ii*) if no address for service has been so specified, his last known address or place of business in the United Kingdom or, if the party is a corporation, the corporation's registered or principal office in the United Kingdom or, in any case, at such address or place outside the United Kingdom as the President or a Regional Chairman may allow;

(*e*) in the case of a notice or document directed to any person (other than a person specified in the foregoing provisions of this paragraph), his address or place of business in the United Kingdom, or if such a person is a corporation, the corporation's registered or principal office in the United Kingdom;

and if sent or given to the authorised representative of a party shall be deemed to have been sent or given to that party.

(4) A party may at any time by notice to the Secretary of the Tribunals and to the other party or parties (and, where appropriate, to the appropriate conciliation officer) change his address for service under these Rules.

(5) The recorded delivery service shall be used instead of the ordinary post:—

(*a*) when a second set of documents or notices is to be sent to a respondent who has not entered an appearance under Rule 3(1);

(*b*) for service of an order made under Rule 4(1)(*iii*) requiring the attendance of a witness or the production of a document.

(6) Where for any sufficient reason service of any document or notice cannot be effected in the manner prescribed under this Rule, the President or a Regional Chairman may make an order for substituted service in such manner as he may deem fit and such service shall have the same effect as service in the manner prescribed under this Rule.

14

(7) In proceedings brought under the provisions of any enactment providing for conciliation the Secretary of the Tribunals shall send copies of all documents and notices to a conciliation officer who in the opinion of the Secretary is an appropriate officer to receive them.

(8) In proceedings which may involve payments out of the Redundancy Fund or Maternity Pay Fund, the Secretary of the Tribunals shall, where appropriate, send copies of all documents and notices to the Secretary of State notwithstanding the fact that he may not be a party to such proceedings.

(9) In proceedings under the Equal Pay Act 1970(a), the Sex Discrimination Act 1975(b) or the Race Relations Act 1976(c) the Secretary of the Tribunals shall send to the Equal Opportunities Commission or, as the case may be, the Commission for Racial Equality copies of all documents sent to the parties under Rule 9(3), (7) and (8) and Rule 10(5).

(a) 1970 c.41.   (b) 1975 c.65.
(c) 1976 c.74.

SCHEDULE 2

REGULATIONS REVOKED

Statutory Instrument	Title	Extent of revocation
1974/1386	The Industrial Tribunals (Labour Relations) Regulations 1974	The whole Regulations except as respects proceedings instituted before 1st October, 1980.
1976/661	The Industrial Tribunals (Labour Relations) (Amendment) Regulations 1976	
1977/911	The Industrial Tribunals (Labour Relations) (Amendment) Regulations 1977	
1978/991	The Industrial Tribunals (Labour Relations) (Amendment) Regulations 1978	

EXPLANATORY NOTE

(This Note is not part of the Regulations.)

These Regulations regulate the procedure of industrial tribunals for England and Wales in relation to all proceedings instituted on or after 1st October 1980 except those where separate Rules of Procedure, made under the provisions of any enactment, are applicable (there are currently separate Rules of Procedure in relation to proceedings brought under the Industrial Training Act 1964 (industrial training levy appeals), the Health and Safety at Work etc. Act 1974 (improvement and prohibition notices appeals) and the Sex Discrimination Act 1975 and Race Relations Act 1976 (non-discrimination notices appeals)).

These Regulations are in place of the Industrial Tribunals (Labour Relations) Regulations 1974 as amended.

Appendix C

The New Equal Pay Procedures

Background

C.1 In 1982 the European Court of Justice decided that the UK had failed to implement the EEC Council Directive (75/117/EEC) on equal pay for equal work. The British government was obliged, therefore, to introduce amendments to the EqPA, (Equal Pay (Amendment) Regulations 1983, SI 1983 No 1794), to comply with EEC law, which came into force on 1 January 1984.

Previously a woman (or a man) could obtain pay equal to the pay of a worker of the other sex where:

two employees were employed on 'like work' in the same employment [*EqPA s 1(2)(a), (4)*]; and/or

they were employed on work 'rated as equivalent' [*EqPA s 1(2)(b), (5)*].

Where an employee, however, was paid less than an employee of the other sex for 'unlike' or dissimilar work of equal value, the EqPA gave no remedy unless their work had been rated as equivalent under a job evaluation scheme. For example, if a female personnel manager was doing work of equal value to the work done by a male production manager and was receiving less pay, she could not obtain equal pay unless either the work was 'like work', i.e. of the same or a broadly similar nature, or the work had been rated as equivalent through a job evaluation scheme. This is the 'equal value' gap which the UK was obliged to fill by amending legislation. In addition, it was necessary to ensure that overt or hidden sex discrimination in job evaluation schemes could be challenged by judicial process.

The new legislation creates special new procedures for taking and defending an equal value claim. The Industrial Tribunals (Rules of Procedure) (Equal Value Amendment) Regulations 1983 (SI 1983 No 1807) which amend the 1980 Regulations are printed in full at the back of this Appendix.

The new procedures

C.2 The procedure in 'like work and work rated as equivalent' claims is similar to that outlined in the body of this book. Some parts of the procedure in equal value claims are the same.

The early procedure described in Part I relating to bringing a claim (Chapters 1, 2, 3, 4 and 5), defending a claim (Chapters 6, 7, 8 and 9), deciding on representation (Chapter 10), knowing the other side's case (Chapter 13), pre-hearing assessments (Chapter 14), ACAS conciliation (Chapter 20) and notice of the hearing (Chapter 18) are all similar.

This is, however, where the similarity ends. There are something like eight definite stages in a normal tribunal case. With equal value claims there are thirteen, including five possible preliminary hearings. In this Appendix the term 'preliminary hearing' is used in the context of a hearing which takes place prior to the full hearing, whether or not it can result in a decision which avoids a full hearing (cf. the preliminary hearing described in Chapter 19). The new Regulations provide the following **additional** procedure, considered in C.3–C.13 below, which will usually be taken by the same tribunal.

Adjournment (Rule 12(2A))

C.3   The tribunal must invite the parties to apply for an adjournment for the purpose of seeking to reach a settlement, and must, if they agree to this course, grant the adjournment, usually to a specified date.

Preliminary hearing 1: reasonable grounds (Rule 7A(1))

C.4   The tribunal must be satisfied that there are reasonable grounds for determining that the work is of equal value. [*EqPA s 2A(1)(a)*]. If the tribunal decides that there are no reasonable grounds for the claim, then they will dismiss the application at this stage. Either the employer can apply for, or the tribunal can on its own initiative require, this first preliminary hearing and the employee must be given a chance to be heard on the issue.

An employer is likely to apply for such a preliminary hearing where the two jobs have already been evaluated under a job evaluation scheme as unequal. [*EqPA s 2A(2)*]. The first IT case under this hearing suggests that the employee will have to show that the study was discriminatory for the case to proceed. (*Neil and others v Ford Motor Co Ltd, 11 June 1984; COIT 1545/117, IRLIB 260.13*).

Preliminary hearing 2: material factor (Rule 8(2E))

C.5   An employer may apply at this stage for a determination by the tribunal of whether the variation in pay is genuinely due to a material factor which is not a difference of sex. Even if the tribunal makes a preliminary finding that there is a material factor defence (MFD), the employee can still insist on the claim proceeding, although there could be a risk of costs being awarded against her/him if the defence was ultimately upheld (Rule 11(1)(1A)). It is thought that the tribunal has power to defer consideration of the matter until a later stage when the facts would be more fully known.

Preliminary hearing 3: referral to expert (Rule 7A(1))

C.6   Unless the claim has been settled, or the tribunal is satisfied there are no reasonable grounds for determining that the work is of equal value, the tribunal must then require an expert to prepare a report on the question. Meanwhile, the hearing is adjourned pending the receipt of the report (Rule 7A(4)). The expert is drawn from a panel nominated by ACAS.

The tribunal's requirement to the expert must be in writing and must set out:

(*a*) the names and addresses of the parties;

(*b*) the address of the establishment at which the woman (or man) is or was employed;

(*c*) the question to be determined; and

(*d*) the identity of the person with the job claimed to be of equal value.

(Rule 7A(2)).

It must also stipulate that the expert shall:

(*e*) take account of all such information supplied and all such representations made to him as have a bearing on the question;

(*f*) before drawing up his report, produce and send to the parties a written summary of the said information and representations and invite the representations of the parties upon the material contained therein;

(*g*) make his report to the tribunal in a document which shall reproduce the summary and contain a brief account of any representations received from the parties upon it, any conclusion he may have reached upon the question and the reasons for that conclusion, or as the case may be, for his failure to reach such a conclusion;

(*h*) take no account of the difference of sex and at all times act fairly.

(Rule 7A(3)).

Copies of the tribunal's requirement will be sent to the parties. The expert is likely to interview both sides and take evidence from them. This will involve details of job descriptions, working conditions and so on. There is no provision, however, whereby the expert can gain access to the workplace against the employer's wishes.

The expert has no direct authority over the parties, but under Rule 4(1A) may apply to the tribunal for an order requiring any person to furnish written information or produce relevant documents. The expert has no power to require a person to give oral information or be questioned by him. The information or documents are given to the assistant secretary of the ROIT and then passed on to the expert. Such an order cannot be made against an ACAS conciliation officer who has acted in the case, or against a person who would have good grounds for refusing to comply were it a requirement made in connection with a tribunal hearing, e.g. a privileged communication between solicitor and client (Rule 4(1B)).

There is no power to strike out an employee's claim or an employer's appearance for failure to comply with an order, although an unjustified refusal carries a fine of up to £200 (Rule 4(3)). But where a refusal to comply prevents the expert from reaching a conclusion on whether the two jobs are of equal value, the tribunal may later hear evidence on matters of fact which would otherwise be excluded by Rule 8(2C) — *see* C.11 below.

There is no express statement in the rules as to the method of comparison to be used by the expert; Rule 7A(1), however, says 'whether any work is of equal value to other work in terms of the demands made on the person employed on the work (for instance under such headings as effort, skill and decision)', and so seems to favour factor analysis rather than non-analytical methods of assessment.

Preliminary hearing 4: undue delay (Rule 7A(5))

C.7   The expert will clearly take some time to prepare a report, and the rules allow a minimum of six weeks. After that time, either side can complain that there has been or is likely to be undue delay. If the tribunal agrees, it can require the expert to provide in writing 'an explanation for the delay or information as to his progress'. Having considered the expert's response and sought representations from the parties, the tribunal may revoke the request to prepare a report, and then commission a report from a different expert, i.e. start the process again.

The expert's report

C.8   The expert's report goes to the tribunal, which then sends a copy to each party and fixes a date (at least 14 days later) for the reconvened hearing (Rule 7A(6)). The tribunal may, at any time after it has received the expert's report require him (or if that is impracticable, another expert) to explain any matter contained in his report, or to give further consideration to the question (Rule 7A(10)). He must be told to reply in writing to the tribunal giving his explanation or setting down his conclusion (with reasons) resulting from that further consideration (Rule 7A(10)). A copy of the reply must be sent to each of the parties (Rule 7A(11)). They must be allowed to make representations which are written representations only. The tribunal may attach such weight to the reply as it thinks fit (Rule 7A(12)).

The hearing

C.9   The report must be admitted as evidence (Rule 7A(7)) unless it is successfully challenged under Rule 7A(8). So at the beginning of the hearing there can be in effect a fifth preliminary hearing where the tribunal will determine whether it will accept the expert's report and admit it in evidence.

Preliminary hearing 5: whether expert's report acceptable (Rule 7A(8))

C.10   The rules allow a limited right of challenge. Rule 7A(8) provides:

'Where the tribunal, on the application of one or more of the parties or otherwise, forms the view—

(*a*) that the expert has not complied with a stipulation in [Rule 7A(3)], or

(*b*) that the conclusion contained in the report is one which, taking due account of the information supplied and representations made to the expert, could not reasonably have been reached, or

(*c*) that for some other material reason (other than disagreement with the conclusion that the applicant's work is or is not of equal value or with the reasoning leading to that conclusion) the report is unsatisfactory,'

the tribunal can decide not to admit the report as evidence.

Turning from the grounds of challenge to the evidence, Rule 7A(9) states that in forming its view whether or not to admit the report, the tribunal shall take account of the parties' representations and may 'permit any party to give evidence upon, to call witnesses and to question any witness upon any matter relevant thereto'.

Furthermore, Rule 8(2A) makes the expert compellable as a witness either on the tribunal's own initiative or on the application of either party. The parties can 'cross-examine the expert on his report and on any other matter pertaining to the question on which the expert was required to report'. In addition, Rule 8(2B) allows each side, on giving 'reasonable notice' to the tribunal and the other party, to call **one** expert witness on equal value. That expert can also be cross-examined.

At this stage, there is no special restriction on the evidence that can be given by or the questions that can be put to these witnesses provided it is relevant to the issues in Rule 7A(8).

If the tribunal rejects the report, it **must** commission a new one and the whole procedure starts again (because a tribunal cannot decide whether two jobs are of equal value without a report).

The resumed hearing

C.11   Only if the report is admitted can the tribunal then decide whether the two jobs are of equal value. At this point, the tribunal may still hear expert evidence, but not factual evidence. Rule 7A(9) ceases to apply, and Rule 8(2C) comes into play which provides that 'no party to a case involving an equal value claim may give evidence upon, or question any witness upon any matter of fact upon which a conclusion in the report of the expert is based'. So tribunals may have to face up to three witnesses on equal value at the resumed hearing — the independent expert and one expert from each side.

Where, however, the expert's report contains no conclusion, on the equal value issue and the tribunal is satisfied that this is wholly or mainly due to the refusal or deliberate omission of a person to supply a Rule 4(1A) order, then a party may give evidence or question any witness upon any relevant matter including findings of fact by the expert (Rule 8(2D)(*b*)).

If the decision goes in favour of the applicant, the employer can raise the material factor defence, whether or not the tribunal considered it at the second preliminary hearing stage (Rule 8(2D)(*a*)). This is the last defence open to an employer under the new procedure. Witnesses can be called and questioned on matters of fact relevant to the defence.

It is likely that this resumed hearing and the fifth preliminary hearing (see C.10 above) will take place at the same time.

The decision

C.12   The expert's report, other than one which was rejected, is attached to the tribunal's decision (Rule 9(3)). Where evidence has been heard in private, any matter bearing on the substance of that evidence contained in the report may be omitted by the tribunal (Rule 9(4A)).

Costs

C.13   Where costs are awarded under Rule 11(1) because a party has acted frivolously, vexatiously or otherwise unreasonably (see 40.6–40.10), the award may include costs or expenses incurred by the other side in or in connection with the expert's investigations (Rule 11(1A)). The costs of the independent expert however are borne out of public funds.

Summary of the new procedure

C.14   If the equal value procedure takes its full course then a claim could take anything from between 26 to 52 weeks to complete.

The procedure is much more complicated than for other tribunal claims and therefore it is likely that early claims (such as the *Ford* case referred to in C.4 above) will be subject to appeals thereby further delaying the implementation of a decision.

1983 No. 1807

INDUSTRIAL TRIBUNALS

The Industrial Tribunals (Rules of Procedure) (Equal Value Amendment) Regulations 1983

Made - - -	*7th December* 1983
Laid before Parliament	*9th December* 1983
Coming into Operation	*1st January* 1984

The Secretary of State, in exercise of the powers conferred on him by paragraph 1 of Schedule 9 to the Employment Protection (Consolidation) Act 1978(a) and after consultation with the Council on Tribunals, hereby makes the following Regulations:—

Citation and commencement

1. These Regulations may be cited as the Industrial Tribunals (Rules of Procedure) (Equal Value Amendment) Regulations 1983 and shall come into operation on 1st January 1984.

Interpretation

2. In these Regulations —

"the Equal Pay Act" means the Equal Pay Act 1970(b), as amended, with particular reference to the amendments made by the Equal Pay (Amendment) Regulations 1983(c);

"the principal Regulations (England and Wales)" means the Industrial Tribunals (Rules of Procedure) Regulations 1980(d);

"the principal Regulations (Scotland)" means the Industrial Tribunals (Rules of Procedure) (Scotland) Regulations 1980(e);

"the principal Rules of Procedure (England and Wales)" means the Industrial Tribunals Rules of Procedure 1980 contained in Schedule 1 to the principal Regulations (England and Wales);

(a) 1978 c.44; Schedule 9 was amended by Regulation 3 of the Equal Pay (Amendment) Regulations 1983, S.I. 1983/1794.

(b) 1970 c.41; section 1 was amended by the Sex Discrimination Act 1975 (c.65), section 8 and Schedule 1, paragraph 1, and was applied by the Employment Protection Act 1975 (c.71), section 122(2), as amended by the Race Relations Act 1976 (c.74), Schedule 3, paragraph 1(5); section 1 was amended and section 2A was inserted by the Equal Pay (Amendment) Regulations 1983, S.I. 1983/1794.

(c) S.I. 1983/1794.   (d) S.I. 1980/884.   (e) S.I. 1980/885.

"the principal Rules of Procedure (Scotland)" means the Industrial Tribunals Rules of Procedure (Scotland) 1980 contained in Schedule 1 to the principal Regulations (Scotland)

and, unless the context otherwise requires, any expression to which a meaning has been assigned by Regulation 2 of the principal Regulations (England and Wales), or, as the case may be, of the principal Regulations (Scotland), shall have that meaning.

Proceedings of tribunals in cases involving equal value claims
  3.   In any proceedings before a tribunal involving a claim by an applicant which rests upon entitlement to the benefit of an equality clause by virtue of the operation of section 1 (2)(*c*) of the Equal Pay Act —

(*a*) in a case in which the principal Regulations (England and Wales) have effect —

  (i) those Regulations shall have effect in relation to that claim subject to the amendments contained in Part I of the Schedule to these Regulations; and

  (ii) the principal Rules of Procedure (England and Wales) shall have effect in relation to the claim subject to the amendments contained in Part II of the Schedule to these Regulations except in so far as such amendments are expressed to apply only to the principal Rules of Procedure (Scotland); and

(*b*) in a case in which the principal Regulations (Scotland) have effect —

  (i) those Regulations shall have effect in relation to that claim subject to the amendments contained in Part I of the Schedule to these Regulations; and

  (ii) the principal Rules of Procedure (Scotland) shall have effect in relation to the claim subject to the amendments contained in Part II of the Schedule to these Regulations except in so far as such amendments are expressed to apply only to the principal Rules of Procedure (England and Wales).

Signed by order of the Secretary of State.

Alan Clark,
Parliamentary Under Secretary of State,
Department of Employment.

7th December 1983.

PART I

AMENDMENTS TO THE PRINCIPAL REGULATIONS (ENGLAND AND WALES) AND TO THE PRINCIPAL REGULATIONS (SCOTLAND)

1. In Regulation 2 (interpretation) —

    (*a*) after the definition of "decision" there shall be inserted —

        " "the Equal Pay Act" means the Equal Pay Act 1970(**a**), as amended, with particular reference to the amendments made by the Equal Pay (Amendment) Regulations 1983(**b**);

        "equal value claim" means a claim by an applicant which rests upon entitlement to the benefit of an equality clause by virtue of the operation of section 1(2)(*c*) of the Equal Pay Act;

        "expert" means a member of the panel of independent experts within the meaning of section 2A(4) of the Equal Pay Act;" and

    (*b*) after the definition of "Register" there shall be inserted —

        " "report" means a report required by a tribunal to be prepared by an expert, pursuant to section 2A(1)(*b*) of the Equal Pay Act;".

PART II

AMENDMENTS TO THE PRINCIPAL RULES OF PROCEDURE (ENGLAND AND WALES) AND TO THE PRINCIPAL RULES OF PROCEDURE (SCOTLAND)

1.—(1) In Rule 4, after paragraph (1), there shall be inserted —

"(1A) Subject to paragraph (1B), in a case involving an equal value claim, a tribunal may, on the application of an expert who has been required by the tribunal to prepare a report,—

    (*a*) require any person who the tribunal is satisfied may have information which may be relevant to the question or matter on which the expert is required to report to furnish, in writing, such information as the tribunal may require;

    (*b*) require any person to produce any documents which are in the possession, custody or power of that person and which the tribunal is satisfied may contain matter relevant to the question on which the expert is required to report;

    and any information so required to be furnished or document so required to be produced shall be furnished or produced, at or within such time as the tribunal may appoint, to the Secretary of the Tribunals who shall send the information or document to the expert.

(1B) A tribunal shall not make a requirement under paragraph (1A) of this Rule —

    (*a*) of a conciliation officer who has acted in connection with the complaint under section 64 of the Sex Discrimination Act 1975(**c**), or

---

(**a**) 1970 c.41; section 1 was amended by the Sex Discrimination Act 1975 (c.65), section 8 and Schedule 1, paragraph 1, and was applied by the Employment Protection Act 1975 (c.71), section 122(2), as amended by the Race Relation Act 1976 (c.74), Schedule 3, paragraph 1(5); section 1 was amended and section 2A was inserted by the Equal Pay (Amendment) Regulations 1983, S.I. 1983/1794.
(**b**) S.I. 1983/1794.   (**c**) 1975 c.65.

(*b*) if it satisfied that the person so required would have good grounds for refusing to comply with the requirement if it were a requirement made in connection with a hearing before the tribunal.".

(2) In Rule 4, after paragraph (2), there shall be inserted —

"(2A) A person, whether or not a party to the proceedings, upon whom a requirement has been made under paragraph (1A) of this Rule, may apply to the tribunal by notice to the Secretary of the Tribunals before the appointed time at or within which the requirement is to be complied with to vary or set aside the requirement. Notice of such application shall be given to the parties and to the expert upon whose application the requirement was made.".

(3) In paragraph (3) of Rule 4, after the words "(1)(iii)", there shall be inserted the words, "or paragraph (1A)".

2. After Rule 7, there shall be inserted —

"7A.—(1) In any case involving an equal value claim where a dispute arises as to whether any work is of equal value to other work in terms of the demands made on the person employed on the work (for instance under such headings as effort, skill and decision) (in this Rule hereinafter referred to as "the question"), a tribunal shall, before considering the question, except in cases to which section 2A (1)(*a*) of the Equal Pay Act applies, require an expert to prepare a report with respect to the question: and the requirement shall be made in accordance with paragraphs (2) and (3) of this Rule.

(2) The requirement shall be made in writing and shall set out—

(*a*) the name and address of each of the parties;

(*b*) the address of the establishment at which the applicant is (or, as the case may be, was) employed;

(*c*) the question; and

(*d*) the identity of the person with reference to whose work the question arises

and a copy of the requirement shall be sent to each of the parties.

(3) The requirement shall stipulate that the expert shall—

(*a*) take account of all such information supplied and all such representations made to him as have a bearing on the question;

(*b*) before drawing up his report, produce and send to the parties a written summary of the said information and representations and invite the representations of the parties upon the material contained therein;

(*c*) make his report to the tribunal in a document which shall reproduce the summary and contain a brief account of any representations received from the parties upon it, any conclusion he may have reached upon the question and the reasons for that conclusion or, as the case may be, for his failure to reach such a conclusion;

(*d*) take no account of the difference of sex and at all times act fairly.

(4) Without prejudice to the generality of Rule 12(2)(*b*), where a tribunal requires an expert to prepare a report, it shall adjourn the hearing.

(5) If, on the application of one or more of the parties made not less than 42 days after a tribunal has notified an expert of the requirement to prepare a report, the tribunal forms the view that there has been or is likely to be undue delay in receiving that report, the tribunal may require the expert to provide in writing to the tribunal an explanation for the delay or information as to his progress and may, on consideration of any such explanation or information as may be provided and after seeking representations from the parties,

revoke, by notice in writing to the expert, the requirement to prepare a report; and in such a case paragraph (1) of this Rule shall again apply.

(6) Where a tribunal has received the report of an expert, it shall forthwith send a copy of the report to each of the parties and shall fix a date for the hearing of the case to be resumed: provided that the date so fixed shall be at least 14 days after the date on which the report is sent to the parties.

(7) Upon the resuming of the hearing of the case in accordance with paragraph (6) of this Rule the report shall be admitted as evidence in the case unless the tribunal has exercised its power under paragraph (8) of this Rule not to admit the report.

(8) Where the tribunal, on the application of one or more of the parties or otherwise, forms the view —

    (*a*) that the expert has not complied with a stipulation in paragraph (3) of this Rule, or

    (*b*) that the conclusion contained in the report is one which, taking due account of the information supplied and representations made to the expert, could not reasonably have been reached, or

    (*c*) that for some other material reason (other than disagreement with the conclusion that the applicant's work is or is not of equal value or with the reasoning leading to that conclusion) the report is unsatisfactory,

the tribunal may, if it thinks fit, determine not to admit the report; and in such a case paragraph (1) of this Rule shall again apply.

(9) In forming its view on the matters contained in paragraph (8)(*a*), (*b*) and (*c*) of this Rule, the tribunal shall take account of any representations of the parties thereon and may in that connection, subject to Rule 8(2A) and (2B), permit any party to give evidence upon, to call witnesses and to question any witness upon any matter relevant thereto.

(10) The tribunal may, at any time after it has received the report of an expert, require that expert (or, if that is impracticable, another expert) to explain any matter contained in his report or, having regard to such matters as may be set out in the requirement, to give further consideration to the question.

(11) The requirement in paragraph (10) of this Rule shall comply with paragraph (2) of this Rule and shall stipulate that the expert shall make his reply in writing to the tribunal, giving his explanation or, as the case may be, setting down any conclusion which may result from his further consideration and his reasons for that conclusion.

(12) Where the tribunal has received a reply from the expert under paragraph (11) of this Rule, it shall forthwith send a copy of the reply to each of the parties and shall allow the parties to make representations thereon; and the reply shall be treated as information furnished to the tribunal and be given such weight as the tribunal thinks fit.

(13) Where a tribunal has determined not to admit a report under paragraph (8), that report shall be treated for all purposes (other than the award of costs or expenses under Rule 11) connected with the proceedings as if it had not been received by the tribunal and no further account shall be taken of it; and the requirement on the expert to prepare a report shall lapse.".

3.—(1) In paragraph (1) of Rule 8, at the beginning, there shall be inserted the words "Subject to paragraphs (2A), (2B), (2C), (2D) and (2E) of this Rule".

(2) In paragraph (2) of Rule 8, for the words "paragraph (1)", there shall be substituted the words "paragraphs (1), (2A), (2B), (2C) and (2D)".

(3) In Rule 8, after paragraph (2), there shall be inserted —

    "(2A) The tribunal may, and shall upon the application of a party, require the attendance of an expert who has prepared a report in connection with an equal value claim in any hearing relating to that claim. Where an expert attends in compliance with such requirement any party may, subject to paragraph (1) of this Rule, cross-examine the expert on his report and on any other matter pertaining to the question on which the expert was required to report.

(2B) In a case involving an equal value claim, at any time after the tribunal has received the report of the expert, any party may, on giving reasonable notice of his intention to do so to the tribunal and to any other party to the claim, call one witness to give expert evidence on the question on which the tribunal has required the expert to prepare a report; and where such evidence is given, any other party may cross-examine the person giving that evidence upon it.

(2C) Except as provided in Rule 7A(9) or by paragraph (2D) of this Rule, no party to a case involving an equal value claim may give evidence upon, or question any witness upon, any matter of fact upon which a conclusion in the report of the expert is based.

(2D) Subject to paragraphs (2A) and (2B) of this Rule, a tribunal may, notwithstanding paragraph (2C) of this Rule, permit a party to give evidence upon, to call witnesses and to question any witness upon any such matters of fact as are referred to in that paragraph if either —

(a) the matter of fact is relevant to and is raised in connection with the issue contained in subsection (3) of section 1 of the Equal Pay Act (defence of genuine material factor) upon which the determination of the tribunal is being sought; or

(b) the report of the expert contains no conclusion on the question of whether the applicant's work and the work of the person identified in the requirement of the tribunal under Rule 7A(2) are of equal value and the tribunal is satisfied that the absence of that conclusion is wholly or mainly due to the refusal or deliberate omission of a person required by the tribunal under Rule 4(1A) to furnish information or to produce documents to comply with that requirement.

(2E) In a case involving an equal value claim, a tribunal may, on the application of a party, if in the circumstances of the case, having regard to the considerations expressed in paragraph (1) of this Rule, it considers that it is appropriate so to proceed, hear evidence upon and permit the parties to address it upon the issue contained in subsection (3) of section 1 of the Equal Pay Act (defence of genuine material factor) before it requires an expert to prepare a report under Rule 7A. Where the tribunal so proceeds, it shall be without prejudice to further consideration of that issue after the tribunal has received the report.".

4.—(1) In paragraph (2) of Rule 9, at the end, there shall be inserted the words "and in a case involving an equal value claim there shall be appended to that document a copy of the report (if any) of an expert received by the tribunal in the course of the proceedings.".

(2) In paragraph (3) of Rule 9, after the words "the chairman" there shall be inserted the words "and any report appended to the document pursuant to paragraph (2) of this Rule", and for the word "it" there shall be substituted the word "them".

(3) In Rule 9 of the principal Rules of Procedure (England and Wales), after paragraph (4), there shall be inserted —

"(4A) In any case involving an equal value claim where evidence has been heard in private, any matter bearing upon the substance of that evidence contained in any report of an expert may, if the tribunal so directs, be omitted from the report appended to the document pursuant to paragraph (2) of this Rule, and in that event a copy of the report without that omission shall be sent to any superior court in any proceedings relating to the decision on the case, together with a copy of the entry.".

(4) In Rule 9 of the principal Rules of Procedure (Scotland), after praragraph (4), there shall be inserted —

"(4A) In any case involving an equal value claim where evidence has been heard in private, any matter bearing upon the substance of that evidence contained in any report of an expert may, if the tribunal so directs, be omitted from the report appended to the document pursuant to paragraph (2) of this Rule, and in that event a copy of the report without that omission shall be sent to any appellate court in any proceedings relating to the decision on the case, together with a copy of the entry.".

5.—(1) In paragraph (1)(*b*) of Rule 11, after the word "tribunals" there shall be inserted the word ", experts".

(2) In Rule 11 of the principal Rules of Procedure (England and Wales), after paragraph (1), there shall be inserted —

"(1A) For the purposes of paragraph (1)(*a*) of this Rule, in a case involving an equal value claim, the costs or expenses in respect of which a tribunal may make an order include costs or expenses incurred by the party in whose favour the order is to be made in or in connection with the investigations carried out by the expert in preparing his report.".

(3) In Rule 11 of the principal Rules of Procedure (Scotland), after paragraph (1), there shall be inserted —

"(1A) For the purposes of paragraph (1)(*a*) of this Rule, in a case involving an equal value claim, the expenses in respect of which a tribunal may make an order include expenses incurred by the party in whose favour the order is to be made in or in connection with the investigations carried out by the expert in preparing his report.".

6.—(1) In Rule 12, after paragraph (2) there shall be inserted —

"(2A) Without prejudice to the generality of paragraph (2)(*b*) of this Rule, in a case involving an equal value claim the tribunal shall, before proceeding to hear the parties on the claim, invite them to apply for an adjournment for the purpose of seeking to reach a settlement of the claim and shall, if both or all the parties agree to such a course, grant an adjournment for that purpose.

(2B) If, in a case involving an equal value claim, after the tribunal has adjourned the hearing under rule 7A(4) but before the tribunal has received the report of the expert, the applicant gives notice under paragraph (2)(*c*) of this Rule, the tribunal shall forthwith notify the expect that the requirement to prepare a report has ceased. The notice shall be without prejudice to the operation of Rule 11(1A).".

(2) In paragraph (3) of Rule 12, after the words "Rule 4(2)" there shall be inserted the words "and (2A)", after the words "Secretary of State" there shall be inserted the words "or, in the case of an application under Rule 4(1A), the expert" and after the word "parties", there shall be inserted the words "(or, in the case of an application by an expert, the parties and any other person in respect of whom the tribunal is asked, in the application, to impose a requirement)".

7.—(1) In paragraph (4) of Rule 17, after the words "conciliation officer" there shall be inserted the words "and the appropriate expert".

(2) In paragraph (5)(*b*) of Rule 17, after the words "Rule 4(1)(iii)" there shall be inserted the words "or (1A)".

(3) In paragraph (9) of Rule 17, the words "1970(a)" and the footnote pertaining thereto shall be deleted.

EXPLANATORY NOTE

(This Note is not part of the Regulations.)

These Regulations amend the Industrial Tribunals (Rules of Procedure) Regulations 1980 and the Industrial Tribunals (Rules of Procedure) (Scotland) Regulations 1980 so as to provide the additional procedure to be followed where a claim is brought before an industrial tribunal involving section 1(2)(*c*) of the Equal Pay Act 1970 (as amended by the Equal Pay (Amendment) Regulations 1983). The principal changes made include:—

    (*a*) provision relating to the duty of the tribunal to require an expert to prepare a report on the question whether jobs have equal value and for admitting or not admitting that report in evidence;

    (*b*) provision for the tribunal to require the supply of information and the production of documents for the use of the expert and for appeal from such a requirement;

    (*c*) provision for the expert to be cross-examined by the parties; for the tribunal to question the expert further in writing; and for expert evidence to be adduced by the parties;

    (*d*) provision for the report of the expert to be attached to the document recording the decision of the tribunal.

Useful Addresses

Addresses of Offices of the Advisory, Conciliation and Arbitration Service

Head Office
11–12 St James's Square, London SW1Y 4LA   Tel: 01–214 6000

Regional Offices
London
Clifton House, 83–117 Euston Road, London NW1 2RB   Tel: 01–388 5100

Midlands
Alpha Tower, Suffolk Street, Queensway, Birmingham B1 1TZ   Tel: 021–643 9911

Northamptonshire	Staffordshire (except	Hereford and
(except Corby)	Burton-on-Trent)	Worcester
Shropshire	West Midlands	Warwickshire
Nottingham Office:		

66–72 Houndsgate, Nottingham NG1 6BA   Tel: Nottingham (0602) 415450

Derbyshire (except	Leicestershire	Lincolnshire
High Peak District)	Corby	Burton-on-Trent
Nottinghamshire		

Northern
Westgate House, Westgate Road, Newcastle-upon-Tyne NE1 1TJ
Tel: Newcastle (0632) 612191

Cumbria	Tyne and Wear	Cleveland
Northumberland	Durham	

North West
Bouton House, 17–21 Chorlton Street, Manchester M1 3HY   Tel: 061–228 3222

Lancashire	High Peak District	Greater
Cheshire	of Derbyshire	Manchester

Merseyside Office:
Cressington House, 249 St. Mary's Road, Garston, Liverpool L19 0NF
Tel: 051–427 8881/4

South East
Clifton House, 83–117 Euston Road, London NW1 2RB   Tel: 01–388 5100

Cambridgeshire	Hertfordshire	Hampshire
Norfolk	Essex	(except Ringwood)
Suffolk	Berkshire	Isle of Wight
Oxfordshire	Surrey	East Sussex
Buckinghamshire	Kent	West Sussex
Bedfordshire		

Useful Addresses

ACAS Regional Offices (cont.d)

South West
16 Park Place, Clifton, Bristol BS8 1JP   Tel: Bristol (0272) 211921

Gloucestershire	Cornwall	Dorset
Avon	Devon	Ringwood
Wiltshire	Somerset	

Yorkshire and Humberside
Commerce House, St Albans Place, Leeds LS2 8HH   Tel: Leeds (0532) 431371

North Yorkshire	South Yorkshire	Humberside
West Yorkshire		

Scotland
Franborough House, 123–157 Bothwell Street, Glasgow G2 7JR   Tel: 041–204 2677

Wales
Phase 1, Ty Glas Road, Llanishen, Cardiff CF4 5PH   Tel: Cardiff (0222) 762636

Addresses of Industrial Tribunals

ENGLAND AND WALES

Central Office 93 Ebury Bridge Road London SW1W 8RE   Tel: 01–730 9161

Regional Offices

London
London (South)
    93 Ebury Bridge Road
    London SW1W 8RE
    Tel: 01–730 9161

London (North)
    19/29 Woburn Place
    London WC1 0LU
    Tel: 01–632 4921

London (Central) as
    London (South)
    Tel: 01–730 9161

Ashford (Kent)
Tufton House
Tufton Street
Ashford
Kent TN23 1RJ
Tel: 0233 21346

Birmingham
Phoenix House
1/3 Newhall Street
Birmingham B3 3NH
Tel: 021–236 6051

Bristol
Prince House
43/51 Prince Street
Bristol BS1 4PE
Tel: 0272 298261

Bury St Edmunds
100 Southgate Street
Bury St Edmunds
Suffolk IP33 1HQ
Tel: 0284 62171

Cardiff
Caradog House
1/6 St Andrews Place
Cardiff CF1 3BE
Tel: 0222 372693

Leeds
Minerva House
29 East Parade
Leeds LS1 5JZ
Tel: 0532 459741

Liverpool
1 Union Court,
Cook Street
Liverpool L2 4UJ
Tel: 051–236 9397

Manchester
Alexandra House
14/22 The Parsonage
Manchester M3 2JA
Tel: 061-833 0581

Newcastle
Watson House,
Pilgrim Street,
Newcastle-upon-Tyne NE1 6RB
Tel: 0632 328865

Nottingham
7th Floor
Birbeck House

Trinity Square
Nottingham NG1 4AX
Tel: 0602 45701

Sheffield
14 East Parade
Sheffield S1 2ET
Tel: 0742 760348

Southampton
3rd Floor
Dukes Keep,
Marsh Lane,
Southampton SO1 1EX
Tel: 0703 39555

SCOTLAND

Central Office St Andrew House 141 West Nile Street Glasgow G1 2RU
Tel: 041-331 1601

Regional Offices

Aberdeen
252 Union Street
Aberdeen AB1 1TN
Tel: 0224 52307

Dundee
13 Albert Square
Dundee DD1 1DD
Tel: 0382-21578

Edinburgh
11 Melvill Crescent
Edinburgh EH3 7LU
Tel: 031-226 5584

Glasgow
St Andrews House
141 West Nile Street
Glasgow G1 2RU
Tel: 041-331 1601

Addresses of the Department of Employment

Head Office
Caxton House Tothill Street London SW1H 9NF Tel: 01-213 3000

Regional Offices

Midlands
2 Duchess Place
Hadley Road
Edgbaston
Birmingham B16 8NS
Tel: 021-455 7111

Northern
Welbar House
Gallowgate
Newcastle-upon-Tyne NE1 4TT
Tel: 0632 327575

North Western
Sunley Buildings
Piccadilly Plaza
Manchester M60 7JS
Tel: 061-832 9111

South Eastern and London
Hanway House
27 Red Lion Square
London WC1R 4NH
Tel: 01-405 8454

Useful Addresses

DE Regional Offices (cont.d)

South Western
The Pithay
Bristol BS1 2NQ
Tel: 0272 291071

Yorkshire and Humberside
City House
New Station Street
Leeds LS1 4JH
Tel: 0532 438232

Scotland
Pentland House
47 Robb's Loan
Edinburgh EH14 1UE
Tel: 031–443 8731

Wales
Companies House
Crown Way
Maindy
Cardiff CF4 3UW
Tel: 0222 388588

Other Useful Addresses

Employment Appeal Tribunal
England and Wales
4 St James's Square
London SW1
Tel: 01–214 6000
     01–214 3367 (inquiries)

Scotland
249 West George Street
Glasgow G2 4QE
Tel: 041–248 6213

Equal Opportunities Commission
Overseas House
Quay Street
Manchester M3 3HM
Tel: 061–833 9244

Commission for Racial Equality
Elliott House
10/12 Allington Street
London SW1
Tel: 01–828 7022

Health and Safety Commission
Regina House
259 Old Marylebone Road
London NW1 5RR
Tel: 01–723 1262

Health and Safety Executive
Baynards House
1/13 Chepstow Place
London W2 4TF
Tel: 01–229 3456

Companies House
England and Wales
55 City Road
London EC1
Tel: 01–253 9393

Scotland
102 George Street
Edinburgh EH2 3DG
Tel: 031–225 5774

Where to find names of solicitors
England and Wales
The Law Society (see 'Legal Aid'),
and the Legal Aid Solicitors List can
be inspected locally at town halls,
libraries and Citizens Advice
Bureaux

Scotland
Law Society of Scotland
26 Drumsheugh Gardens
Edinburgh EH3 7YR
Tel: 031-226 7411

Legal Aid
England and Wales
The Law Society
113 Chancery Lane
London WC2A 1PL
Tel: 01-242 1222

Scotland
Legal Aid Administration
41-44 Drumsheugh Gardens
Edinburgh EH3 7SW
Tel: 031–226 7061

National Association of Citizens Advice Bureaux
110 Drury Lane
London WC2
Tel: 01–836 9231

Wages Councils
12 St James's Square
London SW1Y 4LL
Tel: 01–405 8454

HMSO Bookshops
London
49 High Holborn
London WC1V 6HB

Birmingham
258 Broad Street
Birmingham B1 2HE

Bristol
Southey House
Wine Street
Bristol BS1 2BQ

Manchester
Brazenose Street
Manchester M60 8AS

Edinburgh
13A Castle Street
Edinburgh EH2 3AR

Cardiff
41 The Hayes
Cardiff CF1 1JW

Belfast
80 Chichester Street
Belfast BT1 4SY

Appendix E

Further Reading

Pamphlets on employment law

ACAS, CRE, EOC and DE publish various series of pamphlets on legal rights.

Detailed books on employment law

S D Anderman 'The Law of Unfair Dismissal', Butterworth (2nd Edition), 1984
C Grunfeld 'The Law of Redundancy', Sweet & Maxwell, 1980
J McMullen 'Rights at Work', Pluto Press (2nd Edition), 1983
David Lewis 'Essentials of Employment Law', Institute of Personnel Management, 1983
R W Rideout 'Principles of Labour Law', Sweet & Maxwell (3rd Edition), 1983
Elizabeth Slade 'Tolley's Employment Handbook', Tolley (3rd Edition), 1983
Anthony Lester QC and David Wainwright 'Equal Pay for Work of Equal Value — Law and Practice', TMS Management Consultants, 1984.

Loose-leaf regularly updated encyclopaedias on employment law

B A Hepple and P O'Higgins 'Encyclopaedia of Labour Relations Law', Sweet & Maxwell (three loose-leaf volumes)
'Harvey on Industrial Relations', Butterworth (two loose-leaf volumes)
Croner's 'Employment Law', Croner Publishing (six-monthly updates).

Regular journals on employment law

Incomes Data Services produce fortnightly Briefs and regular Supplements and Handbooks covering short digest on tribunal cases
Industrial Relations Services produce a fortnightly Industrial Relations Legal Information Bulletin which covers similar ground plus detailed guidance notes on specific areas of employment law
The Industrial Law Journal, published quarterly by Sweet & Maxwell, has more academic articles on employment law.

Specialist law reports on employment law

Industrial Cases Reports (ICR)
Industrial Relations Law Reports (IRLR).

Other books on industrial tribunals

M J Goodman 'Industrial Relations Procedure', Oyez, 1979

D B Williams and D J Walker 'Industrial Tribunals Practice and Procedure', Butterworth, 1980

W Leslie 'Industrial Tribunal Practice in Scotland', Green & Son, 1981

Phyllis Bateson and John McKee 'Industrial Tribunals in Northern Ireland, Law in Action Series', Queens University Press, 1981

John McIlroy 'Industrial Tribunals: how to take a case; how to win it', Pluto Press, 1983 (aimed at trade unionists).

Index

References are to chapters, paragraph numbers, figures and Appendices in the book.

Index

Index

Index

Index

Tolley Publications

Tax Annuals
Tolley's Income Tax 1984-85 £12.95
Tolley's Corporation Tax 1984-85 £10.25
Tolley's Capital Gains Tax 1984-85 £11.50
Tolley's Capital Transfer Tax 1984-85 £9.95
Tolley's Value Added Tax £10.50

Other Annual Tax Books
Tolley's Tax Guide 1984-85 £11.95
Tolley's Tax Planning Supplement £10.00
Tolley's Tax Cases 1984-85 £12.95
Grout's Value Added Tax Cases 1983 £12.95
Tolley's Tax Data 1984-85 £5.95
Tolley's Tax Tables 1984-85 £3.95
Tolley's Tax Cards 1984-85 £tba
Tolley's Tax Computations 1984-85 £tba
Tolley's Tax Bumph 1984-85 £18.50
Tolley's Company Car Tax Guide 1984-85 £2.95
Taxwise Taxation Workbook No 1 (IT/CT/CGT) 1984-85 £12.95
Taxwise Taxation Workbook No 2 (CTT/DLT/VAT) 1984-85 £9.95
Tolley's Taxation in the Republic of Ireland 1984-85 £9.50
Tolley's Taxation in the Channel Islands and Isle of Man 1984 £9.95

Other Tax Books
Taxation of Lloyd's Underwriters £17.50
Jersey: A Low Tax Area (paperback) £15.00 (hardback) £18.00
Tolley's Anti-Avoidance Provisions £17.50
Tolley's Taxation in Gibraltar 1982 £8.50
The Isle of Man: A Low Tax Area £21.95
Tolley's Practical Guide to VAT Planning £9.95
Tolley's Development Land Tax 4th Edition £10.50
Tolley's Double Taxation Relief £8.95
Tolley's Stamp Duties 2nd Edition £6.95
Tolley's Stock Relief £4.95
Tolley's US/UK Double Tax Treaty £11.50

Focus Series
Capital Transfer Tax: Discretionary Trusts after the Finance Act 1982 £5.50
The Purchase or Redemption by a Company of its Own Shares £5.50
The Purchase and Sale of a Private Company's Shares £6.95
Interest and Discounts £8.95
Tax Planning for New Businesses £6.95
The Administration of Taxes £5.95
The Construction Industry Tax Deduction Scheme £6.95

Company Law and Practice
Tolley's Company Law £19.50
Tolley's Accounting Problems of the Companies Acts £7.95
Tolley's Companies Act 1980 (paperback) £7.95 (hardback) £11.95

Tolley's Companies Act 1981 (paperback) £8.95 (hardback) £11.95
Tolley's Guide to Directors' Transactions £5.95

Accounting
Tolley's Group Pro Forma Accounts £11.00 per pack of 5 £2.95 per single copy (excl. VAT)
Tolley's Pro Forma Accounts £10.00 per pack of 5 £2.75 per single copy (excl. VAT)
Companies Accounts Check List No. 2 £5.95 per pack of 5 (excl. VAT)
Tolley's CCA Conversion Kit £55.00 (excl. VAT)
Tolley's Reporting under CCA £19.95
Tolley's Factoring £17.50
Tolley's Accounting and Audit Data £5.95

Employment Law and Practice
Tolley's Guide to Statutory Sick Pay £4.95
Tolley's Employment Act 1982 £7.95
Tolley's Health and Safety at Work Handbook £12.95
Redundancy . . . what to do next £tba
Tolley's Employment Handbook 3rd Edition £12.95
Tolley's Industrial Tribunals £14.95

Social Security
Tolley's Social Security and State Benefits 1983-84 £10.95
Tolley's National Insurance Contributions 1984-85 £12.95

Insolvency
Tolley's Liquidation Manual £21.00
Tolley's Receivership Manual 2nd Edition £15.00
Tolley's European Insolvency Guide £19.95
Tolley's Employees' Rights in Receiverships and Liquidations 2nd Edition £25.00

Management and Business
Tolley's Expansion Kit for Business £4.95
Tolley's Survival Kit for Small Businesses (2nd Edition) £4.95
The Independent Director £4.50
Tolley's Business Start-Up Pack for a Limited Company £12.50
Tolley's Business Start-Up Pack for a Sole Trader or Partnership £12.50

Surveys
CSR Survey of Company Car Schemes 1984 £27.00 non-subscribers £18.00 subscribers
Accountants' Remuneration Survey £19.90

Europe
Trading Within the European Community £35.00
Tolley's European Community Institutions £4.50

Pensions
Tolley's Pensions Handbook £tba

You may order any of these titles, or obtain a copy of the Tolley catalogue, by telephoning 01-686 0115/01-686 9141 or by completing the enclosed order form.

Order Form

To: **Tolley Publishing Co Ltd, Tolley House, 17 Scarbrook Road, Croydon, Surrey CR0 1SQ. Telephone: 01-686 9141**

Please send the following to me as soon as possible:

Title	Price per copy	No. of copies	Amount £
	Plus VAT where applicable		
	Total cost £		

My cheque is enclosed ☐

Please invoice me ☐

Please debit my Access/Visa* account number_____

Signature_____

Name _____

Position_____

Firm_____

Address_____

_____ Post Code_____

Telephone No._____ Date_____

*Please delete as necessary

If you would like information on the range of Tolley diaries please tick here ☐

If you would like a copy of the full Tolley catalogue please tick here ☐

Registered No 729731 England. VAT No 243 3583 67

Code 949